Leisure
Program
Planning

and

Delivery

Leisure Program Planning

and

Delivery

Ruth V. Russell, ReD
Indiana University

Lynn M. Jamieson, ReD
Indiana University

Human Kinetics

Library of Congress Cataloging-in-Publication Data

Russell, Ruth V., 1948-
  Leisure program planning and delivery / Ruth V. Russell, Lynn M. Jamieson.
    p. cm.
  Includes bibliographical references and index.
  ISBN-13: 978-0-7360-5733-2 (hard cover)
  ISBN-10: 0-7360-5733-1 (hard cover)
  1. Recreation leadership. 2. Recreation--Management. 3. Leisure--Management. 4. Leisure--
Planning. I. Jamieson, Lynn Marie, 1946- II. Title.
  GV181.43.R86 2007
  790.06'9--dc22

                              2007008569

ISBN-10: 0-7360-5733-1
ISBN-13: 978-0-7360-5733-2

Acquisitions Editor: Gayle Kassing, PhD; **Developmental Editor:** Amy Stahl; **Assistant Editors:** Bethany J. Bentley and Jackie Walker; **Copyeditor:** Patricia L. MacDonald; **Proofreader:** Anne Meyer Byler; **Indexer:** Bobbi Swanson; **Permission Manager:** Dalene Reeder; **Graphic Designer:** Bob Reuther; **Graphic Artist:** Dawn Sills; **Photo Manager:** Laura Fitch; **Photo Office Assistant:** Jason Allen; **Cover Designer:** Keith Blomberg; **Photographer (cover):** © Photodisc (top left), © Human Kinetics (right), © Plush Studios/Blend/Robertstock.com (bottom left); **Photographer (interior):** © Human Kinetics, unless otherwise noted; **Art Manager:** Kelly Hendren; **Associate Art Manager:** Alan L. Wilborn; **Illustrator:** Alan L. Wilborn; **Printer:** Sheridan Books

Printed in the United States of America   10 9 8 7 6 5 4 3 2 1

Human Kinetics
Web site: www.HumanKinetics.com

United States: Human Kinetics
P.O. Box 5076
Champaign, IL 61825-5076
800-747-4457
e-mail: humank@hkusa.com

Canada: Human Kinetics
475 Devonshire Road Unit 100
Windsor, ON N8Y 2L5
800-465-7301 (in Canada only)
e-mail: orders@hkcanada.com

Europe: Human Kinetics
107 Bradford Road
Stanningley
Leeds LS28 6AT, United Kingdom
+44 (0) 113 255 5665
e-mail: hk@hkeurope.com

Australia: Human Kinetics
57A Price Avenue
Lower Mitcham, South Australia 5062
08 8372 0999
e-mail: info@hkaustralia.com

New Zealand: Human Kinetics
Division of Sports Distributors NZ Ltd.
P.O. Box 300 226 Albany
North Shore City
Auckland
0064 9 448 1207
e-mail: info@humankinetics.co.nz

Contents

Preface

One of the best developments of the last century was the emergence of leisure as a tool for enhancing the well-being of individuals and communities. Accordingly, leisure has become a vital concern for government officials, business leaders, social service professionals, educators, parents, and everyone concerned with social problems, human development, health, and wellness. We can trace a striking growth of leisure's usefulness as a major form of civic responsibility, social service, business enterprise, medical treatment, and global commodity. An outstanding feature of this increased use of leisure is programs. Leisure programs are a powerful contributor to the emotional, physical, and social well-being of people and are important resources for accomplishing strong and successful communities.

Purpose of This Book

Leisure programs are central to the work of professionals in leisure services fields. Thus, *Leisure Program Planning and Delivery* is intended to assist with the study, training, and practice of recreation program planning.

Leisure Program Planning and Delivery was written primarily as a text for undergraduate students in recreation, park, tourism, therapeutic, cultural, and sport services. Because its coverage of programming concepts and skills is both basic and in-depth, it is useful to those preparing for professional careers in leisure service organizations and agencies that sponsor programs. This book will give you all the information you need to plan, implement, and evaluate leisure program services. The text can be used for a course on recreation or leisure programming, including event management, and as a supplemental resource for a joint course in leadership and programming or foundations of leisure services. As well, because of its comprehensiveness, *Leisure Program Planning and Delivery* is useful as a basic reference and resource for currently practicing professionals in the fields of recreation, park, therapeutic, tourism, cultural, and sport services.

Organization of This Book

Leisure Program Planning and Delivery is organized into four parts. Part I teaches and reviews the foundations of programming. Chapter 1 defends the role of programmed leisure in promoting the well-being of individuals and communities. Chapter 2 honors the professional programmers who provide leisure program services for agencies and organizations. Chapter 3 reviews the important programming axioms, and chapter 4 summarizes the various recreation program packages, or formats. Finally, chapter 5 examines the steps in the program planning process around which the remaining parts of the book are organized.

Part II features the first step—planning preparations. Chapter 6 offers suggestions on understanding your organization and community. Then, chapter 7 takes the next logical step of explaining how to assess program client needs. Chapter 8 focuses on developing program goals and objectives, and chapter 9 offers information on writing the program plan.

Part III of the book covers the next step of the program planning process—implementation. Chapter 10 describes how to make program operation decisions. Chapter 11 covers leading and supervising programs, and chapter 12 explains why and how to monitor ongoing programs. Chapter 13 features important information on risk management in leisure programs.

Finally, Part IV features the step of program evaluation. Chapter 14 outlines the various evaluation approaches appropriate for measuring program success, and chapter 15 explains how to evaluate programs.

Features of This Book

The text maintains a strong base in the actual professional leisure fields; thus it is about both the study and practice of programming in leisure services. Because of the diversity of field-based examples, you will learn programming skills applicable to your own career goals in public recreation and parks, therapeutic recreation, sport and fitness, commercial recreation, outdoor recreation, or tourism settings. Specifically, *Leisure Program Planning and Delivery* features the following:

- *Balanced perspective.* This book offers a strong conceptual foundation for the rationale of providing programmed leisure, as well as the practical information needed to develop skills in program development. Its basis is in both the "best practices" of award-winning programs across North America and the academic "proofs" of successful programming.

- *Case examples.* Chapters contain a minimum of two case studies each. Every chapter opens with a brief illustrative case—based on real agencies sponsoring real programs representing a wide variety of leisure service settings—that alerts readers to what they can expect to learn in that chapter. As well, a single and consistent case study thread is presented in every chapter to illustrate a specific concept discussed in that chapter. For this, we've chosen the gold medal award-winning parks and recreation department in the city of Westerville, Ohio. A different facet of the department's program services is embedded within each chapter to "tell the story" of leisure program development. Using a single case helps provide breadth and depth in understanding the role of programs in leisure service agencies. Finally, additional illustrative

cases are provided in the chapters to highlight specific content.

- *Systematic approach.* Because the book's organization follows a three-step program planning process, reading it seems a logical and rational progression. As well, since each chapter can stand alone as discrete information, the book can be used as a reference source.

Pedagogy and Supplements

Leisure Program Planning and Delivery goes far beyond most texts of this type in including high-lighted learning objectives, up-to-date reference lists, participatory reflections, explanatory figures and tables, boxed points, photographs, focused summaries, and end-of-the-chapter glossaries.

Additionally, a bound-in CD-ROM is included in the back of this text. For the student, each chapter on the CD-ROM includes programming tips, individual practice exercises using the Internet,* individual programming practice activities, group discussion ideas, a programming issue to solve, exam review questions, and information on building a programming portfolio. An instructor might incorporate these activities into course assignments, and students can also participate in them on their own as an effective way to enrich their reading. Whenever an activity on the bound-in CD-ROM is mentioned in this book, you will find a CD-ROM icon in the text.

*The Web addresses cited in the CD-ROM were current as of April 30, 2007, unless otherwise noted.

Acknowledgments

A book is never the sole effort of the authors. Indeed, this book is the result of the commitment of many people, including more than a century of legacy by leisure programmers from around the world. We began to work together on recreation programs in 1970 when we were employed by the City of San Diego Park and Recreation Department. So, although together we have spent some 75 years learning, practicing, and teaching the programming skills presented in this book, they would never have gotten between two covers without the help of these people:

Jody Stowers, director, City of Westerville Parks and Recreation Department

Phyllis Self, recreation superintendent, and her staff, City of Westerville Parks and Recreation Department

Curtis Wright, facilities superintendent, and his staff, City of Westerville Parks and Recreation Department

Anneka Metcalf, administrative assistant, Department of Recreation, Park, and Tourism Studies, Indiana University

Gayle Kassing and Amy Stahl, our editors at Human Kinetics

PART I

Foundations of Leisure Programming

Programs—directed recreation and leisure experiences—are central to recreation and leisure services. Organized outdoor, sport, game, travel, dance, music, and drama programs play a vital role in the well-being of millions of Americans and Canadians. Thus, program planning, management, and evaluation are essential for the success of leisure services.

Yet, this doesn't happen automatically. Program professionals must have mastered both the knowledge and skills required for their programs to positively contribute to people's individual and collective lives. Many understandings and abilities are required to be successful. Helping you achieve these is the mission of this book.

Before delving into all the details, however, it is important to establish a basic foundation. In this part of the book, our goal is to provide the needed background so that your programming actions are contextually placed.

- Chapter 1 focuses on the role of programmed leisure. How does leisure contribute to people's well-being, and why is it necessary to manage leisure as an organized service?

- Chapter 2 discusses the professionals who plan and present recreation programs. How do they develop a programming career?

- Chapter 3 provides the basic programming principles. What are the best practices by which recreation programs are provided?

- Chapter 4 overviews program areas and types. How are recreation programs categorized and packaged for delivery as services to people?

- Chapter 5 outlines the program planning process. What are the ordered steps required in providing successful recreation programs?

CHAPTER 1

The Importance of Programmed Leisure

In this chapter, you can look forward to the following:

- Developing an appreciation of programmed leisure's ability to make life worth living
- Making a commitment to the worth of directed and organized leisure
- Beginning to develop a personal and professional philosophy about programmed leisure
- Becoming aware of future challenges for programmed leisure

Outward Bound is a leading international outdoor education program. As a commercial agency, it uses such outdoor pursuits as canoeing, sailing, climbing, kayaking, dogsledding, desert canyoneering, and backpacking as a "classroom" for self-discovery. Internationally, more than 40 wilderness schools are in operation; in North America, more than 60,000 people are served annually through four wilderness schools, two urban centers, and a primary and secondary school reform program. Outward Bound's commitment to contributing to people's well-being is front and center in its course catalog—this is Outward Bound's program.

Outward Bound makes a difference in people's lives. Its courses compel you to dig deep. Amid encouragement and support, you transcend perceived limits; find within yourself new strengths; and gain trust, compassion, resolve, respect for the environment, and the energy to put it all to work for yourself and your community.

Outward Bound uses programmed leisure to improve the lives of individuals and communities. Thus, we begin this book by presenting the importance of programmed leisure in contributing to well-being. For additional information on this topic, see worksheet 1.1 in chapter 1 of the CD-ROM.

One of the best developments of the last century was the emergence of leisure as a vital concern for government officials, business leaders, social service workers, parents, and everyone concerned with the well-being of people. From earlier eras when people found simple pleasure in at-home hobbies and village events, we can trace a striking growth of leisure's usefulness as a major form of civic responsibility, social service, business enterprise, medical treatment, and global commodity. As a result, billions of dollars are spent each year on outdoor recreation, sport, tourism, cultural art events, and many other pastimes.

An outstanding feature of this increased organization of leisure is the development of **programs**. Programs are the application of the human, fiscal, and other resources of an agency to the provision of systematic and purposeful recreation activities or events. Leisure programs are central to the work of professionals in the leisure services fields. Programmers not only facilitate leisure experiences by preparing facilities and equipment but also, through their leadership, guide, enhance, extend, and maximize how leisure behavior is expressed. Programs are similar to spreading a delicious icing on an already scrumptious cake—quality of life in one's leisure is improved through programs.

This is not to suggest that all leisure should be preorganized and led by leaders. Indeed, leisure's qualities include solitude, surprise, and spontaneity—expressions more likely associated with individual efforts. Rather, our point is that in contemporary societies, where the pace is hectic and the competition for our interests is steep, leisure programs are sought after by patrons more than ever before. More people need professionals to make arrangements for them as they squeeze their free time into crowded weekends and vacations. This is a social problem—one that can fill a whole book (and has). But as long as people have only two weeks available to see Europe, they'll need an organized tour; or as long as children must be cared for while parents are at work, they'll need an after-school program; or as long as young adults demand more high adventure to satisfy their intense, media-driven upbringing, they'll need a skydiving club.

What exactly is leisure's role in our well-being? Individually and collectively, why do we make the unabashed claim that leisure is important not only for our overall quality of life but also for our very survival? We begin to answer these questions next.

Benefits of Leisure

Leisure is a major force in our lives. Along with sleep, it is what we mostly do with ourselves. Indeed, if you are now 18 years old, Leitner and Leitner (2004) calculate that out of the likely 60 years you have left, even with your major employment years still ahead of you, you will spend the equivalent of 18 full-time years in leisure. You will also spend 17.8 years in sleep, 8.33 in work (40 years, 36 hours per week), 1.0 in formal education, 7.12 in personal care, 5.34

in family obligations, 1.53 in commuting, and 0.80 in miscellaneous activities.

Amazed? You shouldn't be because leisure is our main source of those attributes that make us human and able to live with each other. That is, leisure teaches and provides us with many things that are vital for our growth and development from the day we are born until our death. It is a dominant source of our freedom of choice, intrinsic rewards, happiness, pleasure, play, risk, humor, relaxation, ritual, solitude, commitment, and often spirituality. It is even thought to prevent disease. To the point, leisure gives us wellness, satisfaction, and a high quality of life.

Some leisure expressions are better than others, of course. Leisure has the potential to contribute significantly to our physical, social, and emotional well-being, but it must be wisely chosen. For example, taking a walk with friends on a crisp autumn afternoon is more beneficial than sitting alone in a darkened room in front of the television. Some leisure expressions are so positive that we describe them as peak experiences. Indeed, hiking in the mountains, playing flute in an orchestra, challenging someone to a chess match, and running a marathon are often described as enabling what Csikszentmihalyi (1975) has labeled the **flow** experience, or optimal involvement in an activity. Such ultimate fulfillment through leisure is so vital, in fact, that leisure is often used in therapy.

On the other hand, other ways of using our free time harm us. Unpleasant, as well as pleasant, results are possible through our pastimes. Every day thousands of children require medical treatment for playground injuries; and sport participation can make us feel exhausted, nervous, and frustrated. Even more serious, engaging in dangerous sexual practices can give us serious illnesses, gambling too much can financially ruin us, abusing alcohol can kill us, and hanging out in an urban gang can get us arrested. Yet,

> To a large degree, to experience leisure . . . is to experience a subjective state of health. In this sense, the development of a broad repertoire of leisure skills to facilitate rich, meaningful experiences provides the foundation for extending such holistic quality experiences to all of life. Personal initiative, choice, mean-

By some estimates, you will spend the equivalent of 18 years of your adult life in leisure.

© Human Kinetics.

> ingful involvement, and enjoyable, supportive social networks—key aspects for leisure—also have important implications for well-being. In the more extreme subjective view, distinctions between leisure and health disappear. (Wankel, 1994, p. 28)

In what more specific ways might leisure provide for our well-being? In the following discussion we will review the emotional, physical, and social benefits of leisure.

Emotional Benefits

Much more than the other end of a continuum from mental illness, emotional well-being is an important component for a good life (Stumbo & Peterson, 2004). Mentally healthy people flourish because they are filled with positive emotions (Keyes, 2002). Leisure can provide the conditions necessary for positive emotions.

Leisure does this by serving as a mediator for improving self-definition, self-actualization, and a sense of empowerment. For example, one of the benefits described by Csikszentmihalyi and Kleiber (1991) is that leisure provides ample opportunities for self-exploration of talents, capacities, and potential. Similarly, Haggard and Williams (1991) make a case for leisure and self-affirmation. "Leisure activities, primarily because they are unconstrained, may be particularly good vehicles for identity affirmation" (p. 112).

Iso-Ahola and Park (1996) found that leisure involvement is related to mental health in such a way that as one's perceptions of perceived freedom and intrinsic motivation increase in daily life, positive feelings also increase. Iwasaki and Mannell (2000) found that simply believing leisure contributes to emotional well-being is enough to reduce mental illness symptoms. Yet, Iso-Ahola (1980) qualifies all these emotional advantages by insisting that active recreation is more optimally arousing than passive recreation and thus more conducive to psychological health.

Numerous studies point to leisure's ability to help people cope with the particular threat of **stress** to emotional well-being. Stress results when there is an actual or perceived imbalance between a demand and the capability to deal with it (Hood & Carruthers, 2002). Stress may make us very sick, for most commonly it can lead to heart disease, high blood pressure, strokes, back and neck pain, insomnia, and compromised immune systems. College students seem especially effected by stress. One survey of college freshmen (Cooperman, 2000) found that 30.2 percent feel "frequently overwhelmed by all I have to do" (p. 212). Another survey (reported by Leitner & Leitner, 2004) discovered that college women (38.8 percent) are more stressed than college men (20 percent), attributing the difference to a demonstration that college women spend more time than

Stress by the Numbers

- In the general population, 75 percent of people have some symptom of stress every two weeks.
- Stress is a significant health problem for 43 percent of North Americans.
- Stress-induced problems are the reason for 75 to 90 percent of visits to physicians.
- About one million workers are absent from work each day because of stress.
- The cost of stress at the workplace is estimated to be $200 billion annually.

Compiled from the American Institute of Stress, 2000; Health Resource Network, 2000; Verespej, 2000.

men studying, volunteering, participating in clubs, doing housework, and taking care of children. See the box on this page for more stress statistics. For more information on this topic, see "More Options for Individual Programming Practice," option 4, in chapter 1 of the CD-ROM.

Research directly confirms that enjoying life's pleasures, seeking satisfying social interaction, and pursuing an activity that is self-expressive can lower stress and ultimately have a positive effect on the immune system. To summarize the essence of hundreds of research studies, we draw from an overview by Siegenthaler (1997): Meaningful, fulfilling, and active leisure activities promote psychological well-being because leisure helps balance life's demands by increasing a sense of perceived freedom, especially during times of major life crises.

Physical Benefits

Strongly related to emotional health, our physical health also owes a great debt to leisure (Godbey, Caldwell, Floyd, & Payne, 2005). Staying active in leisure has numerous physiological effects on our cardiovascular, respiratory, musculoskeletal, metabolic, and endocrine systems. Our bodies respond very favorably to physical recreation, with reduced risks of coronary heart disease, hypertension, colon cancer, and diabetes. As well, an active lifestyle decreases fatigue, protects us against obesity, maintains bone density and joint mobility, and even protects us from urinary tract infections.

Consistent physical activity provides enjoyment, support from others, confidence in our ability to regularly participate, and positive beliefs about the benefits of physical activity. It also reduces perceived barriers to being physically active. The ultimate payoff of all this, of course, is that longevity comes from improved health. Yet, incredibly, in North America only about 15 percent of adults and 50 percent of children regularly participate in physical recreation (Stumbo & Peterson, 2004).

Life, in general, has become more sedentary, making the importance of physical activity during leisure that much greater. The chosen activity doesn't matter. It can be ultimate Frisbee, snowboarding, group exercise, or taekwondo. Studies have confirmed that regularly participating in these and numerous other sport and recreational activities provides the necessary aerobic benefit (National Center for Chronic Disease Prevention and Health Promotion, 2002). Activities that raise your heart rate 60 to 90 percent for at least 20 minutes each day will provide the physiological benefit you need to be healthy. See table 1.1 for some ideas for these activities.

Social Benefits

Social development and social well-being are also important benefits of leisure. With the exception of isolating pursuits, such as watching television and playing video games, many leisure expressions contribute to our friendships and ability to get along with others. Social behavior is the reciprocal exchange between two or more individuals, and most of these interactions for both children and adults happen during leisure. Therefore, leisure is largely a social phenomenon (Samdahl, 1992).

A solid record of research demonstrates leisure's social benefits. For example, participation in leisure that is highly social in nature promotes social support. Social well-being requires social support (Larson, 1997), and connections or relationships among individuals can often be best strengthened and tested during leisure experiences. When individuals feel cared for and believe they have adequate support if needed, they feel better about themselves and their lives. Iso-Ahola and Park (1996) found that the higher the leisure friendship and leisure companionship, the higher the perception of being healthy. As well, Orthner and Mancini's (1991) review of research literature suggests that leisure plays a significant role in the development and maintenance of family. They showed that partners who share leisure activities reported the highest marital satisfaction levels.

As with physically active forms of leisure, pursuits that emphasize sociability are becoming rare in contemporary societies (Burns, 1993). Today, the leisure habits of many people detract from socializing. People seem to prefer watching a movie alone at home on a DVD rather than in theaters with others, exercising in the garage on their own equipment instead of with others at a recreation center, or playing games on computers instead of face to face with a competitor.

TABLE 1.1

Active Leisure for Aerobic Fitness

High potential of promoting fitness	Medium potential of promoting fitness	Low potential of promoting fitness
Lap swimming	Basketball	Softball
Jogging	Downhill skiing	Bowling
Power walking	Tennis	Golf
Rowing	Hiking	Volleyball

Leitner & Leitner, 2004.

Today people seem to prefer less socializing in leisure.

© Stockdisc.

Leisure and Well-Being

The many benefits of leisure converge to create an all-around sense of well-being in people. Leisure is of vital importance to the vitality of our neighborhoods, towns, regions, states or provinces, nations, and world. It builds vigorous and caring communities, facilitates a strong and healthy workforce, has the power to create equity among diverse people, builds economies (see "A Sampling of Leisure's Economic Impact"), solves social problems, and makes the environment more aesthetic (Russell, 2005). Several basic concepts capture all this: wellness, life satisfaction, and quality of life.

Wellness

Wellness is an approach to personal health that emphasizes individual responsibility for practicing a health-promoting lifestyle (Hurley & Schaadt, 1992). This definition suggests that well-being is a positive and proactive approach requiring good daily decisions, including eating nutritious food, wearing safety belts, not smoking, and regularly participating in healthful leisure pursuits. This implies a progression toward a higher potential of functioning for the whole being (Travis & Ryan, 2004). Through a healthful lifestyle, we focus on enhancing our well-being rather than on avoiding getting sick or on treating illness when it occurs. The box, "It's More Than a Name," describes one college's commitment to wellness.

A Sampling of Leisure's Economic Impact

On average, Americans annually spend more than $500 billion in pursuit of a good time. This includes purchases of video, audio, and computer products ($89.7 billion); toys and sports supplies ($45.4 billion); and commercial amusements ($46.2 billion) (U.S. Department of Commerce, 1999). It does not include travel, which is estimated to carry an annual price tag of another $500 billion (Cordes & Ibrahim, 2003). In Canada, the growth in leisure expenditures increased by 21 percent between 2000 and 2004 (Euromonitor International, 2005).

It's More Than a Name

More and more colleges and universities are declaring their commitment to student and faculty wellness by attaching the term to their campus recreational programs and services. For example, the Centre for Sport, Recreation and Wellness at Douglas College in British Columbia, Canada, seeks to enhance the lives of its students and employees through programs designed to develop the mind and spirit in addition to the body. One program, the Wellness Challenge, helps patrons get in total shape with activities that "exercise the physical, mental, social, spiritual, and environmental aspects of the individual. Whether you're reading a book with humour (Activity #35), getting a massage (Activity #25), or walking the seawall (Activity #1), the Wellness Challenge will be a rewarding experience."

Reprinted, by permission, from Douglas College, www.douglas.bc.ca/csrw/wellness.htm; accessed November 14, 2005.

Life Satisfaction

Leisure's benefits to us individually can also contribute to life satisfaction. **Life satisfaction** is often thought of as happiness and contentedness about life. If we are satisfied with our lives, we feel good about them—we are happy. Although it is difficult to pin down a precise definition of life satisfaction, we certainly recognize it when we have it! It is an internal, subjective, emotional condition. And it is not static. We must constantly behave, think, and feel in ways that make us happy. Myers (2000) reports that happy people—people who feel satisfied with their lives—are less self-focused, less hostile and abusive, and less vulnerable to disease. They are more loving, forgiving, trusting, energetic, decisive, creative, sociable, and helpful. Companionship, rest, education, good health, family, and a good standard of living, as well as meeting new people, having opportunities for self-expression, and experiencing nature, also make us happy.

Leisure particularly contributes to life satisfaction by providing all these things. Like a rolling snowball, happy people are more likely to engage in wholesome leisure activities, feel positive about their leisure, and believe that leisure is helping them feel happier. If we do not regularly and joyfully participate in positive leisure, we do not necessarily feel worse; we simply do not feel better.

In general, are we satisfied with our lives? Perhaps not yet. According to a *Time*/CNN poll conducted in 1992 (United Way of America Strategic Institute), people are seeking more flexible and shorter work hours, increased vacation time, job sharing, and options for working at home. Even more than they desire more money, people want to slow down and live a more relaxed life, spend more time with family and friends, and generally enjoy life more.

Quality of Life

A third concept that captures the significance of leisure's many benefits is quality of life. **Quality of life** concerns what people are capable of doing and the resources that support them. According to the World Health Organization (2001), quality of life is an individual's position within the context of his culture and value system. It is a combination of his financial status, ability to live in a clean and healthy environment, literacy rate, accessible health services, safety, position in the family and social hierarchies, meaningful work and leisure, and other opportunities he expects and believes to be important. For more information on this topic, see worksheet 1.2 in chapter 1 of the CD-ROM.

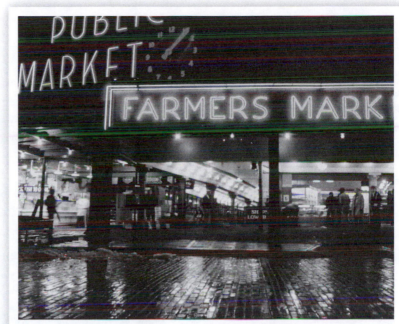

When people have resources that enable them to live according to their expectations, they have a high quality of life.

© Art Explosion.

Programmed Leisure

Leisure can be experienced in multiple ways. A great deal of leisure involvement is unorganized—expressed independently and spontaneously by individuals and groups without any guidance, structure, or sponsorship. People read books, watch television, listen to music, chat through e-mail, have picnics, roughhouse with their pets, play a pickup game of basketball at the park, and enjoy gardening. Of course, to some extent even these leisure expressions require a degree of sponsorship and prior planning. The book was checked out of the library, a corporation made certain decisions about what music to record and market, the grass at the picnic site is regularly mowed, the basketball hoop was put up by a youth-serving agency, and in early spring the garden store nurtured the seeds for the plants in their greenhouse. The level of professional planning for even the simplest pursuit is complex and requires informed decisions.

Beyond being independently expressed, leisure can also be organized. Our label for this is **programmed leisure**. Programmed leisure experiences are sponsored and organized by an agency or business that assesses interests, schedules activities, provides leadership and equipment, maintains the facility setting, and evaluates the result. Programmed leisure can refer to a single activity, such as a bike tour, or an ongoing series of activities, such as a bike safety course. It can be led by leaders, such as a softball tournament, or simply be a supervised open facility, such as softball batting cages. Programmed leisure, or recreation programs, is an integral component in the services provided by public, private, and commercial organizations.

Totally Cool, Totally Art (TCTA) introduces more than 400 children per year to a variety of art media in Austin, Texas. Beach Girls' Cheerleading teaches adolescent girls the sport of cheerleading in Virginia Beach, Virginia. W.I.S.E. trains cancer patients and survivors in fitness-based treatments in Bloomington, Indiana. New Routes, Inc. provides outdoor adventure experiences for survivors of domestic violence and incest. Parks Canada offers nature interpretation to visitors to the national parks. The Gas Station Theatre in Winnipeg, Manitoba, provides drama experiences to both performers and audiences. BackRoads takes tourists on walking or biking tours in interesting areas around the world. For more information on this topic,

The W.I.S.E. program trains cancer patients and survivors in fitness-based treatments in Bloomington, Indiana. Named for an inspiring participant, W.I.S.E. stands for Working out to Increase Strength and Endurance.

see "More Options for Individual Programming Practice," option 1 in chapter 1 of the CD-ROM.

These activities are all examples of programmed leisure. What is central to each program is intention. A professional programmer intentionally conceptualizes how to provide a leisure experience for people who intentionally show up to participate. Programmed leisure is organized; it includes planning, implementation, and evaluation—all intended to bring the benefits of leisure to individuals and groups.

Programmed leisure, of course, is the point of this book. To continue establishing the foundation for developing your knowledge and skill as a programmer, let's now consider how programmed leisure brings about the many benefits discussed earlier. Specifically, we will consider its philosophical premise and its role in engendering well-being.

Philosophical Premise of Programmed Leisure

As professional programmers, how we interpret leisure greatly affects the nature of the programs we offer. Some of us may intend that our programs build self-esteem in children, return convalescent patients to independent living, build positive public relations for the town, pay the bills of the family-run campground, or keep teens out of trouble. On the other hand, some of us may intend for our programs to simply offer rest and diversion, peace and spirituality, risk, play, or a good laugh. Whatever the specific aim, the point is that the program *has* a specific aim.

For example, the Phoenix Parks and Recreation Department, through its At-Risk Youth Division, implemented a Curfew Diversion Program. Instead of taking youth who violate curfew to a local precinct, police take them directly to the nearest community center. There, the paperwork is processed while the staff members offer the detainees recreational activities until parents pick them up. The program has resulted in a 50 percent reduction in curfew violations. In Virginia Beach, at-risk middle school youth have an opportunity to participate in the Questing for Success Camp. Forty youth participants are identified through referrals from school guidance counselors and sent to camp for a week during spring break. There, educational sessions address such topics as

The Programming Process: Achieving the Dream

Let's get acquainted with the City of Westerville Parks and Recreation Department. Located in Westerville, Ohio, the city's population of 36,000 people is spread over 12.5 miles. To serve these constituents, the department annually spends about $212.64 per person for facilities and programs. Under the directorship of Jody Stowers, 55 full-time employees, plus many part-time and seasonal staff and volunteers, take care of the facilities and plan and manage programs.

The program offerings are numerous and comprehensive—the department offers more than 1,140 different programs annually. Serving all age groups, the schedule includes fitness, sport, aquatic, bicycling, hiking, rock climbing, social, gardening, travel, nature, school mentoring, arts and crafts, dance, and theater programs. Why such a focus on programs? City officials and citizens alike believe in the power of leisure programs to create the best possible place to live. This is even reflected in the department's mission:

> Our mission is to enhance our community by providing quality and diverse leisure facilities, programs, and services and by preserving and/or developing our natural areas.

Westerville's commitment—from its mission statement to actual expenditures on facility and staff resources—demonstrates the importance of programmed leisure in providing for the well-being of people. We therefore feature this leisure service organization as a case study in each chapter in this book. Throughout its operations, the department demonstrates a real-world application of the recreation program planning process.

In fact, the Westerville recreation department does such an excellent job of providing program services that it is frequently recognized nationally, for providing such services as sport, aquatics, and nature programs. As a special recognition for "excellence in the field of park and recreational management for agencies in towns of 20,000 to 50,000," the department was awarded the Gold Medal Award by the National Recreation and Park Association.

Jody Stowers, director of the Westerville Parks and Recreation Department, proudly displays the Gold Medal Award.

Photo courtesy of Westerville Parks and Recreation Department, Westerville, Ohio.

This is the highest recognition possible, and each year awardees are selected from among more than 4,800 communities in the United States. For more information on this topic, see "More Options for Individual Programming Practice," option 3, and "Group Discussion Ideas," option 1, in chapter 1 of the CD-ROM.

---

handgun violence, healthy relationships, HIV/AIDS and other sexually transmitted diseases, job interviewing skills, conflict resolution, and money management (Witt & Crompton, 2002). For more information on this topic, see worksheet 1.3 in chapter 1 of the CD-ROM.

Leisure service organizations provide recreation programs because they believe that leisure experiences have positive value in meeting significant human needs. They have a common commitment to the power of leisure to accomplish something worthwhile. Indeed, one of the characteristics of the profession is that it has a social mandate. That mandate is grounded in the fundamental needs of

people and their society—whether the concern is for their physical health, economic vitality, or overall quality of life. As aptly put by leisure advocate Doug Sessoms (1992, p. 47), "Without a mandate, there is no soul, no sense of purpose, no sustaining will, which attracts people to the cause."

In addition to having a social mandate, programming leisure requires you to have a philosophical base. This influences how you see the world and, as a result, how you conceptualize leisure and the nature of the programs you offer. For our purposes, **philosophy** means a set of basic values and beliefs that guide behavior. Over time, different philosophical approaches have developed about programmed leisure, and professional practitioners have adopted some of these approaches as part of the basis for their actions. These philosophical approaches include pragmatism, idealism, realism, humanism, and existentialism.

Pragmatism seeks to resolve questions by tracing the practical consequences. For example, if program A accomplishes the same outcome as program B (i.e., there is no practical difference between them), what does it matter? Yet, if there is a pragmatic difference between the two programs, the better program is to be provided. For leisure programmers, pragmatism raises the following question: Why adopt a particular program service unless it makes a difference? The work of the founders of playgrounds and settlement houses more than 100 years ago was based on the pragmatic philosophy of John Dewey, who argued that leisure was necessary because it made a difference in young people's development (Searle & Brayley, 2000).

Idealism, on the other hand, confirms that there is an eternal set of ideals governing human behavior and that people should work toward perfecting them. Idealists believe that individuals should be goal directed—that the means are as important as the ends. For example, playground leaders in the early 1900s in Toronto believed that their goal was to protect the children from evil and teach them high ideals (Searle & Brayley, 2000). Idealism also supports a contemporary philosophy that some forms of leisure are better than others. Thus, it has been believed for a long time that programmers should focus on providing opportunities for creative and active participation rather than passive or even antisocial activities (Nash, 1935).

The philosophical approach of **realism** is based on the scientific method—life is a matter of cause and effect. Realists believe that things do not just happen; rather, there are causes. To the realist, orderliness is important. Realists believe that something doesn't exist unless it can be observed. An illustration of realism as a basis for professional practice is the development of standards for planning and managing park and recreation areas and facilities. To say that there must be 10 acres of open space per 1,000 citizens is a widely used standard in North America (Searle & Brayley, 2000). It provides an orderly, scientifically based rationale for developing leisure services.

Next, **humanism** is a philosophy that honors the supremacy of the human being. Humanists are concerned about what happens to individuals and seek to enhance their humanism through growth and development. Humanism stresses purposeful living,

higher functioning, and a sense of social consciousness (Searle & Brayley, 2000). In the provision of leisure services, humanists provide ways for participants to realize their potential. In studying the mission statements of the Boys and Girls Clubs, for example, we see the goal is to bring more positive life experiences to youth simply because they deserve this outreach as human beings. For more information on this topic, see worksheet 1.2 in chapter 1 of the CD-ROM.

Finally, we can see indications of **existentialism** in the provision of leisure services. Existentialism maintains that individual freedom is the most important quality in life and that what matters is the present. Therefore, a person's goal is to be responsible to herself and do what she needs to fulfill her life at the moment (Searle & Brayley, 2000). Leisure programmers grounded by an existentialist philosophy hold that if they make a difference in a person's single day, then they have achieved success.

As a professional leisure programmer, the philosophical approach you adopt will influence your understanding of leisure's role in providing for the well-being of individuals and communities. As well, you will often need to articulate your philosophy to employers, advisory boards, professional colleagues, staff, and participants. Although often difficult to do, this task is highly important for providing a useful framework for programmed leisure. For more information on this topic, see "More Options for Individual Programming Practice," option 2, and "Group Discussion Ideas," option 3, in chapter 1 of the CD-ROM.

Providing Well-Being With Programmed Leisure

Does programmed leisure actually provide the benefits presented earlier? Do leisure programs really work? What proof is there that they accomplish what is intended? Here is a sampling of the proof from the research literature.

Brock (1988) reported improved arm and leg coordination from a horseback riding program. Yoder, Nelson, and Smith (1989) found improved range of motion for older adults in a cooking group. Rothe, Kohl, and Mansfield (1990) documented increased effort tolerance and decreased heart rate after a running and swimming program for children who were asthmatic. Riddick (1985) demonstrated that an in-home aquarium program reduced the diastolic blood pressure of elderly individuals.

Meanwhile, Scher (2001) confirmed that participation in a theater group helped Jewish and Arab youth develop more trust and social interest in each other. Boverie (1994) demonstrated an increase in employee job satisfaction and productivity at Eastman Kodak from designated "humor rooms" where employees go to watch videos. Grover (2003) confirmed that community gardening programs revitalize decaying urban neighborhoods. College students enrolled in a leisure education course increased their knowledge of their campus leisure resources (Leitner, 1987).

Even a casual search of the research literature in leisure studies will turn up many more confirmations that programmed leisure can make a difference in individual and community lives. Yes, recreation programs really work. In fact, the commitment to this statement has been so solid that specific projections about exactly what recreation programs can accomplish have been put forth.

For example, Dr. Karl Menninger explored the use of recreation in treating mental illness (in Weiskopf, 1982). According to Menninger, creative activities such as crafts are prescriptive against emotional tension, collecting items such as stamps increases feelings of security, and noncompetitive sports eliminate feelings of inferiority. Menninger saw leisure participation as "miniature victories" to counteract the "miniature defeats" of everyday life (Kraus, 1984).

In spite of this record of success, the challenge for leisure services programmers is to continue to provide leisure experiences that ultimately improve wellness, life satisfaction, and quality of life by contributing to emotional, physical, and social well-being. This mandate is becoming even more challenging as programmers are increasingly responsible for serving a broader range of participants—with widely different interests, personalities, skills, and concerns—according to a larger list of activity options. For more information on this topic, see "Group Discussion Ideas," option 2, in chapter 1 of the CD-ROM.

Research demonstrates that college students enrolled in a leisure education course are more knowledgeable about their campus leisure resources.

© Human Kinetics.

Summary

This chapter focuses on the role of programmed leisure in fostering well-being. You should understand the following key points:

- Leisure is a powerful contributor to the emotional, physical, and social well-being of individuals.
- Contributions to individual well-being lead to increases in wellness, life satisfaction, and quality of life.
- Leisure also makes significant contributions to the well-being of communities.
- Examples of collective well-being from leisure include solving social problems and increasing economic vitality.
- One of the ways to achieve these benefits is to sponsor leisure in organized forms. These are labeled *programs*.
- The philosophical bases for the benefits of leisure programs include pragmatism, idealism, realism, humanism, and existentialism.

For more information on this topic, see "Can You Solve This Programming Issue?" in chapter 1 of the CD-ROM.

Glossary

program—The application of the human, fiscal, and other resources of an agency to provide systematic and purposeful recreation activities or events.

flow—Optimal involvement in an activity.

stress—Actual or perceived imbalance between a demand and the capability to deal with it.

wellness—A personal health approach emphasizing individual responsibility for well-being by practicing a health-promoting lifestyle.

life satisfaction—Feeling happy and content about life.

quality of life—What people are capable of doing and the resources that support them.

programmed leisure—Leisure experiences that are sponsored and organized by an agency.

philosophy—A set of values and beliefs that guide behavior.

pragmatism—A philosophical approach that seeks to resolve questions by tracing their practical consequences.

idealism—A philosophical approach that believes people should work toward perfecting an eternal set of ideals.

realism—A philosophical approach based on the cause-and-effect premise of science.

humanism—A philosophical approach that honors the supremacy of the human being.

existentialism—A philosophical approach that considers individual freedom the most important quality in life.

References

American Institute of Stress. (2000). Stress: America's #1 health problem. Retrieved March 4, 2007, from www.stress.org/americas.htm.

Boverie, P. (1994). Humor in human resource development. *Human Resource Development Quarterly, 5*(1), 75-91.

Brock, B.J. (1988). Effect of therapeutic horseback riding on physically disabled adults. *Therapeutic Recreation Journal, 22*(3), 34-43.

Burns, L. (1993). *Busybodies: Why our time-obsessed society keeps us running in place.* New York: Norton.

Centre for Sport, Recreation and Wellness. (n.d.). The Wellness Challenge. Retrieved November 14, 2005, from Douglas College Web site: www.douglas.bc.ca/csrw/wellness.htm.

Cooperman, K. (2000). Record numbers of the nation's freshmen feel high degree of stress, UCLA study finds. University of California-Los Angeles School of Education and Information Studies, Higher Education Research Institute, press release.

Cordes, K.A., & Ibrahim, H.M. (2003). *Applications in recreation & leisure for today and the future.* Boston: McGraw-Hill.

Csikszentmihalyi, M. (1975). *Beyond boredom and anxiety.* San Francisco: Jossey-Bass.

Csikszentmihalyi, M., & Kleiber, D.A. (1991). Leisure and self-actualization. In B.L. Driver, P.J. Brown, & G.L. Peterson (Eds.), *Benefits of leisure* (pp. 91-102). State College, PA: Venture.

Euromonitor International. (2005, April). Travel and tourism in Canada. Retrieved November 14, 2005, from www.euromonitor.com/Travel_and_Tourism_in_Canada.

Godbey, G.C., Caldwell, L.L., Floyd, M., & Payne, L.L. (2005). Contributions of leisure studies and recreation and park management research to the active living agenda. *American Journal of Preventative Medicine, 28*(2S2), 150-158.

Grover, T.D. (2003). The story of the Queen Anne Memorial Garden: Resisting a dominant cultural narrative. *Journal of Leisure Research, 35*(2), 190-212.

Haggard, L.M., & Williams, D.R. (1991). Self-identity benefits of leisure activities. In B.L. Driver, P.J. Brown, & G.L. Peterson (Eds.), *Benefits of leisure* (pp. 103-120). State College, PA: Venture.

Health Resource Network. (2000). Stress facts. Retrieved April 22, 2002, from www.stresscure.com/hrn/facts.html.

Hood, C.D., & Carruthers, C.P. (2002). Coping skills theory as an underlying framework for therapeutic recreation services. *Therapeutic Recreation Journal, 36*(2), 137-153.

Hurley, J.S., & Schaadt, R.G. (1992). *The wellness lifestyle.* Guilford, CT: Dushkin.

Iso-Ahola, S.E. (1980). *The social psychology of leisure and recreation.* Dubuque, IA: Brown.

Iso-Ahola, S.E., & Park, C.J. (1996). Leisure-related social support and self-determination as buffers of stress-illness relationship. *Journal of Leisure Research, 28*(3), 169-187.

Iwasaki, Y., & Mannell, R.C. (2000). Hierarchical dimensions of leisure stress coping. *Leisure Sciences, 22*, 163-181.

Keyes, C.L.M. (2002). The mental health continuum: From languishing to flourishing in life. *Journal of Health and Social Behavior, 43*(2), 207-222.

Kraus, R.G. (1984). *Recreation and leisure in modern society.* Glenview, IL: Scott, Foresman.

Larson, J.S. (1997). The MOS 36-item short form health survey: A conceptual analysis. *Evaluation and the Health Professions, 20*(1), 14-27.

Leitner, M.J. (1987). The effects of a leisure education course on college students' leisure awareness and attitudes. California State University, Chico, unpublished manuscript.

Leitner, M.J., & Leitner, S.F. (2004). *Leisure enhancement* (3rd ed.). New York: Haworth Press.

Myers, D.G. (2000). The funds, friends, and faith of happy people. *American Psychologist, 55*(1), 56-67.

Nash, J.B. (1935). *Philosophy of recreation and leisure.* Dubuque, IA: Brown.

National Center for Chronic Disease Prevention and Health Promotion. (2002). Physical activity and health: A report of the Surgeon General. Retrieved February 5, 2003, from Centers for Disease Control and Prevention Web site: www.cdc.gov/nccdphp/sgr/summary.htm.

Orthner, D.K., & Mancini, J.A. (1991). Leisure impacts on family interaction and cohesion. *Journal of Leisure Research, 22*(2), 125-137.

Riddick, C.C. (1985). Health, aquariums, and the non-institutionalized elderly. In M. Sussman (Ed.), *Pets and the family* (pp. 163-173). New York: Haworth Press.

Rothe, T., Kohl, C., & Mansfield, H.J. (1990). Controlled study of the effect of sports training on cardiopulmonary functions of asthmatic children and adolescents. *Pneumologie, 44,* 1110-1114.

Russell, R.V. (2005). *Pastimes: The context of contemporary leisure* (3rd ed.). Champaign, IL: Sagamore.

Samdahl, D. (1992). Leisure in our lives: Exploring the common leisure occasion. *Journal of Leisure Research, 24,* 19-32.

Scher, G. (2001). Attitudes, national stereotypes and preparedness for social interaction of Jewish and Arab youth who participated in the joint theatrical project in Tel Aviv-Jaffa. Haifa University, Haifa, Israel, master's thesis.

Searle, M.S., & Brayley, R.E. (2000). *Leisure services in Canada: An introduction.* State College, PA: Venture.

Sessoms, H.D. (1992). Lessons from the past. *Parks and Recreation, 27*(2), 46-53.

Siegenthaler, K.L. (1997). Health benefits of leisure. *Parks and Recreation, 32*(1), 24, 26, 28, 30-31.

Stumbo, N.J., & Peterson, C.A. (2004). *Therapeutic recreation program design: Principles and procedures.* San Francisco: Pearson/Benjamin Cummings.

Travis, J.W., & Ryan, R.S. (2004). *Wellness workbook* (3rd ed.). Berkeley, CA: Celestial Arts.

United Way of America Strategic Institute. (1992). *What lies ahead: A decade of decision.* Alexandria, VA: Author.

U.S. Department of Commerce. (1999). *Statistical abstract of the United States.* Washington, D.C.: Government Printing Office.

Verespej, M.A. (2000). Stressed out. *Industry Week, 249*(4), 30-34.

Wankel, L.M. (1994). Health and leisure: Inextricably linked. *Journal of Physical Education, Recreation and Dance, 65*(4), 28-33.

Weiskopf, D. (1982). *Recreation and leisure: Improving the quality of life.* Boston: Allyn & Bacon.

Witt, P.A., & Crompton, J.L. (2002). *Best practices in youth development in public park and recreation settings.* Ashburn, VA: National Recreation and Park Association.

World Health Organization. (2001). International classification of functioning, disability and health. Retrieved February 21, 2004, from www3.who.int/icf/icftemplate.cfm?myurl=homepage.html.

Yoder, R., Nelson, D., & Smith, D. (1989). Added purpose versus rote exercise in female nursing home residents. *American Journal of Occupational Therapy, 43*(9), 581-586.

CHAPTER 2

The Profession of Leisure Programming

In this chapter, you can look forward to the following:

- Discovering a variety of leisure service delivery systems where programmers might serve
- Adopting the necessary personal qualities and philosophies of a successful recreation programmer
- Making a commitment to the ideas of professionalism and the activities that foster professionalism in the leisure services fields
- Making initial decisions about your own future programming career

The YMCA is a private not-for-profit membership organization that relies heavily on volunteers and fund-raising efforts to support a multitude of programs and services. Facilities that include lodging, food service, gyms, pools, general purpose rooms, weight rooms, tracks, fields, and more are available for the widest range of recreation programs and services. Staffing consists of paid leisure programmers who organize activities around a central theme of core values to be gained through the program and a host of volunteers who work with the staff. Youth and adult members engage in programs delivering a strong message of Christian values, including youth development and family-oriented leisure involvement:

> To put Christian principles into practice through programs that build healthy spirit, mind, and body for all. (YMCA, n.d.)

The YMCA provides opportunities for youth and families to participate in positive activities, where the goal is to enhance self-esteem, values, confidence, and many other attributes. For more information on this topic, see worksheet 2.1 in chapter 2 of the CD-ROM.

At some point in your professional career in leisure services you will be a **programmer**, someone who plans, coordinates, executes, and evaluates recreational opportunities and experiences. Whether you are employed by a hospital, nature center, camp, community center, theme park, resort, national park, rehabilitation clinic, professional sports team, or any of thousands of other agencies and organizations, your responsibilities will at least initially include programming recreational experiences for people. In some situations you will be the only programmer on the staff—planning, creating, implementing, leading, and evaluating all the programs yourself. Other times you will be a member of the organization's programming staff, such as the director of sports, with responsibilities for specific activities. After you've developed some experience and tenure in the organization, you will likely seek promotion to a more supervisory role, where you oversee other staff in the delivery of program services. For more information on this topic, see "More Options for Individual Programming Practice," option 2, and "Group Discussion Ideas," option 3, in chapter 2 of the CD-ROM.

Before delving into the details of how programs are planned, implemented, and evaluated, in this chapter we make a very important pause in our discussion. What can you expect from a career that includes recreation programming? What are the types of agencies, companies, or organizations in which you might try to find employment? As a professional, what is expected of you both in terms of personal qualities and in representing a professional field?

The opportunities to organize programs are many.

Organizational Settings

Some refer to programming as the organized leisure service system (Kraus, Barber, & Shapiro, 2001b). What does this mean? The term **system** is used to identify any assembly of entities that share purposes and processes. Further, in a system, the various elements are interrelated so that what happens in one affects all others. Thus, in the organized leisure service system, or **leisure service delivery system**, various agencies, companies, and organizations have in common such processes as staffing, facilities, and fiscal operations. And, although there are some differences, they all have as their purpose the provision of leisure opportunities and options for consumers.

One characteristic of the leisure service delivery system that stands out is its diversification. Such specific enterprises as a cruise ship, a playground, a Boy Scout troop, and a theater are all considered "members" of the system. So is an international park, your campus recreational sport services, Walt Disney World, and the neighborhood tavern. Some of these members are so complex and expansive that they themselves can be considered subsystems. For example, armed forces recreation and therapeutic recreation services represent a complex systematic structure of many different agencies.

Another prominent characteristic of the leisure service delivery system is its pervasiveness. You can test this yourself. Board a city or town bus; as you ride the entire route, jot down all the different buildings, properties, agencies, companies, and so on that have something to do with people enjoying themselves. You'll be amazed! In our small town, for example, in a stroll from the campus up the four blocks of the main street, we counted 42 different leisure-related sites. For more information on this topic, see "Group Discussion Ideas," option 1, in chapter 2 of the CD-ROM.

To reflect this diverse magnitude, the leisure service delivery system can be organized into major categories. We'll adopt the 10 categories presented by Kraus, Barber, and Shapiro (2001b) because they represent the most common understanding of the field. Even though these can be summarized, as in table 2.1, some types of leisure service organizations have not been captured here, and some organizations can arguably be placed in more than one category. In other words, this summary is neither complete nor conclusive. Notice, for example, that some categories describe the type of sponsorship (such as government, commercial, and private membership), while others are categorized according to recreation activity (such as sport, tourism and hospitality, and therapeutic recreation). Let's discuss each category in more detail.

Governmental Recreation and Park Agencies

Public, or governmental, organizations provide networks of parks, community centers, and sports facilities for all citizens of a particular local, state, or federal locale. Governmentally sponsored agencies also directly support such important leisure services as libraries, museums, public gardens, concert halls, and nature centers. Often at state (or provincial) and federal levels, the service reach includes such travel and hospitality entities as lodges, cabins, campgrounds, tour buses, and dining rooms. Program services by governmental agencies are typically supported by tax funds as well as fees and charges, grants, and other sources of financing.

Programming positions are available in a wide variety of government-sponsored leisure activity areas. These positions are usually filled by means of the **civil service** procedure of awarding jobs—based on education, experience, or skill requirements. Governments are major employers of persons with the appropriate skills and education. Both of us began our careers as family fitness programmers and leaders for the San Diego Park and Recreation Department.

Nonprofit Community Organizations

Nonprofit community organizations offer recreation services as part of a total multiservice approach that may also include education, job training, leadership development, companionship, and other socially beneficial functions. Sometimes referred to as voluntary agencies, such organizations as the Boys and Girls Clubs, Camp Fire USA, the Police Athletic League, Boy Scouts and Girl Scouts, and the YMCA rely heavily on volunteer leadership, donations, and other community agency partnerships. Although not restricted to youth-serving goals, nonprofit community agencies do place a high priority on offering recreation programs for youth development. You'll want to consider a programming career within this category of the leisure service system if you enjoy helping people and society meet social needs primarily through sports, outdoor recreation, and hobbies. For an example of nonprofit services, see the box on page 21. For more information on this topic, see "Group Discussion Ideas," option 6, in chapter 2 of the CD-ROM.

TABLE 2.1

Categories of the Leisure Service System

Organization type	Organization description	Program services range	Example
Governmental recreation and park agencies	Services sponsored by federal or national, state or provincial, and local governments	Primarily tax-supported services for the public at large	Westerville Parks and Recreation Department
Nonprofit community organizations	Services provided by the voluntary efforts of community residents	Primarily youth-serving advocacy services	Big Brothers/Big Sisters of Greater Montreal
Private membership organizations	Services provided for and by members	Usually according to socioeconomic class, special interests, or residential status	Phuket Country Club, Thailand
Employee services	Services provided by industry and corporation employers to employees	Usually focused on health-related functions	Chase Manhattan Bank's corporate challenge running series
Armed forces recreation organizations	In the United States, services provided by the Morale, Welfare, and Recreation (MWR) branch	Recreational programs focused on maintaining combat readiness and reenlistment	Fort Benning MWR
Campus recreation organizations	Services for students, faculty, and staff of colleges and universities	Primarily physical, social, and cultural recreation pursuits	Butler University's Culture Club
Commercial recreation businesses	Varied services for paying customers	Primarily sport, outdoor recreation and adventure, cultural arts, entertainment, and media pursuits	Sun Peaks Ski Resort, British Columbia
Therapeutic recreation services	Services offered by many different kinds of sponsors for persons with disabilities or illnesses	Use of recreation skills and participation for treatment of illness or disability	Inclusion Services, City of Henderson, Nevada
Sport services	Services offered by many kinds of sponsors in sports, athletics, and games	Sports	Disabled Women in Sport, Feminist Majority Foundation
Tourism and hospitality	Tour, lodging, dining, and entertainment services	Vacation-related	Windjammer Barefoot Cruises

Based on R. Kraus, E. Barber, and I. Shapiro, 2001a.

Private Membership Organizations

Private membership organizations are similar to nonprofit agencies, but with some important differences. For example, although the Girl Scouts is also a membership-based organization, its membership is not very restrictive, and its primary mission is to serve the developmental needs of girls and communities. On the other hand, the Catholic Youth Organization; the South Hills Tennis Club in Charleston, West Virginia; and Leisure World retirement villages are more restrictive in membership and are focused primarily on giving members what they want. Programming positions in private membership organizations might

Girl Guides Respond to Tsunami Disaster

In most of the world, *Girl Guides* is the name attached to the program sponsor that Americans call Girl Scouts. The following report was written by a Girl Guide from Malaysia after the devastating tsunami that struck southeastern Asia in late December 2004. Programs sometimes simply present themselves.

The tsunami hit the northern side of Kedah on 26 December 2004 at 1:30 p.m. Two districts in Kedah were badly affected and with fatalities. A total of 4,278 victims from 1,048 families were placed at eight relief centers. Girl Guides of Kedah Branch visited the relief center at Sekolah Kebangsaan Juala Muda on 28 December and Sekolah Kebangsaan Hj Sulaiman on 29 December. Guides asked the elderly victims what they need and immediately started collecting the items and distributed the next day. Guides also provided service to the elderly by preparing food for them, feeding them, assisting them to the toilet, and comforting them. Two families were adopted as a special project by the Girl Guides of Kedah. One of them is an elderly lady, Embon bt Ahmad, 85 years old from the Padang Salem village. This lady stays alone and the guides will assist her in the process of moving back to her house.

Reprinted from World Association of Girl Guides and Girl Scouts, www.wagggsworld.org/newsroom/tsunami_relief/index.html.

Raytheon Missile Systems

In 2002, Raytheon Missile Systems of Tucson, Arizona, received national recognition as the most outstanding employee services program from the Employee Services Management Association, a professional society that provides companies with ideas and resources for creating employee leisure services. Raytheon's WorkLife and Wellness Program earned the award based on its well-rounded offerings, which tie into its corporate culture and bottom-line goals. Included in the distinction are the fitness facilities, diversity organizations, volunteer program, commuter services, and dependent care program.

Adapted from a news release by the Employee Services Management Association, www.esmassn.org/2003raytheon.pdf.

professional development has become the Employee Services Management Association (ESMA), a professional organization with more than 2,300 companies as members. The term **coordinator** is often used for those providing employee recreation programs.

Armed Forces Recreation Organizations

Within the armed forces, the system of leisure services in the United States is labeled Morale, Welfare, and Recreation (MWR). Supported by Congress, as well as by user fees, the Navy, Army, Air Force, and Marine Corps assign thousands of both uniformed and civilian employees to recreation responsibilities at installations around the world. Programs in sport, outdoor recreation, hobbies, travel, entertainment, and special events are designed to make such a positive contribution to the military life of soldiers and sailors that they will be combat ready as well as want to reenlist. If you are interested in civilian employment in armed forces MWR programs, explore the possibilities through the wide range of internship opportunities available through your college. This applies to the Canadian Armed Forces and the military systems in other countries as well.

Campus Recreation Organizations

Do you enjoy campus life? Well, why not stay around? Campus recreation is a major area for career possibilities in leisure programming. Every college and

oversee sports, recreation skills classes, social events, and cultural activities.

Employee Services

Originally known as industrial recreation, contemporary employee services provide programs ranging from holiday events, sports leagues, and special interest activities aimed at building a sense of camaraderie and loyalty among company employees, to charter travel arrangements, stores, fitness centers, and even high school equivalency diploma classes. The point is to help employees lead more healthful and productive lives, as with Raytheon's employee services programs, described in the second box on this page. Today, typical programs include stress management, weight control, and substance abuse cessation. The payoff for the company, of course, is healthier employees, which both increases work productivity and decreases insurance costs. Since few college and university curricula offer specialized options in employee services, the main source of

Colleges and universities have excellent recreation facilities and programs.

martial arts studios offer a wide range of program-based employment options. Yet, unlike most governmental and nonprofit leisure service organizations in a community, recreation businesses do not often have clearly classified job descriptions or hiring procedures. In many cases, acquiring a programming position will depend on being at the right place, being there at the right time, and knowing the right people. An important exception to this, however, is commercial enterprises that require certified programmers and leaders, such as fitness centers and outdoor leadership schools. Also, in such settings as campgrounds, tennis centers, and bowling centers, the term **event specialist** is often used for those who plan major recreation programs that are more extensive than routine programming.

university campus offers recreation programs for students, faculty, and staff. Primarily, these programs involve active forms of recreation, such as intramural sports, club sports, and outdoor recreation. Similar to armed forces recreation in purpose, campus recreation programs are designed to promote student well-being and morale so that academic and other developmental tasks can be achieved—and ultimately so that students remain in college to graduate. Some colleges organize dormitory-based programs, while others have a campuswide department labeled "campus life." Student unions also typically sponsor a great deal of programming for the campus. While you are in college is an excellent time to become acquainted with the campus recreation system by serving in a leadership, part-time employment, or volunteer role.

Commercial Recreation Businesses

Another common way of categorizing organizational settings is as commercial recreation businesses, which provide recreational programs for the purpose of making a profit. Enterprises such as billiard and bowling centers, dance studios and commercial ballrooms, golf courses, tennis centers, outdoor leadership schools, video arcades, flying centers, campgrounds, hunting and fishing services, health and fitness spas, white-water rafting companies, and

Therapeutic Recreation Services

Therapeutic recreation is a major component of the leisure service delivery system. This sector is a melting pot of various sponsor and program types. For example, commercial hospitals, private rehabilitation centers, nonprofit extended-care services, public recreation and park departments, colleges and universities, and many other different kinds of sponsors include recreation programming within their service reach for persons with illnesses or disabilities. If you are interested in these employment opportunities, you will be able to choose a job situation either according to the nature of the client, such as working with hospitalized children, or according to the type of recreation experience, such as outdoor recreation in a community. Regardless, you will use recreation programs as a tool for the cure, adjustment, accommodation, or improvement of an illness or disabling condition. In certain clinical settings, programmers who have majored in therapeutic recreation in an accredited college or university are usually hired.

Sport Services

Some opportunities are available to provide programs within a sport services subsystem. Sport represents a huge force in the lives of millions of North Americans. This field has immense economic implications as well as growth and development potential. It is also an entertainment business, offering active direct participation as well as spectator roles. As with the therapeutic recreation category, sport programs are not provided by a single type of agency. Schools and colleges, public recreation departments, nonprofit and voluntary organizations, private clubs, employee services departments, and commercial businesses all offer sport as an integral part of their programming. Many different kinds of programming employment opportunities are available in sport, including coaching and officiating, athletic conditioning and fitness coordination, sports facilities management, sports league directing, sports manufacturing and sales, and even sports journalism. For example, the U.S. Armed Forces provide extensive sport programming for both enlisted personnel and officers, as well as their families. This program, overseen by the Department of Defense, includes annual worldwide championships in 18 different sports.

Tourism and Hospitality Services

Finally, the leisure service delivery system includes tourism and hospitality. Although we may have correctly included this category within commercial recreation businesses, we've singled it out because collectively it represents a major industry for the entire world. In fact, for 83 percent of countries, tourism is one of the top five elements of the economy (World Tourism Organization, n.d.). Tourism itself represents a complex system encompassing holiday and vacation travel, sports travel, cultural travel, beaches and theme parks, hotels and resorts, conferences and conventions, cruise lines, restaurants, airlines, and retail shops—just to name a few. There are many low-paying entry-level positions in tourism that often serve as a threshold to more responsible and financially rewarding career positions (Kraus, Barber, & Shapiro, 2001b). For an example of employment information in tourism, see the box on this page.

Many communities have extensive leisure service for-profit centers such as this fitness facility.

© Human Kinetics.

Audition Call-Out for Sesame Place

Sesame Place, near Philadelphia, Pennsylvania, is a commercial playground themed around the popular children's television program *Sesame Street*. Here is an excerpt from a recent employment newsletter:

> Seeking performers who are 16 and older to entertain families and children. Entertainers will be hired for 110 positions from all performing disciplines. There are many opportunities, including dancers who perform as Elmo and Cookie Monster and singers who perform in live stage shows. General entertainers performing as Big Bird are also sought to greet visitors throughout the day. Says Michael Joyce, director of entertainment, "It is so important for the staff playing these lovable characters to be able to perform with a smile as that will come right through the costume!"

Reprinted from Sesame Place, 2004, www.sesameplace.com/sesame/pa/news/new_auditions_2004.html.

For more information on this topic, see worksheet 2.2 in chapter 2 of the CD-ROM.

One term in use within tourism is that of **concierge**, one who coordinates many guest- or patron-centered events and opportunities when tourists visit areas. For more information on this topic, see "Individual Programming Practice," option 3, "Individual Programming Practice," option 4, and "Group Discussion Ideas," option 4, in chapter 2 of the CD-ROM.

Personal Qualities

Your exact role as a recreation programmer will be determined by the size and type of your organization, the amount and qualifications of other staff, the organizational mission and goals, the budgetary and physical resources, and such other factors as your own interests. Beyond all these differences, however, is a common set of qualities that programmers must possess in order to be successful. These include empathy, energy, integrity, and vision.

Empathy

Because programmers base their efforts on the needs and interests of constituents and consumers, they must be able to empathize with them. Even if your mission is to make a profit, such as for a commercial recreation company, you will fail if you are not focused on the problems and desires of the end users. The program planning procedure is foremost based on your willingness to listen and learn—to determine what it is like to "be in another person's shoes." Some describe this as having people-centered qualities. At its root, empathy means having a genuine respect and liking for others and enthusiasm for their differences.

Energy

You've no doubt already guessed from the size of this book that recreation program planning is a major professional endeavor. Thus, it takes energy, or the ability to be a self-initiator and maintain a sustained effort. Programming for recreation requires vigor and enterprise to meet and creatively master constant new challenges. In other words, you must be willing to work hard, often putting in long hours. Other people's free hours are typically the recreation program professional's working hours. It is not uncommon for programmers to work on office-related responsibilities during the day and then supervise programs

Programming coordination requires a great deal of personal investment and energy.

© Human Kinetics.

in the evening, or to work regularly on weekends and holidays, when many recreational activities are scheduled.

Integrity

Integrity is another important quality of successful programmers. In a world increasingly bombarded with accusations of impropriety, it is crucial that professionals in the leisure service delivery system maintain a high level of ethical care. For participants to believe they are being treated with dignity and fairness, they must first be treated this way by their programming professionals. This means being forthright, truthful, ethical, and responsible to participants. Particularly if you are working in sport programs, you'll discover the power of your efforts to help people learn to treat each other graciously. Integrity abuses are not inherent in sport, but they do come about frequently, perhaps because of pressures to win.

Vision

Finally, the quality of vision, or an ability to project the intended direction of a programming plan, is necessary. To be able to "do it," you must first be able to visualize its positive outcome. When vision is lacking, the task is nearly impossible. This suggests that your contributions to recreation program services will be greatly hampered if you cannot at first dream them. For example, the campus recreation department at Loyola University Chicago has this vision for its program constituents:

> We are committed to recognizing and appreciating our customers as unique. We encourage them to expect excellent service and we seek to exceed their expectations. When we make a mistake, we admit it and learn from it. When we have dissatisfied customers, we listen to them very carefully, without being defensive, and treat them with respect.

Loyola University, Chicago, n.d., www.luc.edu/depts/campusrec/home.shtml#mission.

There are other important programmer qualities as well. Our list could also include competence, creativity, authenticity, organization skills, courage, maturity, willingness to take risks, sense of humor, problem-solving skills, love of life, affability, and many others. From your own experiences as participants in recreation programs, we're sure you can think of some additional qualities. Perhaps what all these boil down to, regardless of the organizational setting, is a service-to-people philosophy. For more information on this topic, see "More Options for Individual Programming Practice," option 1, and "Group Discussion Ideas," option 2, in chapter 2 of the CD-ROM.

Professionalism

By now you realize that leisure services programmers are professionals. We are members of a profession, and we personify qualities that reflect professionalism. Sounds simple enough, but what does it actually include? As you can see from the career paths of Phyllis and Curtis in the case on page 26, many avenues are available for becoming a professional in leisure programming. These include developing specific attributes, acquiring a college specialist degree, taking courses and attending professional association conferences, receiving in-service training, and becoming certified.

Specific Programmer Attributes

Although there are many specializations inherent in programming leisure services, we believe that once an individual has adopted the professional skills for program management, she is capable of programming any type of service she is assigned. That noted, it is important to identify the attributes that may be inherent in specialized programs in order to create awareness of some of the unique aspects of particular programs. Table 2.2 shows examples of

TABLE 2.2

Programmer Skills

Programming types	Certification needed	Other skills
Aquatics	Yes	Swimming, diving, rescue skills, and so on
Cultural arts	No	Aesthetics and technical skills
Sport	Often; in fitness programs, for example	Sport-specific and coaching skills
Outdoors	Often; in wilderness programs, for example	Risk awareness and technical skills
Performing arts	No	Aesthetics and technical skills
Therapeutic recreation	Yes	Adaptation and modification skills
Youth	Yes	Social service, group dynamics, youth development skills

The Programming Process: The Professionals

Meet Phyllis and Curtis. Phyllis Self is the recreation superintendent and Curtis Wright is the facilities superintendent for the Westerville Parks and Recreation Department. Phyllis programs services for preschoolers, youth, and adults in art, fitness, sport, special event, and therapeutic recreation. Curtis, meanwhile, is responsible for facilities, including buildings, parks, and baseball fields. Even though they have separate responsibilities for the city's recreation services, they meet together daily to combine their individual efforts into a coordinated planning process.

Phyllis and Curtis have chosen different routes to their careers in leisure programming.

How did Phyllis and Curtis get such important careers? Through very different paths, actually. Both professionals illustrate the range and variety of choices and directions available within the leisure service delivery system.

Phyllis began as a programmer in the United States Air Force, first working at a NATO base in Turkey and then as a recreation program supervisor in Okinawa, Japan. After returning to the United States, she noticed an advertisement for a part-time recreation program position with the city of Kettering, Ohio. She jumped at the opportunity and, within six months, became a full-time program supervisor, remaining for 14 years. Her only reason for moving to Westerville was the opportunity to work with director Jody Stowers. Phyllis intends to stay a recreation programmer for the rest of her career.

Curtis followed a different career path. While completing his bachelor's and master's degrees in recreation from Eastern Kentucky University, he gained some hands-on programming experience with the YMCA and through camping. After graduation, he worked as a youth programmer for the Westerville Parks and Recreation Department, soon receiving a promotion to community center operations manager. Promotion to his current position as superintendent of all facilities followed, and Curtis sees his next career move to be either an agency director's position at a similar-sized department as Westerville or a facilities superintendent position with a larger organization. His goal is to use his programming skills and know-how to move up the organizational ladder. For more information on this topic, see worksheet 2.3 in chapter 2 of the CD-ROM.

what specialized skills may be necessary for those who provide direct leadership in programs. The program planner can then hire personnel with the appropriate backgrounds for that direct leadership requirement.

College Degrees

Many of you are probably enrolled in a college or university degree program in one of the recreation fields. Recently, the Society of Park and Recreation Educators listed 381 leisure-related curricula in the United States and Canada (NRPA, n.d.a). Available degrees include associate, bachelor's, master's, directorate, and doctorate in such majors as park and resource management, outdoor recreation, therapeutic recreation, sports management, tourism management, recreation programming and leadership, and youth services management. These degree programs teach students about their roles in the leisure service delivery system, including necessary technical skills and theoretical and philosophical guidelines. Typically, colleges and universities establish special institutes and provide workshops and learning events that enhance working professionals' knowledge and service delivery skills. They also offer certification assistance to practitioners already working in the field, as well as a menu of online professional preparation and continuing education courses.

The National Recreation and Park Association offers many professional support and enhancement opportunities.

Continuing Education

Professional associations regularly provide **continuing education** workshops and courses. For example, in just one month, the National Recreation and Park Association (NRPA) directly offers or cosponsors an average of 20 conferences and courses, including the National Playground Safety Institute Program and the Aquatic Facility Operator Course. The International Association of Amusement Parks and Attractions sponsors professional education programs in financial management, risk management, merchandising, and insurance coverage. State and provincial professional societies, such as the LRPA (Louisiana Recreation and Park Association), also conduct annual conferences that offer educational sessions.

In-Service Training

Leisure service agencies typically provide **in-service training** to their own employees. In-service training can include agency-sponsored instructional presentations, technical assistance, or hands-on experiences that provide continual professional development for staff. These can range from the spring orientation for new playground leaders to a comprehensive and ongoing training regime, such as that provided by the YMCA, Boy Scouts, armed forces, and Police Athletic League. For example, the YMCA sponsors an extensive range of courses and certification authorization, including aquatics, camping, child care, health and fitness, sports, teen leadership, and youth and community development. As well, organizations focused on particular aspects of programming provide educational opportunities for staff and members. For example, the Catholic Youth Organization sponsors conferences and workshops designed to upgrade the level of youth sports coaching and league management.

Certification

For many in the leisure fields, all this education and training culminate in **certification**. The purpose of certification is to assess competence according to a set of performance standards to determine if practitioners have the needed skills and abilities for particular types of employment opportunities. In a sense, the professional certification process is an agreement of verification, accountability, and control between society and the leisure professions. Its ultimate point is to protect the leisure services consumer.

Professional certification is a voluntary process in which an individual submits her credentials for review based on identified competencies or standards. In the leisure services fields, certification provides individual recognition and enhances self-esteem, but it also promotes respect for the profession itself. It enhances the credibility of the individual professional and the profession at large by providing a reward system for those who achieve a high level of professionalism.

Some programs offer certification for programmers and leaders, including aerobics, personal fitness training, swimming and boating safety, scuba, sports refereeing, rock climbing, and wilderness rescue. Certification requirements also apply in many of the service delivery system categories. For example, for a number of years, the Employee Services Management Association (ESMA) has authorized certification of recreation services directors in companies throughout the United States. In therapeutic recreation, the National Council for Therapeutic Recreation Certification (NCTRC) is a nonprofit organization founded in 1981 to develop and manage professional certification standards for these program professionals. Today, there are more than 16,000 actively certified therapeutic recreation specialists (NCTRC, n.d.).

In Canada, many national and provincial professional societies have initiated certification procedures (Kraus & Curtis, 2000). For example, the Coaching Association of Canada (CAC) has a five-stage certification process that determines eligibility to coach sports according to community, school, or club levels.

In 1981, in the United States, the NRPA instituted a national certification plan. For example, to qualify as a certified park and recreation professional (CPRP), you must have one of the following combinations of education and experience (NRPA, n.d.b):

- A bachelor's degree from an NRPA/AAPAR-accredited (American Association for Physical Activity and Recreation) program, verified by official transcript, plus successful completion of the CPRP examination

or
- A bachelor's or higher degree from a non-NRPA/AAPAR-accredited program, verified by official transcript; with a major in recreation, park resources, and leisure services; and no less than two years of full-time experience in a recreation, park resources, and leisure ser-

vices position after the degree, plus successful completion of the CPRP examination

or
- A bachelor's or higher degree from a non-NRPA/AAPAR-accredited program, verified by official transcript; with a major other than recreation, park resources, and leisure services; and no less than five years of full-time experience in a recreation, park resources, and leisure services position after the degree, plus successful completion of the CPRP examination

For more information on this topic, see "Group Discussion Ideas," option 7, in chapter 2 of the CD-ROM.

Summary

This chapter focuses on the careers of programmers—professionals who design and deliver programmed leisure. You should understand the following key points:

- There is a wide variety of settings, roles, and career paths for recreation programmers.
- Organizational settings include governmental, nonprofit community, commercial business, private membership, employee services, armed forces, college campus recreation, therapeutic recreation, sport, and travel and hospitality.
- Many options are available to those preparing for a career in leisure programming, including college degree specialization, in-service and continuing education events, and online course work.
- This education often culminates in professional certification.
- Regardless of the road taken to become a professional leisure programmer, you will foremost need the qualities of energy, empathy, integrity, and vision.

For more information on this topic, see "Can You Solve This Programming Issue?" in chapter 2 of the CD-ROM.

Glossary

programmer—One who plans, coordinates, executes, and evaluates recreation opportunities and experiences.

system—Any interrelated entities that share purposes and processes.

leisure service delivery system—The organizations that provide recreation program opportunities.

civil service—An impartial means of classifying and awarding government jobs based on education, experience, or skill requirements.

coordinator—One who organizes details of leisure programming.

event specialist—One who coordinates major program areas that are more extensive than routine programming.

concierge—In the accommodations setting, the person who coordinates guest activities.

continuing education—Learning events that enhance working professionals' knowledge and service delivery skills.

in-service training—Agency-sponsored instructional presentations, technical assistance, and hands-on experiences that provide continual professional development for staff.

certification—A process of assessment to determine if practitioners have the needed skills and abilities for particular types of employment positions.

References

Employee Services Management Association. (2003, June). Raytheon missile systems wins top honor for employee services that recruit and retain top employees. Retrieved June 17, 2003, from www.esmassn.org/2003raytheon.pdf.

Kraus, R., Barber, E., & Shapiro, I. (2001a). *Creative management in recreation, parks, and leisure services* (6th ed). Boston: McGraw-Hill Companies.

Kraus, R., Barber, E., & Shapiro, I. (2001b). *Introduction to leisure services: Career perspectives.* Champaign, IL: Sagamore.

Kraus, R.G., & Curtis, J.E. (2000). *Creative management in recreation, parks, and leisure services* (6th ed.). Boston: McGraw-Hill.

Loyola University Chicago. (n.d.). Campus recreation home page. Retrieved February 5, 2007, from www.luc.edu/depts/campusrec/home.shtml#mission.

NCTRC. (n.d.a). Home page. Retrieved January 11, 2005, from www.nctrc.org.

NRPA. (n.d.b). Accreditation/certification. Retrieved January 11, 2005, from www.nrpa.org/content/default.aspx?documentId=26.

NRPA. (n.d.). Certification levels defined. Retrieved February 4, 2007, from www.nrpa.org/content/default.aspx?documentID=1063.

Sesame Place. (n.d.). Anheuser-Busch Adventure Parks career opportunities. Retrieved January 11, 2005, from www.sesameplace.com/sesame/pa/news/new_auditions_2004.html, site now discontinued.

World Association of Girl Guides and Girl Scouts. (n.d.). Tsunami report. Retrieved January 10, 2005, from www.wagggsworld.org/newsroom/tsunami_relief/index.html, site now discontinued.

World Tourism Organization. (n.d.). Why tourism? Retrieved January 11, 2005, from www.world-tourism.org/aboutwto/eng/menu.html.

YMCA. (n.d.). Home page. Retrieved November 15, 2005, from www.ymca.net.

CHAPTER 3

Programming Principles

In this chapter, you can look forward to the following:

- Appreciating the role of overarching professional beliefs or principles in shaping high-quality leisure programs
- Developing an understanding of principles of leisure programming such as service quality, customer service, customer satisfaction, diversity, public good, environmental compatibility, efficiency, and continuous improvement
- Developing a commitment to adopting these principles

ort Benning MWR supports a major infantry unit of the U.S. Army. *MWR* stands for Morale, Welfare, and Recreation; and for Fort Benning in Georgia, this department serves the leisure and well-being needs of more than 165,000 active-duty military personnel and their family members, as well as retirees and civilian employees. As the name suggests, MWR programs directly use planned leisure services to boost the morale and enhance the overall welfare of the base community.

For example, on the southwestern side of Fort Benning is a place to enjoy tall trees, cool and deep waters, and abundant wildlife. This is Uchee Creek Army Campground and Marina—a getaway where military staff and their families can spend a weekend or an entire vacation along the scenic Chattahoochee River.

At Fort Benning, MWR leisure program services such as the campground and marina are grounded in programming principles that include quality, customer service, public good, diversity, and environmental compatibility.

Once you've read more of this book, you'll realize that successful programming of leisure experiences requires a great deal of complex knowledge and abilities. Gone are the days (thankfully) of tossing out a playground ball and seeing what happens. Today's professionals apply a system of approaches and techniques, including tested procedures, so that the recreation programs they offer to constituents are the very highest quality and accomplish their goals.

For this reason, it is important to consider the basics of high-quality professional practice. In this chapter we focus on the most important principles in programming leisure experiences. Wholeheartedly abiding by these best practices is enough to ensure solid professional practice, even if you don't master all the techniques taught in this book—they're that important.

Such overarching principles are called axioms. An **axiom** connotes something worthy—a self-evident truth. Axioms are widely accepted by professionals in all corners of the leisure services fields simply on their intrinsic merit. We consider the axioms of quality, customer service, customer satisfaction, diversity, public good, environmental compatibility, efficiency, and continuous improvement. For more information on this topic, see worksheet 3.1 in chapter 3 of the CD-ROM.

Quality

The first axiom of programming leisure is quality. Programmers must achieve and deliver excellent quality. This means being and doing the best you can—emulating those who are outstanding in the field and striving for world-class services. Consumers of recreation programs have the right to receive professionally prepared services that are of the highest quality. Although many of the principles that follow (such as customer satisfaction and continuous improvement) could be considered aspects of this first axiom, we feature quality here—front and center—to emphasize its role in all that programmers seek to accomplish.

What do we mean by *quality*? Many schools of thought exist, and many have established reputations for themselves by proposing various theories about quality. For example, over the years the concept has carried such labels as quality inspection, quality control, and quality assurance. Lately, the idea has been tagged with the label of total quality management, or TQM, suggesting a philosophical approach to managing that emphasizes such techniques as the empowerment of employees (Dale, 1999).

Therefore, there are numerous ways of defining quality. We define it as excellence. This means that quality is more than catering to the needs of program participants and achieving the mission of the program's sponsoring organization. It is doing these things in a way that goes beyond what is minimally required. It is providing the very best programs via the very best programming practices. It is what Berry, Zeithaml, and Parasuraman (1985) call the "service surprise." For more information on this topic, see "Group Discussion Ideas," option 4, in chapter 3 of the CD-ROM.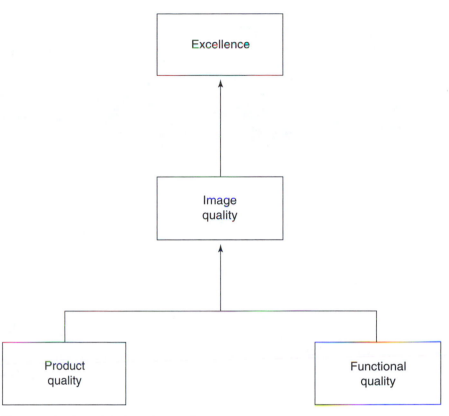

To extend this idea, we can adapt a simple model of quality from Gronroos (1990). In this perspective, excellence is made up of three kinds of quality (see figure 3.1). The first is **product quality**, which is the "what" of the recreation program. It is the quality of the specific recreational pursuit, event, or program service, and it is usually measured by customers' opinions. The second type of quality is **functional quality**, which is the "how" of the recreation program. It is the quality of the method of delivering the program, the abilities of the staff, the sufficiency of the funding, the suitability of the location, and so on. Functional quality is measured in a variety of ways including cost analysis, staff evaluations, and site inspections.

According to the model, both product quality and functional quality are filtered through **image quality**, which includes the quality of the reputation of the program and organization and perceptions of these qualities from the past. Through image quality, then, excellence is ultimately achieved. Yet image quality can either enhance or detract from product and functional qualities; therefore, excellence is not stationary—it must be constantly sought.

Leisure services programmers pay attention to all three of the quality factors—product, functional, and image. Yet the filtering action of image quality can create perceptions of product quality and functional quality that may or may not be accurate. Thus programmers often devote significant time and energy to creating positive image quality. Indeed, many things must be done to create the perception

Figure 3.1 A model of service quality.

Adapted from Gronroos, 1990, p. 38.

of excellence in service quality. For example, image quality itself requires planning and evaluation. Image quality must be sought by being innovative, seeking constant improvements, having a future orientation, getting things right the first time, attending to detail, and taking pride in and caring about the work. Staff must assume personal responsibility for quality. For more information on this topic, see "More Options for Individual Programming Practice," option 1, in chapter 3 of the CD-ROM.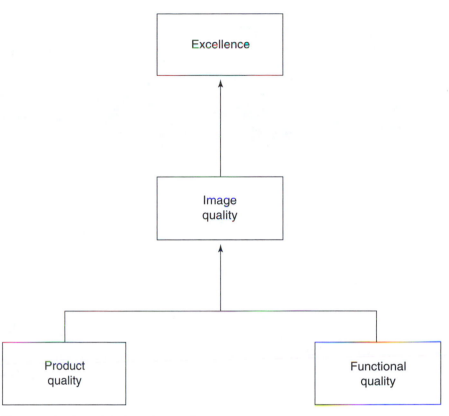

Customer Service

Recreation programs serve people—consumers, clients, constituents, customers. A commitment to customer care is not new, but it is perhaps more important than ever. Without people to participate in leisure program services, there *are* no leisure program services and likely no leisure service organizations. For this reason, the belief that the customer is paramount, and that the customer is to

Both the external customer and the internal customer must be treated with care and respect for leisure program success.

sponsoring organization must be cared for, too. For example, the marketing department of a theater is an internal customer. Behind-the-scenes staff especially deserve respect and attentiveness. Internal customers are just as important as external customers for successful programming. Their satisfaction and support may make or break a program.

Customer service is based on respecting the expectations of program participants. Customer expectations include the following:

- *Value for the money.* The value of the programmed leisure experience depends on many things. Even if the program is free, participants expect a certain level of worth. A program's worth is defined by many nonabsolute elements, including personal experience, preferences and tastes, amount of money available to spend, and perception of benefits received. These are all very tricky elements to manage. For example, customers may assign a higher importance to certain parts of the experience (restaurants available during the car trip to the trail head) than does the programmer (the five days of backpacking). As well, different customers may perceive the same experience differently, and the same customer may view an experience differently from one time to the next. Sometimes people see what they want to see and have a good time (or a miserable time) because they were determined to.

be treated well, is central to our best programming practices (see the box on page 35). A customer-service-oriented programmer has a "high degree of responsiveness, attentiveness and willingness to help others" (Albrecht & Zemke, 1985, p. 39). This ethic is tempered, by the way, with an understanding that customers do not always know what they want, how to make choices, or where to find resources. This is why you plan and offer the program!

Two types of customers are important to the professional leisure programmer: external customers and internal customers. **External customers** are the participants, users, buyers, patients, patrons, athletes, spectators, visitors, and tourists—the people directly served by the recreation program. The Walt Disney Company is so careful about customer service that employees refer to their customers as guests. This label reflects their commitment to hospitality—courteously placing the needs of their customers first. For more information on this topic, see "Group Discussion Ideas," option 1, in chapter 3 of the CD-ROM. ⊙

The designation of **internal customers** acknowledges that the people working within the program-

- *The experience as described.* Participants in recreation programs expect to experience what was promised. This means that advertising, brochures, catalogs, and Web sites must be up to date and accurate in their descriptions of programs. It also means program managers and leaders must deliver the services described there. Consumer protection legislation and contract law apply as well to make sure program services are not misrepresented. The expectation for receiving what was promised is so

• *A feeling of appreciation.* Every customer must be made to feel special, admired, and appreciated. In the daily life of a programmer, this at times means prioritizing assistance to a customer over attention to the tasks on that day's to-do list. Participants in programmed leisure expect an atmosphere of positive energy and zestfulness. No matter how many times program leaders have offered the program, each participant, every time, must be made to feel special.

• *Advocacy.* Programmers must go beyond serving customers, clients, and participants and be proactive advocates for them. Often this means serving as a spokesperson and champion for their interests and needs, as well as "blowing the whistle" when customers are not being treated fairly or adequately.

Customer Satisfaction

Basically, the axiom of high-quality service and the axiom of customer service lead to a third axiom of customer satisfaction. Participants in recreation programs are satisfied when they judge the service itself and how they were treated in the service as equal to or exceeding what they expected. The third best-practice principle of customer satisfaction, then, refers directly to the mix of quality service and customer service.

To illustrate, Oliver's theory (Oliver & DeSarbo, 1988) claims there are three potential satisfaction levels:

• **Negative disconfirmation** occurs when the service is worse than expected.
• **Positive disconfirmation** occurs when the service is better than expected.
• **Simple confirmation** occurs when the service is as was expected.

This means that customer satisfaction depends on achieving expectations in all aspects of the service delivery process as well as in the outcomes of the experience itself. For example, one outcome of a recreation program is obviously "having a good time." Satisfaction comes from knowing you've had the good time you expected. Swarbrooke and Horner (1999) refer to this as arousal and consider it a main satisfaction element in recreation programs. Programs that result in arousal create "delighted" customers—that is, their expectations have been exceeded (positive disconfirmation), and they feel satisfied. For more

strong that participants will sometimes blame the weather on programmers if it keeps them from the leisure experience they thought they'd have.

• *A means for complaining if necessary.* Establishing and communicating complaint procedures and frequently asking for opinions will go a long way to creating customer service. According to Grainger-Jones (1999), it is generally accepted by the tourism industry that 90 percent of dissatisfied customers never complain directly to the organization, but they tell nine other people about their dissatisfaction. Handling customer complaints means actually paying attention to them. Customers must not only be satisfied with the program but also, if they do complain, dealt with graciously and appropriately. At minimum, this means solving the problem that inspired the complaint in the first place. It might also mean giving the customer something extra, such as a free ticket to the next show.

Customer satisfaction depends on the perception that expectations for the service were met.

before and after. It is very difficult for a programmer to know (and thus manage) the participants' perceptions. Two participants can formulate totally different perceptions of an identical program experience (Williams & Buswell, 2003) because perceptions are affected by such personal factors as mood, health, personality, and even what was eaten for breakfast.

Dissatisfaction occurs when customers' perceptions of a program do not meet their expectations. This happens when their needs and wants are not met by the program, the advance information about the program gave a false expectation, staff members are not able to deliver the program as planned, or unsafe situations and even bad weather arise. Professionally prepared recreation programs go a long way to reduce the impact of such occurrences. Indeed, avoiding customer dissatisfaction is what this text is all about. For more information on this topic, see worksheet 3.2 in chapter 3 of the CD-ROM.

information on this topic, see "More Options for Individual Programming Practice," option 2, and "Group Discussion Ideas," option 3, in chapter 3 of the CD-ROM.

Where do program participants' expectations come from? Zeithaml, Parasuraman, and Berry (1990) propose that word of mouth, personal needs, advertising, and past experience can influence the formulation of expectations. The expectations of a frequent user of a recreation program would likely rely more on the influence of past experiences than on an advertisement. However, a first-time participant may be more informed about what to expect in the program by the opinions of already attending friends.

Potential participants may also form expectations based on the program's reputation. For example, golfers typically have higher expectations for a round of golf at a private course because private courses are generally perceived by golfers to be of higher quality than public courses.

Therefore, expectations play a major role in determining customer satisfaction in a program service. And, as you can see from the golf example just given, so does perception. Whether or not a good time was experienced is in the mind of the participant. Customer perceptions about the experience are formed throughout the programming process—including

Diversity

The United States, Canada, Australia, and many other nations of the world are made up of immigrants from a wide array of regions, ethnic backgrounds, languages, and traditions. And each census confirms that such countries are becoming more and more diverse. In the United States by the year 2050, citizens from Asian cultures are predicted to increase by 213 percent, and those from Spanish-speaking cultures are likely to increase by 188 percent, while people from European origins are predicted to increase by only 7 percent (Armas, 2004). For more information on this topic, see "Can You Solve This Programming Issue?" in chapter 3 of the CD-ROM.

Recreation programs are often an integral way to bring equal opportunity to such diverse peoples. A programmer's clientele may include gay men and lesbians, grandparents raising their grandchildren, single mothers and single fathers, young retirees, those living in poverty, teenage parents, people coping with terminal illness, and many others with an ever-widening diversity of motivations and needs for programmed leisure.

Recreation program services must also show awareness of the needs of people with differences of ability. At least 54 million people in the United States have disabilities (Cordes & Ibrahim, 2003). For people with physical, emotional, or learning disabilities, recreational activities may be not only a necessary part of a balanced life but also an integral element of a treatment or rehabilitation regime. For them, recreation programs may provide a way of coping, overcoming, and thriving.

For professional leisure programmers to be successful, they must be proactive in serving all populations effectively and in using recreation experiences as a tool to correct inequities, stimulate understanding of cross-diversity, overcome traditions of segregation, and advocate for genuine respect. Indeed, according to a 1998 study of university professors in leisure studies (Kraus, 2000), the axiom of diversity will become more important in the coming decades.

Table 3.1 presents some of the findings from this study. The higher the score, the more important that challenge for the future. Notice from the table the dominance of those challenges relating to diversity. For more information on this topic, see "More Options for Individual Programming Practice," option 3, in chapter 3 of the CD-ROM.

Public Good

As outlined in chapter 1, programmed leisure provides numerous benefits for both individuals and communities. The axiom of **public good** is a direct recognition of this. By reemphasizing the point here, we maintain that professional programmers should always focus on how their program services improve people's lives. Indeed, programmers should focus foremost on accomplishing public good. This best-practice principle is vital because through recreation programs, communities can become more attractive places to live by offering individuals a higher quality of life.

Realistically, most participants in leisure programs probably do not consciously think of all this. They

TABLE 3.1

Ranking of Future Challenges for Leisure Services Professionals

Challenge	Weighted score
1. Serving an increasingly diverse society (race, age, gender, and so on)	453
2. Working with at-risk youth, serving persons with disabilities, promoting community development	437
3. Achieving fuller understanding of the value of recreation and the leisure services profession	434
4. Upgrading recreation programs and facilities, particularly in inner cities and for minority groups	417
5. Adopting a benefits-based approach to delivering services focused on the positive outcomes of recreation	411
6. Promoting recreation's identity as healthful	392
7. Developing partnerships with environmental organizations to protect resources	386
8. Employing a marketing approach to achieve fiscal self-sufficiency and public respect	378
9. Expanding family-centered programs and facilities	373
10. Promoting higher ethical practices in youth sports	363

Adapted from Kraus, 2000, p. 354.

likely make recreational choices largely because of specific personal motives such as sociability, creativity, challenge, and rest. Yet professional leisure programmers, in addition to being committed to addressing these individual intentions, must also be dedicated to the broader social service reach of their efforts.

Ironically, this must be accomplished while knee deep in the financial and political requirements of sponsoring organizations. Today, organized leisure often must at least break even financially and retain a high level of political support. Programmed leisure is now part of an entrepreneurial strategy where participants are viewed not simply as users of services but as paying customers. Many of the operational methods of business are rapidly becoming full-fledged principles in park and recreation agencies. Even for a city or county government-sponsored program, the marketing approach is a necessity as tax-based support is reduced (Kraus, 1997). Nonetheless, within such political and financial requirements, professional leisure programmers must still be dedicated to the public good.

What exactly is public good? Dustin, McAvoy, and Schultz (1991) refer to the public good axiom as the "standard of goodness." They argue that recreational pursuits that preserve life, promote life, and help life achieve its highest destiny are morally superior to those that do not. Certainly programmers are obligated, then, to provide leisure options that are just "right." This sometimes means resisting the temptation to offer programs that, although popular, "consume nonrenewable resources, are destructive of other life forms, or in some way contribute to personal or social problems" (Kraus, 1997, p. 79). It's this public good principle, for example, that makes the question of providing off-road vehicle trails in public forests such a controversial one.

The axiom of public good has been a long-standing principle for the leisure professions. In fact, more than 30 years ago, leisure scholars David Gray and Seymour Greben (1976) summed it up with a list of goals for leisure program professionals:

- Adopt a social conscience focused on the supremacy of the human being.
- Take action to solve social problems.
- Emphasize human welfare.

Public good, then, means programmers work from such core values as citizenship, fairness, steward-ship, charity, and other qualities necessary for looking out for the greater good. An apt expression for this is *noblesse oblige*, which conveys the message of obligation to community. For more information on this topic, see worksheet 3.3 in chapter 3 of the CD-ROM. ◉

Environmental Compatibility

The standard of goodness extends to the viability of our natural world, too. Obviously, park, recreation, sport, and tourism organizations play an important role in conserving and preserving the natural environment. Many leisure pursuits require a clean, aesthetic, and healthy forest, river, beach, cave, mountain, lake, trail, ocean, or sky. As well, outdoor recreation and tourism in particular pose serious threats to the quality of the environment (see the box on page 39 for examples). Resorts are built in fragile natural areas, water parks destroy marsh habitat, and power boaters pollute lakes and damage vegetation. Thus, an important principle for professional leisure programmers is a sound environmental **ethic**.

Environmental concerns of all forms continue to besiege the world, especially North America—by far the largest user of nonrenewable natural resources. Global warming, acid rain, biodiversity losses, abandoned nuclear waste products, water and air pollution, and fossil fuel depletion will need to be foremost on the minds of everyone. In spite of this, interest and participation in outdoor recreation and tourism will increase. Accordingly, participant conflicts are likely. Hunters will interfere with bird watching, snowmobilers will aggravate cross-country skiers, and jet skiers will terrorize canoeists. Those who favor resource-consuming motorized pursuits will increasingly become at odds with others—including professionals working toward the preservation of natural areas.

For professional leisure programmers, developing an environmental ethic will likely mean major adjustments, such as closing parks when visitor capacity has been reached and charging entrance and user fees for outdoor recreation areas and programs. It will also require small changes, such as eliminating campfires at evening camp programs and keeping children indoors on high-alert pollution days at after-school recreation programs. Eco-vacations will need to be encouraged. Parties that use fewer disposable

Is Recreation Killing the Planet?

- More whales are killed each year by collisions with ships, including whale-watching boats and cruise ships, than by any other cause.

- The growing sport of rock climbing severely damages plant ecology; regularly climbed rock faces have up to 80 percent less plant coverage and 80 percent fewer native plants than do unclimbed cliffs.

- Yellowstone National Park rangers are forced to wear gas masks to prevent headaches and nausea caused by snowmobile exhaust; unfortunately, there are no respirators for the park's bison, elk, trumpeter swans, and other wildlife.

- Site preparation for Hong Kong's future Disney theme park has resulted in massive water pollution, already driving away local fishers and fish farms.

- Scientists warn that melting glaciers, less snow, and shorter and warmer winters due to global warming could make future Winter Olympics impossible.

- Too many sport anglers in Canada are causing a rapid decline of trout, walleye, and pike stocks.

Adapted from *Earth crash—documenting the collapse of a dying planet: Population–environmental impacts of recreation and "eco-tourism,"* http://eces.org/archive/ec/population/recreation.shtml (accessed 5/5/04; site now discontinued).

Achieving the best-practice principle of environmental compatibility extends to the rehabilitation and creative programming of urban areas.

decorations must be planned. Camps will recycle, resorts will wash bedding only once per guest, and sports leagues will "hand down" trophies. Programmers must become advocates of what has been labeled "conserver leisure" (Spry, 1991).

This calls for an all-out "green" appeal in recreation programs—one that will likely include an educational component. Environmental education and leisure education will need to be more pervasive in every agency's program offerings. Customers and clients need to become better educated about the out-of-doors so that they contribute to its survival.

Concern for the urban environment is also necessary. Abandoned factories, degraded housing, and deteriorated waterfront areas present a unique opportunity for programmers. As urban planners and officials rehabilitate more and more such sites, creating new programs in sport, the performing arts, and tourism will be possible.

To sustain the axiom of environmental compatibility, professionals will need to uphold these ethical values:

- The recreation program helps the environment remain healthy over time.
- The recreation program experience enriches participants' appreciation of the environment.
- The recreation program improves the environment.

Presenting the leisure services fields with this challenge, Fox (1991) declared that,

for all our concentration and fascination with management principles, marketing strategies, and satisfying the client, we are, in the final analysis, an idealistic profession and it is time we included an ethic of respect and protection for the ecosphere in our mission. (p. 30).

For more information on this topic, see "More Options for Individual Programming Practice," option 5, in chapter 3 of the CD-ROM.

Efficiency

The principles presented up to this point might all be viewed as having to do with effectiveness. Quality, customer service and satisfaction, the public good, and human and environmental diversity and worth are centered on accomplishing something worthwhile through recreation programs. Yet, in spite of what might seem like an unbridled enthusiasm for these, we should warn you that none of these markers of effectiveness should come at the cost of efficiency.

Efficiency means producing results through economical use of talent, energy, time, and resources. Whereas effectiveness refers to results and the ability to achieve the desired outcomes through recreation programs, efficiency means these results are accomplished with minimal needless expenditure of effort. For professional leisure services programmers, this calls for accountability and innovation. Adopt a Playground, described in the box on this page, is one example of a program that is innovative and efficient.

Adopt a Playground

Here's an idea for being innovatively efficient. Right to Play, a nonprofit volunteer organization based in Louisiana, is committed to creating an inclusive playground for every child. The organization's mission is to build playgrounds so that all children, including those with physical, sensory, or developmental disabilities, can play together. One of the ways it accomplishes this is through the Adopt a Playground Structure program. For example, here's some pieces of play equipment and the cost of their adoption:

- Flat pipe climber: $1,000
- Vertical climbing wall: $3,000
- Crow's nest with mini maze: $675
- Big foot slide: $2,500

- Talk tubes: $675
- Funnel bridge: $2,000
- Tire swing: $4,725

For their donation, adoptive "parents" receive a plaque placed on or near their adopted structure, honoring them or a loved one.

From Right to Play, Inc., www.righttoplay.org/adopt.php3.

The Programming Process: Do What's Best

In 2004, Westerville opened a bark park. The staff went to a lot of effort to provide for both its canine and human citizens with this facility and program. After holding dozens of planning meetings, recruiting 17 volunteer park consultants and supervisors (including two veterinarians), and raising more than $25,000 in corporate and organization donations, the Westerville Bark Park opened.

The park features a fenced one-acre area for large dogs; a fenced quarter-acre area for small dogs; drinking fountains for both humans and dogs; a dog shower; a paved plaza for viewing; an information kiosk; and even such agility equipment as jumps, a ramp, a tunnel, a window, and an A-frame. Phase II plans call for adding a doggy wading and spray pool and a woodland trail.

Why did the staff go to so much trouble for the town's nonvoting, non-tax-paying pet citizens? For Westerville, the answer is rather automatic. Following a philosophy of best practices, the staff realized that contributing to public good, as well as to the principles of customer service and service quality, meant the extension of their efforts to those with an interest in enjoying recreational activities with their pets. "Even I'm amazed at how much time and effort we put into envisioning, planning, constructing, and even programming that little park, but in order to truly call ourselves professionals, we felt we had to reach out to meet these needs too," said director Jody Stowers at the park's grand opening.

Did you say programming, Jody? Indeed, programming staff are planning such dog park programs as obedience, pet first aid, and vaccination sessions; pampered pet day, with dog washes and nail clipping; pet trick demonstrations; a dog show and pet fair; and a dog Olympics.

The Westerville Bark Park.

Photo courtesy of Westerville Parks and Recreation Department, Westerville, Ohio.

How many clients does the program serve? How many staff members are required? Does this program take a facility away from other users? Do we have enough time to fully plan the program? Do our leaders have the skills needed to carry out this program? All these are questions of efficiency. Professionals in leisure services are no longer able to offer programs that are not efficient.

Originally, government-sponsored recreation programs were considered a free public entitlement comparable to highways, police services, and fire protection—paid for by taxes. Parks, playgrounds, and community centers provided programs without charge to participants. Gradually, as more facilities were needed to meet the increasingly sophisticated interests of clientele by offering a wider array of programs, it became necessary to charge a fee for registration, instruction, admission, use of equipment, and other services. This has become even more necessary since the 1980s era of fiscal austerity. Now all types of leisure service agencies, including public, private, and commercial, are responsible for more cost-effective ways to support programs.

Continuous Improvement

Finally, leisure programmers are faced with the mandate of constantly improving. For many reasons, including the dynamic nature of leisure itself, competition from other programming organizations, and the ever-present tug of change in society, no one can provide the same program services year after year and remain professionally viable. Innovations in technology often drive the need to change recreation programs and how they are planned and delivered to clients.

Clients and participants also have vibrant expectations for more and better. When a particular program meets their expectations, the level it must achieve next time goes up. The need for continuous improvement also comes from the complexity of the clients themselves. Programs are intended to solve problems and have a positive impact on people. As people and their problems become ever more complex, so does meeting their needs. The challenge for the programmer is staying alert to people's changing needs and creating responsive programs. For all these reasons, to remain the same is, in effect, to fall behind (McCarville, 2002). Consequently, continuous improvement lies at the heart of all successful recreation programs.

Improvement requires proactive change. Programmers, their organizations, and their customers must be willing to adapt and change. This is sometimes difficult to do. Whatever the nature or extent of the change needed, it is virtually certain it will be resisted. Even changes that seem positive, desirable, and rational will involve loss and uncertainty for someone. Change initiatives can threaten the status of an employee, bring a sense of loss of control to participants, and cause even supervisors and directors to feel incompetent in their successes. Thus, programmers must also work toward creating a readiness for change in their organization and among their constituents. Even this is difficult, which is why so many books about leadership include a focus on managing and leading change. Essentially, changes will be more successful if they possess the following basic characteristics: relative advantage, compatibility, complexity, trialability, and observability (Rogers, 1983).

First, **relative advantage** refers to the perceived or actual superiority of the change compared with the status quo. In order to desire or at least accept change, people must believe the change will improve their situation—that it is fair and appropriate to them (Welch, 2000). The second characteristic of **compatibility** suggests there must be a fit between the change and the existing situation. The change must be appropriate for the culture of the program, the organization, and the community. Changes that fit well within existing situations are more likely to be accepted. Third, **complexity** is how well the change can be understood by those involved. Complex changes are more difficult to understand and thus more likely to be resisted. The characteristic of **trialability** is the process of trying out the change gradually. In particular, if ideas for new or different programs are difficult to understand, programmers should implement them in increments—testing and experimenting with the idea so that improvements can be made before a full-fledged implementation. Finally, **observability** refers to the visibility of the results of the change. The more people are able to see the positive effects from a change, the more likely they are to adopt it.

Continuous improvement is at the heart of all successful programming. It is so critical that an entire section later in this book is devoted to one of the tools for making continuous improvement—evaluation. In addition, programmers can take personal responsibility for continuous improvement by staying professionally up to date. Successful programmers remain well informed of emerging professional practice. Professional knowledge has a very short life span, so to keep current, professionals must remain informed by reading, participating in conferences, and networking with colleagues. Program participants deserve the services of professionals who are on the cutting edge. See table 3.2 for a to-do list for staying well

TABLE 3.2
___

How to Remain on the Professional Cutting Edge

Weekly	Monthly	Trimonthly	Annually
• Visit at least one Web site related to recreation programming. • Participate in the chat room. • Post questions. • Download usable information.	• Read at least one professional leisure services book or article. • Read at least one research-based article.	• Contact and visit related agencies and organizations to share ideas and program solutions. • Participate in a professional conference, workshop, or training session.	• Serve on the special interest committee of a professional organization. • Join a research team sponsored by faculty or students of a university. • Present a paper or educational session at the annual meeting of a professional organization.

informed. For more information on this topic, see "More Options for Individual Programming Practice," option 4, in chapter 3 of the CD-ROM.

Summary

This chapter presents several important principles for successful recreation programs. You should understand the following key points:

- Quality means excellence in program services. Excellence requires product quality, functional quality, and image quality.

- Recreation programs serve people. A commitment to their care is more important than ever. Customer service includes advocacy, value, honesty, and appreciation.

- Program participants are satisfied when they judge that the service and their treatment equal or exceed what they expected. Customer satisfaction is the mix of perceptions and expectations.

- Programmers must be proactive in serving all populations effectively and in using recreation experiences as a tool to correct inequities, stimulate understanding of cross-diversity, overcome traditions of segregation, and advocate for wholehearted respect.

- Ultimately, programmers provide recreational pursuits that preserve life, promote life, and help life achieve its highest destiny; they are obligated to provide the right leisure options for people—to contribute to public good.

- Programmers must also be guided by an environmental ethic, helping the natural world achieve its highest destiny.

- Efficiency means producing results economically.

- At the heart of successful programs is continuous improvement—changing for the better.

Glossary

axiom—A principle widely accepted for its own merit.

product quality—The "what," or the quality of the specific recreation event or program.

functional quality—The "how," or the quality of the method for carrying out the recreation program.

image quality—The reputation of the recreation program.

external customers—Participants served by the recreation program.

internal customers—Staff working within the organization that sponsors the recreation program.

negative disconfirmation—When the program service is worse than expected.

positive disconfirmation—When the program service is better than expected.

simple confirmation—When the program service is as was expected.

public good—Something that is positive for everyone.

ethic—A guiding philosophy or belief.

efficiency—Skillfulness in avoiding wasted effort.

relative advantage—Perceived or actual superiority of a change compared with the existing situation.

compatibility—A fit between a change and the existing situation.

complexity—How well a change can be understood by those involved.

trialability—The process of trying out the change gradually.

observability—The visibility of the results of a change.

References

Albrecht, K., & Zemke, R. (1985). *Service America!* Homewood, IL: Dow Jones-Irwin.

Armas, G.C. (2004, May 1). Asian population surging as diverse groups settle. *Bowling Green (Kentucky) Daily News*, p. A10.

Berry, L.L., Zeithaml, V.A., & Parasuraman, A. (1985). Quality counts in services, too. *Business Horizons, 28*(May/June), 44-52.

Clayton, M. (2004). In a national park, the call of the wild: Is it cellular? *Christian Science Monitor.* Retrieved October 4, 2004, from www.usatoday.com/tech/wireless/phones/2004-09-30-parkcells_x.htm.

Cordes, K.A., & Ibrahim, H.M. (2003). *Applications in recreation and leisure for today and the future.* Boston: McGraw-Hill.

Dale, B.G. (1999). *Managing quality.* Oxford, UK: Blackwell.

Dustin, D., McAvoy, L., & Schultz, J. (1991). Recreation rightly understood. In T. Goodale & P. Witt (Eds.), *Recreation and leisure: Issues in an era of change* (pp. 97-106). State College, PA: Venture.

Earth crash—Documenting the collapse of a dying planet: Population–environmental impacts of recreation and "eco-tourism." (n.d.). Retrieved May 5, 2004, from http://eces.org/archive/ec/population/recreation.shtml, site now discontinued.

Fox, K. (1991). Environmental ethics and the future of parks and recreation. *Recreation Canada, 49*(2), 28-31.

Grainger-Jones, B. (1999). *Managing leisure.* Oxford, UK: Butterworth-Heinemann.

Gray, D., & Greben, S. (1976). Future perspectives. *Parks and Recreation, 9*(6), 49.

Gronroos, C. (1990). *Service management and marketing: Managing the moments of truth in service competition.* Lexington, MA: Lexington Books.

Kraus, R. (1997). *Recreation programming: A benefits-driven approach.* Boston: Allyn & Bacon.

Kraus, R. (2000). *Leisure in a changing America: Trends and issues for the 21st century.* Boston: Allyn & Bacon.

McCarville, R. (2002). *Improving leisure services through marketing action.* Champaign, IL: Sagamore.

Oliver, R.L., & DeSarbo, W.S. (1988). Response determinants in satisfaction judgments. *Journal of Consumer Research, 14,* 495-507.

Right to Play. (n.d.). Adopt a playground structure. Retrieved January 19, 2006, from www.righttoplay.org/adopt.php3.

Rogers, E.M. (1983). *Diffusion of innovations.* New York: Free Press.

Spry, I.M. (1991). The prospects for leisure in a conserver society. In T.L. Goodale & P.A. Witt (Eds.), *Recreation and leisure: Issues in an era of change* (3rd ed., pp. 141-153). State College, PA: Venture.

Swarbrooke, J., & Horner, S. (1999). *Consumer behavior in tourism.* Oxford, UK: Butterworth-Heinemann.

Welch, R.J. (2000). Monitoring conditions for staff acceptance of organizational change: A case study at St. Lawrence Islands National Park. University of Waterloo, Waterloo, Ontario, unpublished master's thesis.

Williams, C., & Buswell, J. (2003). *Service quality in leisure and tourism.* Wallingford, UK: CABI.

Zeithaml, V.A., Parasuraman, A., & Berry, L.L. (1990). *Delivering quality service: Balancing customer perceptions and expectations.* New York: Free Press.

CHAPTER 4

Leisure Program Components

In this chapter, you can look forward to the following:

- Learning how activity areas commonly used in leisure programs are classified
- Learning how formats commonly used in leisure programs are classified
- Discovering how activity areas and program formats can, through activity analysis, be clustered, modified, and substituted to create programs

The Neal-Marshall Black Culture Center (NMBCC) at Indiana University (IU) in Bloomington offers programs focused on celebrating the educational, cultural, and social achievements of African American students, faculty, and community members. Its program mission is to "promote public awareness about the Black experience" (NMBCC, 2001-2006). Dedicated in January 2002 and named in honor of the first male and female African American graduates of IU, the center features a grand hall, library, lounge, and arts institute available for programs. Although leisure programmers have a wide variety of activity areas and formats available, the Neal-Marshall Black Culture Center features cultural festivals. The Sound the Drum and Family Fest is held annually in celebration of Black History Month; Culture Fest welcomes new students to campus each fall; the Kwanzaa Celebration is featured in December; and the Africana Festival honors the cultural heritage from Africa.

Leisure programs come in a wide variety of shapes and sizes. Over the past weekend, for example, you may have competed in intramural volleyball, attended a meeting of your scrapbooking club, worked out on your own in the recreational sports facility, and attended a play. This seems like a lot, but these represent only a very small portion of the leisure program possibilities most likely available to you.

From the service delivery perspective, this means there are many different ways of providing programmed leisure to achieve an organization's purposes. As the professional programmer, your responsibility is to creatively "juggle" the many recreational options for maximum effect. Think of it as playing with pieces of a puzzle. In this chapter, we consider these pieces—or components—as composed of activity areas and program formats. Further, in concluding the chapter, we discuss how these components can be clustered, modified, and substituted through a task known as activity analysis.

Activity Areas

Because recreation includes a wide range of activity opportunities, and because people have varied backgrounds and interests, agencies responsible for providing leisure program services have had to develop planned programs as broad as humanity itself. This diversity is not meant to cause dismay but instead to encourage you to creatively use the possibilities.

To assist, we begin with a discussion of the most typical recreation activity areas that appear in leisure service delivery systems. Such a classification will necessarily mean some reduction of the limitless possibilities, yet recreation program professionals have found it useful to catalog recreation behavior into **activity areas**, or activity sets (see table 4.1). For more information on this topic, see "More Options for Individual Programming Practice," option 2, in chapter 4 of the CD-ROM.

The means of this classification is arbitrary because there is no universal definition for leisure. Thus, it is possible to classify any one activity in a number of different ways. For example, in table 4.1 the activity of snorkeling could be placed in the aquatics, outdoors and nature, and adventure classification groups. Also, some activities don't seem to fit well into any category. Where in table 4.1 would you place video games? In spite of these imperfections, these categories of recreation program areas make some intuitive sense. If you ask a person what he or she typically does for recreation, the answer is usually given in terms of a set of activities (e.g., "I'm into sports"). For more information on this topic, see worksheet 4.1 in chapter 4 of the CD-ROM.

As well, within each classification, leisure programmers have numerous ways of organizing the activities. Some activities require higher levels of planning and structure, while others are more informal. In some categories the recreational pursuits are typically done in a group, while others are mostly experienced individually. Some recreation activity areas require active involvement, and others are more passive. The programmer can provide programs either indoors or outdoors; at beginner, intermediate, or advanced skill levels; inexpensively or expensively; and in only one or all seasons of the year. This diversity of programming options within the activity areas is also reflected in table 4.1. Now let's consider recreation activity areas in more detail.

TABLE 4.1

Sampling of Recreation Activity Areas

Category	Examples	Organization level (L = low, H = high)	Participant groupings (I = individual, G = group)	Participant skill level (B = beginner, I = intermediate, A = advanced)	Cost ($ = cheap, $$ = moderate, $$$ = expensive)
Sports	Team athletics (basketball, softball)	H	G	All levels	$$–$$$
	Individual athletics (golf, horseback riding, gymnastics)	H	Both	All levels	$$–$$$
	Dual athletics (table tennis, wrestling, racquetball)	H	G	All levels	$–$$
	Physical games (dodgeball, tag)	Both	G	B	$
	Fitness (Pilates, yoga, weightlifting)	Both	Both	B, I	$–$$
	Walking and biking (stationary cycling, speed walking)	L	Both	All levels	$–$$
	Extreme sports (in-line skating)	Both	I	A	$$
Aquatics	Swimming and diving	H	I	All levels	$–$$
	Water sports (water polo)	H	G	A	$$
	Underwater activities (snorkeling)	Both	I	A	$$–$$$
	Water fitness and aerobics	H	Both	All levels	$
	Boating (sailing, rowing, windsurfing)	Both	Both	I, A	$$–$$$
Adventure	Ropes courses (challenges)	H	G	All levels	$$–$$$
	Team and initiative activities (games)	H	G	All levels	$

(CONTINUED)

TABLE 4.1 *(CONTINUED)*

Category	Examples	Organization level (L = low, H = high)	Participant groupings (I = individual, G = group)	Participant skill level (B = beginner, I = intermediate, A = advanced)	Cost ($ = cheap, $$ = moderate, $$$ = expensive)
	Rock climbing	Both	Both	I, A	$$–$$$
	Hang gliding	L	I	A	$$$
	White-water kayaking	L	Both	I, A	$$
	Snow skiing	H	Both	All levels	$$$
	Surfing	L	Both	All levels	$$
Dance	Ballroom	Both	G	All levels	$
	Tap	L	Both	All levels	$
	Social	L	G	B, I	$
	Folk, square, and traditional	L	G	All levels	$
	Jazz and modern	L	Both	I, A	$
	Ballet	H	Both	I, A	$$
	Hip-hop	L	Both	All levels	$
	Interpretive	L	Both	All levels	$
Drama	Films and videos	L	I	All levels	$$
	Television	L	I	B	$
	Plays, musicals, and variety shows	H	Both	I, A	$$–$$$
	Pantomime and mime	L	I	I, A	$
	Puppetry	Both	Both	All levels	$$
	Storytelling	L	G	All levels	$
	Historical reenactments	H	G	I, A	$$–$$$
Fine arts	Painting and drawing	L	Both	All levels	$–$$
	Sculpture and clay modeling	L	Both	All levels	$$–$$$
	Paper making and printing	H	Both	I, A	$$
	Photography	H	I	I, A	$$–$$$
Crafts	Needlecraft and sewing	L	Both	All levels	$–$$

Category	Examples	Organization level (L = low, H = high)	Participant groupings (I = individual, G = group)	Participant skill level (B = beginner, I = intermediate, A = advanced)	Cost ($ = cheap, $$ = moderate, $$$ = expensive)
	Weaving	H	I	I, A	$$–$$$
	Jewelry making	H	I	I, A	$$$
	Model building	L	Both	I, A	$–$$
	Pottery and ceramics	H	Both	All levels	$$–$$$
	Cooking and baking	H	I	All levels	$–$$$
	Flower arranging	L	Both	All levels	$$
Music	Instrumental	Both	Both	All levels	$$–$$$
	Vocal	Both	Both	All levels	$–$$
	Listening and appreciation	L	I	I, A	$–$$
	Composition	L	I	A	$
	Rhythm games	L	G	B	$
Hobbies	Collecting	L	Both	All levels	$–$$$
	Gardening	L	Both	All levels	$$–$$$
	Education (computers, wellness)	Both	Both	All levels	$$–$$$
Outdoors or nature	Camping	Both	Both	I, A	$–$$
	Backpacking	Both	Both	I, A	$$–$$$
	Bird watching	L	Both	I, A	$
	Conservation	L	Both	All levels	$
	Nature crafts	L	Both	B, I	$
	Stargazing	L	Both	I, A	$
	Nature interpretation	L	Both	I, A	$
Intellectual or literary	Reading and study (book club)	L	Both	I, A	$
	Writing	L	Both	A	$
	Debating	H	G	A	$
	Visiting museums	L	Both	All levels	$$
	Puzzles	L	Both	All levels	$

(CONTINUED)

TABLE 4.1 *(CONTINUED)*

Category	Examples	Organization level (L = low, H = high)	Participant groupings (I = individual, G = group)	Participant skill level (B = beginner, I = intermediate, A = advanced)	Cost ($ = cheap, $$ = moderate, $$$ = expensive)
	Card and board games	L	G	All levels	$
	Retreats and conferences	H	G	A	$$$
	Genealogy research	L	Both	I, A	$$
Travel	Tours	H	G	I, A	$$$
	Independent trips	L	Both	A	$$-$$$
	Field or day trips	H	G	All levels	$-$$
	Cruises	H	Both	All levels	$$$
	Eco-tourism	H	Both	I, A	$$-$$$
	Travelogues	L	G	All levels	$
	RVing	Both	Both	A	$$$
Social recreation	Parties	Both	G	All levels	$-$$$
	Picnics and potlucks	Both	G	All levels	$-$$
	Social dances	Both	G	All levels	$$
	Mixers (receptions, open houses)	Both	G	I, A	$$-$$$
	Visiting and conversation	L	G	All levels	$
Volunteer service	Coaching	H	G	A	$-$$$
	Youth activity leadership	H	G	A	$-$$
	Fundraising	H	Both	A	$-$$$
	Service learning	H	Both	I, A	$

Sports

Growth in sports, probably the single largest recreation program area, presents a remarkable trend. The category also represents limitless possibilities for programmers. For example, a list of all sports currently programmed by leisure service agencies (including archery, trapshooting, crew, curling, horseshoes, casting, boche ball, rope jumping, water skiing, karate, billiards, ice hockey, and synchronized swimming) would occupy several pages.

Specific programming procedures and considerations for sport activities vary with local customs, agency resources, and geographic location. But, above all, it is important for programmers to remember that through sports, recreation programmers should seek to open the door to enjoyable physical movement. How might this be accomplished? Here are some planning principles you'll find useful for programming sport activities for your organization (Russell, 1982):

- *Offer programs at all skill levels.* In addition to providing activities for the highly skilled, offer participants at beginner and intermediate levels comparable opportunities to run a marathon, play lacrosse, cast a line into a stream for trout, and water ski.

- *Feature lifetime sports.* Your programming mission is to provide participants with options for enjoying physical activity throughout life. You are not training elite athletes. Therefore, although local customs may dictate that you provide football, softball, basketball, and soccer for school-age participants, sports that can be enjoyed throughout life, such as swimming, tennis, bowling, cross-country skiing, badminton, bicycling, walking, and weightlifting, should receive at least equal programming focus.

- *Pay attention to safety.* The very nature of sports— participants often place themselves in physical jeopardy—calls for offering sport experiences that reflect sound safety practices. Schedule regular maintenance of equipment and facilities, always enforce player rules, and make sure officials are well trained.

Aquatics

Sport, fitness, and outdoor recreation activities on water require even more careful planning. As a programmer in aquatics, you may be preparing programs for indoor and outdoor pools, water parks, beaches, lakes, oceans, or rivers. These could include boating safety clinics, swim and dive teams, water polo tournaments, fitness classes, sailing regattas, individualized therapy sessions, supervised lap swimming, evening family socials, and swimming lessons. People participate in aquatics to fulfill a wide range of needs, including risk, adventure, health, therapy, and self-esteem. Thus, programmers must not only have technical expertise to ensure safe and beneficial water experiences but also be sensitive to the diversity of participant needs. Here are some programming principles to help achieve this:

- *Aquatic programming should provide participants with enough knowledge, attitude, and skill to enable them to play in the water safely.* Programming in aquatics requires a great deal of responsibility for the safety of participants. Part of this increased responsibility should be assumed by participants themselves. They should have ample opportunities through your programming to learn how to swim, understand waterfront safety procedures, and handle emergencies.

- *All staff working within the aquatics program should be appropriately trained and*

Sport programs are appropriate for participants of all ages and skill levels.

The Programming Process: Program Components

Westerville has a major aquatics program. Its outdoor swimming complex is the largest municipal swimming facility in central Ohio. It contains seven swimming pools, including two instructional pools, two tot pools, two competitive pools, and a diving well. Other amenities include a triple-loop water slide that is 20 feet (6 meters) high, two diving boards, a spray fountain, sand volleyball, basketball, a picnic shelter, a concession stand, and sunbathing and shade areas. At the community center, the indoor Watering Hole pool complex includes a leisure pool, competition pool, and whirlpool. The leisure pool has a body slide, a tube slide, fountains, a shallow play area, a water playground, and a lazy river.

Programs for all these excellent facilities include swimming lessons, open-lane lap swimming, water fitness classes, and such special events as "family night." Wow! Who could ask for anything more? But that's exactly what aquatics director Tim Moloney is doing.

Tim believes the extensive and well-maintained aquatic facilities are underprogrammed. Yes, the swimming lessons for children and youth are popular, and open-swim days and times are always in high demand. But what else might be offered at the pools besides the activity of swimming and the formats of open facility and instructional class?

For starters, more frequent and more imaginative special events could be planned. Currently, there are only three: family night, teen splashdown (a party), and an appreciation night for season pass holders. Also, what about the other formats? For example, could aquatic-based clubs be formed? What about competition?

What water-based activities besides swimming can be offered? Scuba? Board diving? Synchronized swimming? In what ways can options in the water fitness classes be enhanced? Are formats other than instructional useful for water fitness? What programs might be planned around the water slides, the lazy river, and the sunbathing areas?

Aquatics programming sponsored by the Westerville Parks and Recreation Department.

Photo courtesy of Westerville Parks and Recreation Department, Westerville, Ohio.

---

certified. Certification and training in lifeguarding, scuba, small craft, and other aquatic-based activities are provided through the YMCA, American National Red Cross, Royal Lifesaving Society Canada, colleges and universities, and such private associations as the National Outdoor Leadership School.

Adventure

The adventure category of activities has also expanded dramatically. This reflects not only rising interest in such long-standing activities as rock climbing, kayaking, snow skiing, and surfing but also extensions and inventions of new pursuits such as spelunking, geocaching, and kiteboarding. This popularity has also resulted in nontraditional efforts to bring these usually outdoor activities indoors (e.g., indoor climbing walls) and to create simulated versions (e.g., constructed white-water courses and virtual hang gliding).

Activities in the adventure category usually make more demands on planning time and effort. For example, some outdoor pursuits, such as wilderness trekking, require lengthy and specialized leadership training. To get you started, here are some important programming principles (Russell, 1982):

- *A major ingredient is dynamic and competent leaders.* Whether they come from your own agency or from outside professional services, by the force of their enthusiasm, the leaders will establish the nature and goals of the adventure program and ultimately its success. Usually this also requires technical skills, strong safety skills, and sharp judgment.

- *A thorough familiarity with logistics is required.* Such elements as area guides and maps, planned locale reconnaissance, and emergency planning should be of prime planning consideration.

- *Participant readiness should be appropriate for the activity.* Participant abilities need to be carefully assessed. Participants should also be given adequate lead-up training, safety briefing, and skill practice as part of risk management efforts.

Dance

Dance is a form of personal expression through rhythmic movement. Thus, it is appealing to both participants and spectators, making it a useful programming option for a wide range of people. Dance programs offer physical fitness, social interaction, aesthetics, relaxation, and cultural understanding. In the programs of most leisure service agencies, dancing consists mostly of instructional classes for children. Yet, this activity area contains much more potential for creating intriguing and exciting experiences. Here are some programming guidelines (Russell, 1982):

- *Talented and motivated dance leaders are vital for program success.* Trained dance teachers—who are able to present, adapt, coach, and control program quality without forfeiting the element of fun—are necessary, particularly for instructional programs.

- *Appropriate facilities are required.* Although dance programs don't usually require costly equipment and venues, a minimum standard must be met. The basics are a well-ventilated area with good acoustics and an adequate floor space and floor surface. Too small an area makes movement difficult and destroys the quality of the dance experience. On the other hand, in social dancing too large an area destroys the spirit of the group. Further, ballroom dancing requires a hard, smooth surface, while popular dance forms can be programmed for almost any flat surface—even a sandy beach.

- *Appropriate musical accompaniment is a must.* CDs, music videos, a pianist, a drummer, or a large dance band? How the music is presented for dancing must be adequately prepared, including providing sufficient amplification.

Drama

Drama imitates life. Yet, unlike life, when provided through programming, drama allows performers and audiences to try out new personalities, thoughts, and relationships without consequences. Drama activities can be as simple as reading aloud at a children's story hour, playing a game of charades at a party, or watching television from a hospital bed. Or it can be as elaborate as a historical reenactment involving hundreds of performers and acres of land. Drama is rich with potential, and there is no community, organization, or group that is unable to include drama in its programming. Here are some suggestions for planning (Russell, 1982):

- *Provide a progression of dramatic activities.* Each dramatic participation or performance should provide a step-by-step range, from the simple to the sophisticated.

- *Use both active and passive formats.* Drama can be programmed to offer a quiet, thoughtful, introspective activity as well as energetic and vigorous action.

- *Be flexible and innovative in the nature and size of facilities.* Even complex and elaborate dramatic programming can take place almost anywhere: a private home, the gymnasium, a vacant store, the steps of a public building, an art museum, a garden, or a swimming pool.

Fine Arts

In some programming settings, it is important to distinguish between the fine arts and crafts in order to best serve participant interests. Fine art may be viewed as the use of materials to demonstrate a concept or perception, while crafts use materials to make useful items. Participants in art programs often want to express themselves via an aesthetic response. Participation can therefore call for individual as well as group involvement. But, unlike such other activity areas as social recreation and certain forms of sport and drama, arts participation does not require others to cooperate. Here are some planning considerations for fine arts (Russell, 1982):

- *The amount of planning complexity is determined by the level of the art.* The more advanced the artistic expression, such as tapestry weaving or silver molding, the greater the scope and talent of the leadership, the material and equipment resources, and the required skill levels of participants.

- *Multiskilled leadership is key.* An arts specialist is just as important for the effectiveness of an art program as a coach is for the success of a sports team. Although the major role of an art program leader is to stimulate quality workmanship, originality, and free expression, at least some technical expertise in the art form is also necessary.

- *Providing quality art materials is an important planning consideration.* Fine arts require materials. Whether it be paper, rocks, paints, clay, wood, yarn, wax, or sand, programming requires locating, purchasing, maintaining, storing, and cleaning often expensive and dangerous products.

Crafts

People engage in crafts to create something useful for themselves, family, or friends. They also participate to test and expand their creative potential. Historically, crafts emerged from utilitarian needs for furniture, food containers, and clothing, but craft programming seeks to create opportunities for refinements and ornamentation of what is useful. Being able to say, "I made it," provides a pride of accomplishment that is the goal of the craft programmer. Here are some planning considerations (Russell, 1982):

- *Be alert for ways to incorporate crafts into other recreation activity areas.* Crafts can enhance programs in dance, drama, and music as well as in social and nature recreation.

- *Focus on respect for individual originality.* Even though participants in craft programs strive to make something useful, the creative expression of the experience should always outweigh the functionality of the result.

- *Adaptability of location can extend programming options.* Many craft projects can be completed almost anywhere—in a moving vehicle, in a janitor's closet, in the middle of a forest. However, some crafts do require special facilities and equipment, such as a kiln and sink for ceramics.

- *Preplan for safety and cleanup.* Safety considerations include proper storage of flammable materials, adequate ventilation, fire extinguishers, safety areas for power tools, and a first aid kit. Cleaning up may require running water, soap, and towels.

Music

Combinations of sounds stir our emotions. People feel music—this is its basic function. Because of music's mood-setting quality, it is often used to set the tone for other recreation activities. Music at a party, ice hockey game, and evening campfire is considered an absolute requirement. Music can be used in programs to control behavior, develop group unity, and provide therapy. And music programming is useful for its own sake. Appreciation of its form, balance, and rhythm helps people express joy, sorrow, and love. Here are a few basic planning considerations (Russell, 1982):

- *Technical knowledge and ability are required.* Qualified leadership is a must for music programs. For participants in music programs to enjoy and be satisfied with the experience, they must be guided to achieve higher levels of results.

Crafts are often combined with other recreation activity areas, such as outdoors or nature.

- *Use available community resources.* Recruit the expertise, facilities, and supplies of other organizations. Both private and commercial music organizations have extensive instructional and performing music programs that can be tapped into and coordinated with your agency's music programming.

- *Seek to serve all interests.* Because music appeals to everyone, a wide variety of music preferences exists. Be sensitive to the different tastes of the clientele in order to select, organize, and introduce appropriate music experiences.

Hobbies

Hobbies are a more important activity area than many leisure programmers realize. Because hobbies are more readily identified as individual pursuits, not requiring agency resources, they are often ignored in leisure services. Yet, even though hobbies are based on independent exploration, programmed services can support and extend the hobby interests of constituents. Such services as beginning instruction, club meetings, shows and exhibitions, demonstrations, and supplies can greatly enhance the hobby experience. Some planning considerations follow (Russell, 1982):

- *Focus on linking hobbyists with each other.* Programs that help the hobbyist meet and interact with other hobbyists in the same field are most useful. Sometimes this simply means providing a place where hobby groups can meet.

- *Provide assistance for initiating hobbies.* This could include learning about the scope of the hobby and providing information on how to get started, sources for materials, and help for continued interest.

Outdoors or Nature

Outdoor recreation is not just playing outdoors. Activities in this category must have a meaningful and intentional relationship with the natural environment. Because outdoor activities are resource based, they depend strongly on the wise use of natural resources. How people pursue resource-based recreation depends on varying factors, including their skill and opportunities. For example, when cost and performance requirements are low (such as hiking in the woods), more people will partake of the activity. Conversely, when the requirements of an outdoor activity are many and demanding (such as backpacking), there are fewer participants. Here are some general suggestions for programming (Russell, 2005):

- *Be alert to the leadership requirements of conducting programs.* Many activities require special training in safety procedures or the natural sciences. For example, knowledgeable leadership most likely will require course work in the natural sciences as well as first aid and perhaps even campcraft.

- *Look for opportunities to program even within urban areas.* When developing outdoor programs, enthusiastic and competent leaders can sometimes compensate for the lack of large and remote outdoor areas.

- *Plan for balance and simplicity.* Plan programs that caution the overly bold and encourage the overly timid. Build activities around local materials and the common, everyday, unseen miracles of nature. Base the program on discovery and firsthand experience.

- *Strive for a conservation ethic.* In every outdoor or nature program, include messages and experiences in natural resource conservation. Helping participants understand what is ecologically happening around them is the goal. See the box on this page for an example of conservation in outdoor recreation.

Earthwatch Expedition: Butterflies of Vietnam

The Earthwatch organization exists through a combination of the outdoor recreation and travel activity areas. For close to $2,000, tourists are able to help naturalists in Vietnam better understand butterflies as sensitive indicators of ecological health by monitoring and collecting more than 100 species of butterflies in the Tam Dao National Park.

Prized by collectors, butterflies are also sensitive indicators of ecological change. Thanks to their astounding diversity, high visibility, short life cycles, and specialized host-plant requirements, these living bursts of color provide a window into the health of an ecosystem. That window is desperately needed for Tam Dao National Park, which is struggling against a growing human population and a history of exploitation for timber, wildlife, and slash-and-burn agriculture.

Reprinted, by permission, from Earthwatch, www.earthwatch.org/expeditions/vu.html.

Intellectual or Literary

Even though mental-type recreation offerings occupy a relatively small place in comprehensive leisure programs, such activities are becoming an increasingly vital element—think of the current interest in sudoku. Many intellectual activities require "no audience, no teammate, no partner, and no special facility" (Russell, 1982, p. 154). In fact, studying, creative writing, and reading can often best be experienced in solitude. Nonetheless, programmers should include literary opportunities for clientele in a comprehensive program for the following reason:

- *Many activities are inexpensive.* Mental and literary activities typically require minimal resources (such as facilities, leaders, equipment) yet appeal to a wide range of people. All you may need to provide is a quiet corner, a computer station, or a table and chairs.
- *Many activities are convenient to the recreator.* They can be engaged in at home, at work, in the yard, and in many other areas.
- *Many activities appeal to a wide range of people.* Programming activities in this activity area are not restricted according to age, gender, or ethnicity. Indeed, reading a good book together can often bridge difference gaps among people.

Travel

Whether it is an afternoon outing to a nearby woods or a three-week trip to Kathmandu, travel programs should be carefully planned. The degree of effort required, of course, will depend on the destination and the number of participants. By and large, however, there are some basic planning considerations (Russell, 2005):

- *Trips should not be extemporaneous.* No matter how short and near, they should be carefully planned.
- *Make sure travelers are well oriented to the trip's purpose and logistics before departure.* Plan pretrip briefings, or develop other recreational programs to support the trip. For example, before a trip to Italy, take the teen group to a local Italian restaurant to practice ordering in Italian and to sample foods they have never tried.
- *Do not attempt to include too much activity in one trip.* Travel is inherently tiring, even for youth, so pacing trip activities to allow ample free time for rest or self-exploration is important.

- *Make contingency arrangements.* Even for the most thoroughly planned trip, alternative transportation modes, restaurant choices, and event tickets may be required. Also plan for the possibility of last-minute cancellations by the travelers themselves.
- *Successful tour leadership is critically important.* The tour guide must show integrity by following the customs and rules of the destination, by remaining pleasant regardless of any problems that arise, and by handling these problems firmly and cheerfully.

Social Recreation

Social recreation activities bring people together for the purpose of socializing. At its best, a social recreation program provides a relaxed experience. Unlike some other activity areas where challenge, skill development, and winning are primary, social recreation tends to feature the ordinary and the familiar (Russell, 1982). Further, social recreation is also unique in that it relies on all other program areas to meet its social interaction objective. For example, a party may include experiences in sports, drama, music, crafts, and dance. Here are some planning considerations (Russell, 1982):

- *The most important factor is appropriateness.* Programming for social interaction requires attention to the nature of the group and the purpose of the gathering. For example, is this an introductory gathering of strangers, a ladies luncheon, a high school class reunion, or a company picnic?
- *Pay attention to the social action curve.* This means there should be a subdued level of excitement as the participants arrive for the event. The excitement builds to a higher level about midway through, then returns to a lower level toward the event's end. The social program should have a definite beginning and end.
- *Plan for leadership appropriateness.* The social recreation facilitator must be able to study the group and the situation and recognize when to insert direct stimulation or control and when to allow the natural flow of events to occur.

Volunteer Service

Volunteering is a special activity that also applies to all the recreation activity areas. Within sport, aquatic, adventure, dance, drama, fine art, craft, literary, travel, and social programs, there are participants who receive primarily altruistic benefit by volunteering their time and energy to help others in the program. Serving as a Girl Scout leader, coaching a youth basketball team, and reading to patients in a convalescent center are examples of recreation programs in and of themselves. As a programmer, a portion of your planning needs to focus on your program volunteers according to these principles (Russell, 1982):

- *Purposefully recruit volunteers.* The most effective volunteers are those recruited for their special talent, training, or interest in the program.

- *Be clear about volunteer assignments.* Discuss exact arrangements with all volunteers at the time of their recruitment. Provide a specific job description, and outline the time commitment and duration of the volunteer service.

- *Supervise volunteers.* As you would do for paid employees, regularly observe and assist volunteers. Be alert to their motivations and their need for a meaningful challenge. Recognize volunteers for their achievements.

Volunteering in a recreation program in and of itself provides recreational benefit. These adult volunteers are lending their expertise to a youth soccer program.

Program Formats

Within every activity area, recreational experiences can be conducted according to specific structures. These **program formats** show how activities are organized for participation. Usually the programmer can choose the format, which should be selected according to the objectives of the program. Further, and ideally, participants in comprehensive program services should be able to select from a variety of formats. For example, a person interested in the sport activity of basketball should be able to choose from a basketball league, a basketball clinic, a trip to a college or professional basketball game, or pickup basketball play at the gym.

The most frequently used program formats are competition, open facility, special event, special interest group, and instructional. The experience of a recreational activity will be different according to the format provided. For more information on this topic, see worksheet 4.2 in chapter 4 of the CD-ROM.

Competition

In the **competition** program format, a participant's performance is judged by and compared with his own previous performance, the performance of other participants, or an established standard (Russell, 1982). The competition format itself may take different forms. Organizational patterns such as tournaments, contests, meets, and leagues are the most common forms (see table 4.2).

Nearly every recreation activity can be competitively structured. Although sports have traditionally dominated competition program services, the capable programmer realizes that drama, music, fine arts, and even intellectual activities easily lend themselves to the competition format. For example, a Saturday afternoon watercolor painting contest at a state park, a "battle of the bands" at the community center, and a one-act play competition at dusk on the beach are

TABLE 4.2

Structures of the Competition Format

Form of competition	Definition	Examples
Tournament	Competitors take part in limited–time events that rely on specific organizational configurations for determining winning and losing.	Single-elimination softball tournament, round-robin badminton tournament, consolation Monopoly tournament
Contest	Competitors compare ability through parallel performances, with a set standard determining the winner.	Spelling bee, dance contest, street ball tour, chili cook-off
Meet	Competitors participate in a series of contests involving the measurement of skills against those of all participants. If team based, individual scores are combined for a total team score.	Track meet, gymnastics meet, figure skating competition
League	Teams or individuals play one another over an extended period of time. The ultimate winner is determined as the one with the most wins.	Bowling league, Little League baseball, slamball league

Too Much Competition?

The following excerpt is taken from an essay by a college student:

> As a child I participated in numerous sports. However, the only sport in which I did large amounts of traveling was during AAU basketball. Looking back on my years of AAU basketball, they were fun at the time, but I wish I hadn't played for so many years. We would have at least four games per week and tournaments on the weekends. During a typical tournament, we played seven games in two days. We the players became so burned out on weekends that it carried over into the school week. Our focus was considerably lacking because we were just so tired. Also, our parents had to sit through all of our games which I am sure was not fun, especially sitting on bleachers. Overall, participating in sports this way was not as beneficial as everyone thought it was going to be.

For more information on this topic, see "More Options for Individual Programming Practice," option 4, in chapter 4 of the CD-ROM.

programs that provide participants with an opportunity to test themselves on a variety of levels. When well planned and well led, competitive recreation can serve as a motivator for continued interest and improvement in an activity. This requires providing for skill development, along with respect and dignity in play. For more information on this topic, see "More Options for Individual Programming Practice," option 1, in chapter 4 of the CD-ROM.

Yet, programming in the competition format can be frustrating. For example, even when your programming philosophy is focused on the recreational values of competition, participants, as well as parents and coaches, can push for a more "win at all costs" posture (see the box on this page). Thus, for the competition experience in recreation programs to be fulfilling for the participants, these two principles should be kept in mind (Russell, 1982):

- *Participants in a competition should always be matched with others with similar skills, ability, and size.* If this is not possible, such mechanisms as handicapping could be used to equalize the competition. Activities themselves can also be modified to equalize competition. For example, in tennis, less-experienced players could be allowed two bounces instead of one before the ball is returned over the net.

- *Participants in a competition should be able to expect a fair and safe environment.* Safety is both physical and emotional and is a high priority in competition. Participants need to feel in control of their own situations and believe they are being treated equitably. Rules of the game must be fair and enforced.

For more information on this topic, see "Group Discussion Ideas," option 3, in chapter 4 of the CD-ROM.

The programming principles of the competition format can be applied to all the recreation activity areas. For example, this sand castle–building contest in San Clemente, California, is an annual event.

© Nik Wheeler/CORBIS.

Open Facility

The **open facility** format facilitates casual, drop-in activity participation. Also known as informal, it is a program format that encourages spontaneous involvement by assigning a certain portion of time for a facility or part of a facility to be available for unstructured, self-directed play. For example, open swims at the pool, practice putting greens at the country club, open bowling lanes, music practice rooms at the community center, and open courts and gymnasium times at the high school are easy opportunities for participants to experience programmed leisure—no classes to enroll in, clubs to join, or teams to try out for. Thus, we recommend you give this format careful consideration for its usefulness in creating a comprehensive program service.

Open facility is frequently an overlooked or underplanned format (Russell, 1982)—the time set aside is often limited to what is left over after scheduled programs. Yet, for many participants, such informal participation is the most satisfying because it doesn't require any advance commitment.

For the programmer, however, open facility programs do require planning and preparation. We recommend that you first study a facility's use and determine when people are most likely to want to drop in. The resulting open facility schedule should then be communicated widely. Your agency may decide to provide supervisory staff to maintain order and facilitate safe play, as well as to provide assistance or information when requested by participants. Some agencies have also found it more beneficial to supply the equipment needed for open-play programs. Here are some planning tips:

• *Establish a conducive environment for meaningful play, and then provide general supervision if necessary for safety.* Even drop-in programs have specific goals for participants. For example, a well-run program of free play for children might aim to select toys, materials, and an environment appropriate for arousing children's curiosity or practicing sharing.

• *Constantly monitor and evaluate use of the open facility and equipment so that the best possible environment can be provided.* When participants leave activities prematurely, raise their voices, lose interest, or resort to arguing, reprogramming for the time and space is needed.

YMCA Basketball/Volleyball Court Rules

- Game ends when one team gets 10 baskets
- Winners can stay, but only two consecutive games
- Each new game must have at least 5 new players
- The next team to play must have a representative on the floor and ready for the next game
- Full court games on both courts only during the following:
    - Weekdays, 11:30am to 1:30pm
    - Sundays 8:00am to Noon
    - Special circumstances designated by staff
- If class/ program or a full court game is occupying one court then: only half of remaining court may be used for game play.
- One basket must always be available as a shooting basket except:
    - Weekdays, 11:30am to 1:30pm
    - Sundays 8:00am to Noon

Please ask for Building Supervisor assistance in regard to the above rules. The supervisor has the authority to enforce rules deemed appropriate. Supervisor decision is final.

ABSOLUTELY NO PROFANITY OR ABUSIVE BEHAVIOR WILL BE TOLERATED

Managing gym users' behavior in an open facility format means creating policies such as these posted at a YMCA in Monroe County, Indiana.

In some cases, it may be necessary to plan for inappropriate uses of the open facility format. For example, programmers should be alert to the problem of absent parents using this option for drop-off child care for their young children. Also, you may need to prepare for issues of gang actions, fighting between participants, and use of the space as shelter from bad weather by persons who are homeless. This often requires creating use policies for the drop-in program.

Special Events

The program format of **special events** gives both programmers and program participants opportunities for unique and celebratory recreation activities. Special events are "planned occurrences designed to entertain, inform, or provide enjoyment and/or inspiration to audiences and/or spectators" (Jack-

Types of Special Events

Banquets	Hunts
Campfires	Jamborees
Carnivals	Open houses
Ceremonies	Openings
Dedications	Pageants
Demonstrations	Parades
Exhibits	Races
Fairs	Rallies
Fests	Roundups
Field days	Sales
Fiestas	Shows

son, 1997, p. xii). A pizza party in the bleachers at the end of youth basketball season, a style show at the Girls Inc. clubhouse, a volunteer-appreciation banquet—these are all examples of special programs that deviate from the norm (see the box on this page for more examples).

The number of special events is increasing. For example, each year in the United States alone, more than 20,000 regularly recurring community festivals are held—a figure that is growing at about 5 percent each year (Janiskee, 1996).

The purpose of this program format is to change the pace, ignite enthusiasm, reward accomplishments, honor talents, announce new things, or end old things (Russell, 2005). Indeed, leisure service organizations frequently rely on the special event format to attract interest to their regular program services. Programmers can use shows, roundups, pageants, parades, Olympics, exhibitions, fairs, and festivals to raise funds, recruit new participants, unify different program activity areas, and deliver a message to people outside their organizations' usual service reach.

The most prominent planning factor for special events is that they are bigger than usual. In fact, bigness is what makes the event special. An extreme example is the "World's Largest Barbecue," an annual community event held in Abilene, Texas. Sponsored since 1965 by the city of Abilene and the Dyess Air Force Base MWR department, the event has grown to rely on more than 225 volunteers to dish up 1,000 pounds (450 kilograms) of Texas beef and a truckload of coleslaw and baked beans to more than 10,000 hungry people (Bailey, 1995).

Now consider the monthly art exhibit held at Charleston Gardens assisted living facility in Charleston, West Virginia. The watercolor painting class of usually five students displays their month's work in the dining room during lunch on the fourth Friday of that month. About 35 admirers view and comment on the paintings. In both examples, the point is not about absolute bigness, it's about relative bigness. Special events are always bigger than regularly offered program services.

Relative bigness requires more planning effort and makes the planning more complex. Crowd control, intricate scheduling, provision of extra facilities and services (such as parking and restrooms), and extra cleanup details are issues programmers are not usually required to accommodate on a daily basis. As well, the provision of instructional signs, roped-off areas, wheelchair access, foul weather options, and even extension cords require more preplanning time and list making. All this often means that the planning effort goes beyond the single-handed efforts of the programmer, with various subfunctions assigned to separate committees. Here are some tips to help:

- *Begin planning well in advance of the event.* Some events require that planning be initiated months and even years ahead of time.

- *Coordinate your event date with other community special events to ensure they do not conflict.* Or collaborate with other same-date events to create more interest. Plan on alternative rain dates or alternative rain locations.

- *Form a planning committee and, if necessary, various subcommittees.* Individual subcommittees could take responsibility for facilities, safety, publicity, concessions, fund-raising, cleanup, and so on.

For more information on this topic, see "Group Discussion Ideas," option 2, in chapter 4 of the CD-ROM. 💿

Special Interest Groups

Participants who wish to experience a recreational activity in an ongoing, focused way are often attracted to programs in the **special interest group** format. This format offers participants in a particular activity

The "pirate invasion" is a special segment of the weeks-long Gasparilla, a festival held annually in Tampa, Florida, that attracts 500,000 people for just one day.

© Ruth V. Russell

continuous support and opportunity for socialization. The euchre club, biking club, gourmet cooking club, book club, and quilting club are examples of special interest groups formed around a specific activity. A senior citizen club, teen club, wives club, and neighborhood association are examples of special interest groups formed around other unifying factors such as age, family role, and locale.

In the special interest group format, diverse needs and interests can be met simultaneously. The format provides a communication and inspiration contact point that helps create and reinforce individual interests. Information is traded, challenges are generated, and collective group energies are constructed. All this is accomplished with only minimal planning and leadership efforts by the sponsoring organization.

The organizational pattern of these clubs usually provides for self-direction by members. As a programmer, you will often provide assistance in establishing a club, after which the various activities become the responsibility of the club's officers and members (Russell, 1982). Your assistance may include developing written agreements such as bylaws or constitutions, selecting leadership, defining financial needs, and providing a space or facility. This latter effort depends, of course, on the nature of the club. A model train club, for example, will likely have high demands for an appropriate facility, including a designated indoor room, elevated platforms, and extra electrical outlets; a model airplane club will likely need only the temporary use of a sports field or meadow. Here are some guiding programming principles for special interest groups:

- *Ensure that membership in the club is open.* All interested participants should be included in the club activities sponsored by your organization.

- *Volunteers often operate specific club programs, but professional programmers are ultimately responsible for overseeing their quality.* Remain attentive to club activities and decisions. Although special interest groups offer an easy way to extend program services, never relinquish control over their agreement with the programming philosophy of your organization.

Instructional

Finally, we consider the **instructional** program format. Perhaps most organized recreation activity participation uses this instructional, or class, format. Why might this be so? Recreational participation is likely to achieve its fullest potential when skills and knowledge are at least adequate. As you know, it's difficult to enjoy photography if you don't know how to operate a camera, or softball if you haven't mastered throwing the ball, or being in a swimming pool if you can't swim. Since we are societies of the "quick fix" and immediate results, the instructional class format is a good way to get our recreational abilities in order. We sign up for a Friday afternoon cross-country skiing class before embarking on a weekend cross-country skiing tour.

The instructional format for programming is a highly structured learning situation in which individuals or groups meet in order to be taught specific recreational skills or knowledge. The purpose is to learn, practice, and improve with the guidance of a teacher. For example, a senior center might offer classes in investing for retirement, genealogy, tai chi, using the Internet, and woodcarving. Even though learning occurs during participation in all program formats, opportunities for teaching and learning are explicit in a class setting. An important advantage for the teacher is that in the recreational class, students are often participating voluntarily and therefore have learning readiness and enthusiasm (as with students attending Mini University, described in the box on page 63).

The instructional format specifies a high degree of leadership, a limited number of participants, a series of meeting dates and times, and regular occupancy of a particular facility or equipment. An enrollment fee is also common. Following are some suggestions for planning an instructional format program (Russell, 1982):

- *For optimal recreational value, keep class size to a reasonable number.* This may mean 20 participants or fewer, depending on the number of teachers.

- *Scheduling of class sessions should allow for sufficient time between sessions for outside practice.* Also, depending on constituent needs, the length of class "seasons" should be limited to four to six weeks.

Participants look to the instructional format to get them ready as quickly as possible for recreational experiences.

- *Teachers must have sound credentials.* Program leaders in the instructional format are teachers who are able to choose and deliver the most appropriate means of instruction for the situation.

- *Class sessions should build on each other.* Participants should be able to move through the class, progressively becoming more capable in the skill taught.

Workshops, seminars, institutes, clinics, conventions, and conferences are special cases of the class format. The purpose is still instructional, but because there is usually involvement in a single subject over a short time period, these forms provide participants with an intense and singularly focused recreation experience. For example, a one-day softball batting clinic held for middle school girls in February initiates interest for the upcoming softball season and begins preparing potential players for team tryouts. For more information on this topic, see "Group Discussion Ideas," option 4, in chapter 4 of the CD-ROM.

Putting the Components Together

Now that you know the possible recreation activity areas and formats for programs, let's talk about how to mix and match them. That is, recreation activity areas and formats can be clustered, modified, and substituted to create program services that are tailored to meet constituent needs and interests as well as reflect agency objectives and philosophy.

To illustrate, let's assume you've decided to offer a sport program for youth. Depending on your goals for the program, you'll need to select the specific sport activity. Will it be soccer, basketball, lacrosse, or tee ball? Further, you'll need to match the sport activity with an appropriate format. Will the lacrosse program, for example, be instructional, competitive, or a special event? How are such programming decisions made? One tool is activity analysis.

Activity analysis breaks an activity or format into parts so that its structure and characteristics can be analyzed. Its purpose is to provide a rational means of determining the best activity and format combination for meeting programming goals. For example, a game of checkers usually requires mental abilities. Players must understand the rules and strategy of play and must be able to concentrate. Socially, checkers requires taking turns and respecting others. It also demands sitting still and emotional control (Stumbo & Peterson, 2004).

As a result of even this quick analysis, you will realize that checkers is not appropriate for all program clients, such as preschool children or patients with back pain. Following are a few general principles for activity analysis (Farrell & Lundegren, 1978; Russell, 1982):

- *Analyze the activity as it is normally carried out.* Understand the activity in its truest form, without accommodation for any specific type of constituent, time of day, or location.

- *Analyze the activity according to the minimal level of ability required.* For example, when analyzing golf, consider the ability level needed for recreational participation, not that of a tournament professional. Further, what is the usual degree of body contact? The normal amount of risk?

- *Analyze the activity according to four behavioral domains.* What are the physical, emotional, intellectual, and social demands of the activity? For example, bingo makes low demands on social interaction, neuromuscular control, and emotional maturity. Yet some intellectual ability is required to listen for and find numbers on the card.

• *Analyze the activity according to its resource requirements.* What facilities, equipment, and leadership are needed? Ice hockey, for example, requires significantly more facility and player equipment resources than does soccer. And special events usually make more demands on equipment and leadership than the open facility format.

• *Analyze the activity according to its duration requirements.* How long does an activity take to complete? A game of basketball, for example, has specific timing demands, while a game of Monopoly does not.

• *Analyze the activity according to participant characteristic requirements.* Does the activity require a certain number of participants? Is it age, gender, or culture specific?

Refer again to table 4.1 on pages 47-50 for additional dimensions against which to compare activities. Activity analysis can be based on organizational level, participant groupings, participant skill level, and cost. As well, dimensions such as use of rewards and punishments, space requirements, rules complexity, and interactiveness (Farrell & Lundegren, 1991) can be the basis of activity analysis. For more information on this topic, see "Group Discussion Ideas," option 1, in chapter 4 of the CD-ROM.

Activity analysis helps the programmer customize programs by determining the most appropriate activities and formats. When it's established that an activity or format is not suitable for a client or group, activity analysis can help you determine how to cluster, modify, or substitute to make it more appropriate.

Activity Clustering

Activity clustering is the identification of recreation activities or formats that yield similar benefits or that belong together for particular reasons. Programmers are interested in this information because participants tend to confine themselves to certain clusters of activity.

Activities can be clustered into many domains. For one, they can be reasonably grouped by action level—active or passive. As illustration, within the drama activity area, such activities as dramatic games and clowning could be clustered together as active, and storytelling and dramatic readings might be grouped together as passive.

Bishop (1970) also suggests a clustering factor based on potency, where "virile" activities are those in which individuals attempt to prove themselves, such as mountain climbing, solo sailing, bow hunting, and rugby. Status could also serve as a clustering factor, grouping activities according to level of sophistication or cost. Program formats can also be grouped together. For example, combining competition with a special event could produce a chili cook-off program.

Using the results of activity analysis, programmers can choose activities and formats that have a high association with each other, then group them together into the same program service to best match constituent characteristics. Bishop (1970) found that diversity of activities was more popular with younger participants.

Activity Modifying

From activity clustering, programmers are able to modify and substitute activities. **Activity modification** is the changing of an element or elements of an activity so that it can be adapted to participant ability or need. For instance, through equipment modifications persons who use wheelchairs can play golf, downhill snow ski, compete in a basketball league, compete in marathons, and successfully participate in just about any sport activity available. Activity modification has become increasingly used by recreation programmers as a means of complying with the Americans with Disabilities Act (ADA). Passed in 1990, the ADA makes it illegal in the United States to discriminate against a person on the basis of a cognitive, physical, or sensory limitation.

Typically, activities are modified by changing procedures or operations of play, such as modifying the rules; by making environmental adaptations, such as adjusting the play boundaries; by making equipment adaptations or changing equipment, such as using tennis rackets with bigger heads for beginners; and by adding human assistance, such as verbally guiding a woodland hiker with a visual disability. Smith, Austin, and Kennedy (1996) offer these guidelines for modifying activities:

• Change as little as possible.
• Involve participants in the modification process.

- Avoid making unfounded assumptions about a person's abilities.
- Consider all levels of involvement.
- If activity modifications are made, apply them to all participants rather than just to a subgroup.
- Give participants opportunities for free choice.

Activity Substituting

Another mix-and-match tool for the programmer is **activity substitution**, which involves determining which activities may be replaced with other ones while still meeting the same needs and providing essentially the same leisure experience. For example, a person's need to take risks could be met by hang gliding, rock climbing, gambling, and even giving a first public performance. Substitution is based on the idea that a particular activity meaning can be met by a different activity. For more information on this topic, see worksheet 4.3 in chapter 4 of the CD-ROM.

In some programming situations, this may be very useful. Suppose several campers at a resident camp are interested in drama. There are not enough people for formal play productions, so instead the programmer substitutes miming. Miming provides a similar dramatic performance opportunity and can be learned and expressed with as few as one participant. For more information on this topic, see "Can You Solve This Programming Issue?" in chapter 4 of the CD-ROM.

Summary

This chapter focuses on recreation program activity areas and formats for how leisure experiences are typically put together as services delivered to people. You should understand the following key points:

- Leisure experiences can be categorized by activity areas and by program formats.
- There are many ways to group activities; the most common is according to types of leisure behaviors, such as sports, aquatics, adventure, dance, drama, fine arts, crafts, music, hobbies, outdoors or nature, intellectual or literary, travel, social recreation, and volunteer service.
- Activities within these categories can be formatted differently; the most common formats are

competition, open facility, special event, special interest group, and instructional.

- Recreation activity areas and program formats are components that can be combined in many ways to achieve the sponsoring agency's programming goals.
- To accomplish this, activities and formats are selected, clustered, modified, and substituted for their greatest potential.
- A tool for helping in this "juggling act" is activity analysis.

Glossary

activity areas—A set or grouping of similar recreation behaviors.

program format—The organizing structure of recreational activities.

competition format—A participant's performance is compared with that of other participants or an established standard.

open facility format—Casual, drop-in participation.

special event format—A special treatment of a regular program.

special interest group format—People are organized around an activity or purpose.

instructional format—A structured learning situation.

activity analysis—Breaking a recreational activity into parts.

activity clustering—Identification of recreation activities or program formats that yield similar or compatible benefits.

activity modification—Changing elements of an activity or format so that it can be adapted to participant ability or need.

activity substitution—Replacing activities with other ones that provide essentially the same recreation experience.

References

Bailey, S. (1995). The world's largest barbecue. *Parks and Recreation, 30*(1), 50-51.

Bishop, D.W. (1970). Stability of the factor structure of leisure behavior: Analysis of four communities. *Journal of Leisure Research, 2*(3), 160-170.

Earthwatch Institute. (n.d.). Butterflies of Vietnam. Retrieved January 5, 2005, from www.earthwatch.org/expeditions/vu.html.

Farrell, P., & Lundegren, H. (1978). *The process of recreation programming: Theory and technique.* New York: Wiley.

Farrell, P., & Lundegren, H. (1991). *The process of recreation programming: Theory and technique* (3rd ed.). State College, PA: Venture.

Jackson, R. (1997). *Making special events fit in the 21st century.* Champaign, IL: Sagamore.

Janiskee, R. (1996). The temporal distribution of America's community festivals. *Festival Management and Event Tourism, 2*(1), 10-14.

NMBCC. (2001-2006). Our mission. Retrieved February 27, 2007, from www.indiana.edu/%7Enmbcc/home.htm.

Russell, R.V. (1982). *Planning programs in recreation.* St. Louis: Mosby.

Russell, R.V. (2005). *Leadership in recreation* (3rd ed.). Boston: McGraw-Hill.

Smith, R., Austin, D., & Kennedy, D. (1996). *Inclusive and special recreation: Opportunities for persons with disabilities* (3rd ed.). Dubuque, IA: Brown & Benchmark.

Stumbo, N., & Peterson, C. (2004). *Therapeutic recreation program design: Principles and procedures* (4th ed.). San Francisco: Cummings.

CHAPTER 5

Overview of the Program Planning Process

In this chapter, you can look forward to the following:

- Identifying the common overall models for the provision of programmed leisure today
- Learning the three steps required to achieve these structures: preparation, implementation, and evaluation
- Making a commitment to approaching recreation program planning as a systematic and accountable process
- Becoming familiar with the program planning steps to establish a readiness for the remaining chapters in the book

The Special Olympics program illustrates the social advocacy model, a philosophical structure for providing leisure programs that we explore later in this chapter.

© Rick Stewart/Allsport/Getty Imagses.

Special Olympics is an international nonprofit organization "dedicated to empowering individuals with intellectual disabilities to become physically fit, productive and respected members of society through sports training and competition" (Special Olympics, n.d.). Through 26 Olympic-type summer and winter sports, Special Olympics currently serves more than 2.25 million children and adults with intellectual disabilities in more than 150 countries. Truly global, with more than 500,000 athletes in China, more than 4,400 in Rwanda, and more than 600 in Afghanistan, this program helps participants grow through improved motor skills, greater self-confidence, and a more positive self-image. It also creates positive public attitudes toward a population that is often rejected or forgotten. The Special Olympics organization can be seen as illustrating a particular philosophical goal, or model, for what leisure program services will accomplish.

Planning year-round programs for a large city park and recreation department is more complicated than planning an overnight camping trip for a Girl Scout troop. These two program efforts differ as well in their philosophical premise. Yet, committing yourself to providing people with quality leisure experiences and thereby serving the needs of society and individuals in both situations is a professional challenge requiring an understanding of the basics of planning theory and process.

Much of what recreation programmers do and why we do it is based on basic approaches from other disciplines (Russell, 1982). For example, we incorporate the field of social work when we view program planning as a means for solving problems, and we rely on business fields when we see planning as a way of managing change. Planning anything, including leisure program services, involves choices about not only what but also why. What goals do we pursue through recreation programs? Why are we willing to maximize people, money, expertise, facility, and equipment resources to achieve these goals? And what's the best way to maximize them?

Accordingly, in this chapter we establish the basis for all remaining chapters by presenting leisure program models and the program planning process.

Program Models

At the outset you must be clear about your overall strategy, or model, for providing programmed leisure. A **program model** is the overall structure for a program. It is based on the philosophical goals of what the program services will accomplish. This means programs will differ in their approach depending on which model you adopt. For example, in certain models, such as community development, competitive sport is inappropriate, while for other models, such as marketing, competitive sport will be useful. One way to see this difference is to consider program planning strategies as a continuum (see figure 5.1.)

The most commonly adopted program models in leisure service organizations are social advocacy, social planning, marketing, and community development. As they are listed, a continuum of the degree of direct involvement by the programmer is suggested. In the social advocacy model, at one end of the continuum, programmers are considered the expert authority and are usually directly involved in all aspects of the program. At the other end of the continuum, the community development model uses the programmer only as a facilitator. Here participants identify their own needs and solutions, and

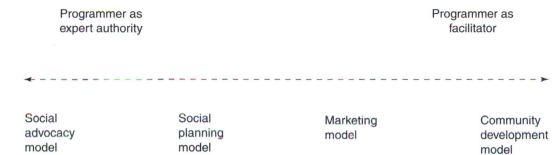

Figure 5.1 The continuum of common program models in leisure services.

the programmer and agency assist with resources as required. For more information on this topic, see "Group Discussion Ideas," option 2, in chapter 5 of the CD-ROM.

Social Advocacy Model

The **social advocacy model** is an approach that views leisure programs as promoting a cause, idea, or policy. As illustrated in the chapter's opening case of Special Olympics, the social advocacy model seeks to promote underrepresented groups. This programming approach has a prominent history in our fields. More than 100 years ago, social reformers such as Jane Addams and Ellen Starr, founders of the Hull House settlement in Chicago, advocated for the improvement of life for disadvantaged groups of people through the provision of recreation programs. They primarily used social recreation, special events, and cultural art classes to help immigrants adjust to their new lives in industrial America. For more information on this topic, see worksheet 5.1 in chapter 5 of the CD-ROM.

Social Planning Model

The **social planning model** focuses on helping communities identify strengths and weaknesses and determine ways to improve the quality of life in the community. This approach balances the distribution of resources according to need. Programmers adopting the social planning model strategically plan, organize, and deliver program services according to rational professional-inspired principles. Needs are identified, and programs are developed to meet these needs. The Boys and Girls Clubs of Metro Atlanta, Georgia, for example, has identified the need of employability for its members. Accordingly, career readiness workshops, community service clubs, and workplace exchange programs help the children and teen members explore their future work interests, set

goals, and develop skills for successfully achieving these goals (Boys and Girls Clubs of Metro Atlanta, 2004). For more information on this topic, see "Can You Solve This Programming Issue?" in chapter 5 of the CD-ROM.

Marketing Model

The **marketing model** of programmed leisure focuses on giving people what they want. Market-driven programs are customer oriented. Sometimes referred to as planning according to "expressed desires," this approach requires extensive attention to whom the programs serve and how best to match program services to them.

The cruise industry provides an example. Dining onboard has become an experience of options. Traditionally, cruise dining meant eating in the same dining room, at the same table, with the same people, and at the same time every evening. Yet for Princess Cruises, "personal choice was top priority when the Princess fleet was created. Your 'what you want, when you want it' cruise gracefully unfolds with an endless array of options. You can choose between an Italian trattoria and a southwestern cantina, in addition to our regular dining room" (Travel Reservations Center, 2006).

Community Development Model

The **community development model** is a grassroots empowerment process where people are partners in creating their own leisure programs. This approach builds communities on a local level, with emphasis on building the economy, forging and strengthening social ties, and developing the nonprofit sector. Under the community development model, recreation programs are used to stimulate local initiative, which means the programmer serves as an enabler, helping people and communities identify their own programs.

For example, in Bloomington, Indiana, the city parks and recreation department, local radio and television stations, the United Way, the Indiana Criminal Justice Institute, the telephone company, and the county tobacco prevention coalition have all joined forces to provide a facility and expert support for teens in a youth radio program. The format used is open facility as future disc jockeys, news reporters, and music critics are given a chance to learn about the inner workings of a radio station, spin their own musical selections, promote youth activities, and discuss youth and community issues. For more information on this topic, see "Group Discussion Ideas," option 1, and worksheet 5.2 in chapter 5 of the CD-ROM.

Program Planning Process

The philosophical approach chosen for leisure program service delivery also dictates the procedures followed to create programs. Program planning requires that programmers follow a step-by-step process of procedures to the degree dictated by the program model. The social advocacy model, for example, requires more comprehensive adherence to the steps, while the community development model uses the steps to a lesser degree.

This weekly shuffleboard program is part of a comprehensive array of offerings at Ja-Man North Travel Park in Port Richey, Florida – all planned and implemented by the residents themselves. The result is a strong sense of community, even though residents are seasonal.

© Ruth V. Russell.

Regardless of the program model, however, all leisure programming efforts require these three basic steps: preparation, implementation, and evaluation (see figure 5.2). The **program planning process** is ordered and cyclical. Each step is a necessary prerequisite for the next step, and once completed, the entire cycle begins again. The sequence of steps is logical, and the programmer can return to any of the steps midprocess to make a correction or adjustment. This cyclical and rational nature is what makes the process of delivering organized leisure to people so successful. The task is vital; without a systematic approach, the programmer's efforts—indeed the entire profession—lack accountability.

The remainder of this book is organized according to these three steps of the program planning process. Although each of these steps has multiple substeps, or suggestions for how to accomplish them, all you really need to remember is to first prepare for the program, then deliver the prepared program to constituents, and finally, determine if the program accomplished what it intended. For more information on this topic, see "More Options for Individual Programming Practice," option 4, in chapter 5 of the CD-ROM.

Preparation

The first step is preparation. To provide the best possible program, what must you learn, decide, think through, and advocate beforehand? Basically, the more advanced the preparation, the more likely the program will succeed. Thorough and considered planning gives programs a better chance to accomplish good things. It's like eating a meal—the food will taste and look best with advance preparation.

To help you prepare the program, one of the first things you'll need is a thorough understanding of your organization and community (see chapter 6). Even though organized leisure is targeted to customers, clients, and participants, it always happens within the context of the sponsoring agency and community. If the program doesn't reflect or match the agency and community cultures, it will not be as useful.

As a planner, you should understand your agency's mission and philosophical base (see chapter 6). Sometimes the mission is made explicit in a constitution or set of bylaws, a charter, or an enabling legislation. Additionally, many organizations have formal mission statements as well as strategic and long-range planning documents that identify their visions and most important goals. Most leisure service organizations also have policies and procedures that must be fully understood by the planner at the outset. And, of course, a review of the program records from the past would be very helpful. All these things make up the agency's culture. What does the agency value most and therefore expect its programs to contribute?

In comparison to the other actions in program planning, this task is relatively static. Once you are thoroughly educated in your agency's philosophy and overall program goals, your base for planning will remain fairly stable. Yet, every time your organization develops a self-study report, holds a visioning session, or organizes a long-range planning task force, be involved. That way, you not only learn more about what's important but also, as a professional programmer, have a voice in establishing what's important.

Similarly, you should understand the nature of the community (see chapter 6). What does it value most? What is planned for future development in the public, private, and commercial sectors? What is the philosophical base of other agencies delivering leisure services in the community? What are the ideas of community leaders and officers? To answer these questions, you may need to conduct such diagnostics as an environmental scan, collect economic and demographic data, perform an existing conditions analysis, or undertake a trend analysis. The general task is to understand the social and political atmospheres of your program's community context.

Also critically vital to your preparation of recreation programs is a thorough understanding of potential participants (see chapter 7). Programs must be appropriate for the health, abilities, gender, age, race, ethnicity, lifestyle, residential situation, socioeconomic status, and other qualities of constituents. Who are the current participants, and who are the potential participants? Why haven't potential participants been involved before? What clients are not currently being served?

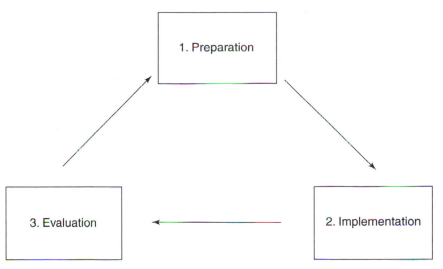

Figure 5.2 The three steps of the program planning process.

These key questions are so important that frequent formal assessment, called a **needs assessment**, is necessary (see chapter 7). Needs assessments employ questionnaires, interviews, observations, library data searches, or other research procedures to identify the needs, interests, and problems of constituents. The goal is to collect, analyze, and interpret information about customer behaviors, attitudes, interests, aspirations, and values so that you understand what programmed leisure services need to accomplish. From year to year, and from target population to target population, the need for programmed leisure differs. Constituent need must therefore be regularly identified so that your programs will be timely, desired by clients, and within their capabilities.

In terms of considering clients and customers, we also suggest you take steps to garner their support and involvement in the program preparations themselves (see chapter 6). This may take a long time, however. For example, before making major decisions about new or altered programs, such agencies as the U.S. Forest Service regularly conduct public meetings and forums to assess the reaction of users. Other strategies for involving participants in the preparations are task forces, citizen advisory boards, and advocacy groups. Gaining the support of politicians and other community agencies may also be called for at this point. These efforts might lead to very useful **interagency partnerships**. For more information on this topic, see "More Options for Individual Programming Practice," option 1, in chapter 5 of the CD-ROM.

Now we have come to the point in our preparations where goals and objectives for the program or program series can be determined (see chapter 8). What are the specific desired outcomes of the program? Goals and objectives validate the impetus for program service initiatives and changes. Priorities and time lines are agreed to. The programmer establishes a program rationale; the benefits the program will provide; and specifications for resource use, which may include program cost, length, and staffing and facility requirements.

In general, **goals** are broad statements of purpose or desired outcomes, while **objectives** are concrete, short-term, measurable statements of specific intentions. Usually there are two types of goals and objectives:

1. *External,* representing the goals or objectives the programmer and organization seek to meet for individual participants or the community at large
2. *Internal,* relating to operational efficiency, fiscal solvency, attendance or membership, and so on (Kraus, 1997)

Sometimes the establishment of goals and objectives for programs is the responsibility of the professional programmer. Other times they are determined by all the staff of an agency, by officials in the "home" office, or even by national or professional standards.

Regardless, the best advice is to get it all in writing. Purpose statements, goals lists, and individualized objectives should be set down on paper and made widely available. No matter how small and brief the program, having a written target helps you take better aim with the program you are planning. As well, these goals and objectives provide a basis for evaluating the program later on. For example, if a program objective is that participants learn to swim, develop a program design that focuses on this objective and then later assess whether participants really did learn to swim.

A final preparation is developing the actual design, or plan, of the program(s) (see chapter 9 and the box on page 73). The range of possibilities for programmed recreation activity is immense. There are thousands of different types of sports and games, outdoor recreation pursuits, high adventure, cultural arts, social events, and hobbies, in a host of varied formats, such as instructional classes or competition (see chapter 4). Based on all the other preparations that have been made up to this point, what exactly will the program be? What will best meet the goals and objectives, client interests and needs, and agency and community culture? Will the program be a rock climbing class? Or a watercolor painting exhibit? Or a trip to a Major League Baseball game? Hard choices and decisions are made.

The result is often referred to as the program plan—it contains the content and format of the program. In fact, there are many types of plans, including master plans, comprehensive plans, site-specific plans, seasonal plans, and individual participant plans (see chapter 9). As well, this last effort of preparation might include making and defending program proposals and writing progress reports for supervisors or governing authorities. For more information on this topic, see "More Options for Individual Programming Practice," option 2, in chapter 5 of the CD-ROM.

A swim instruction program must have clear objectives so that the agency can be held accountable for assessing whether participants really did learn to swim.

Canada's Big Plans

Managing nationally significant outdoor areas in Canada falls under the jurisdiction of Parks Canada, a unit of the federal Department of Canadian Heritage. Parks Canada manages the largest national park and historic site system in the world (Searle & Brayley, 2000), yet officials still consider the system incomplete. How are national parks established in Canada? According to a plan, of course. In fact, according to many plans!

The National Park System Plan classifies Canada into 39 distinct terrestrial natural regions. The intent is to establish at least one national park within each of these regions. Currently, of the 39 regions, 16 (primarily in the Arctic, British Columbia, and Quebec) remain unrepresented. Yet commitment to another plan—the Green Plan, a federal policy on the environment—has initiated a phased development approach to completing the national parks system early in this century.

Besides the national parks program, Parks Canada is also responsible for more than 100 nationally significant cultural heritage sites reflecting native, fur trade, and prairie settlement history. These themes, and their prioritization of significance, are based on the National Historic Sites System Plan. As well, the Canadian Heritage Rivers System Plan is a cooperative program of the federal, provincial, and territorial governments to acquire and manage scenic waterways.

Several written plans govern programming for the national parks of Canada.

© Altrendo Travel/Getty Images.

Implementation

Step two in the recreation program planning process is implementation. Depending on the scope of the program, this service-delivery phase of the programming process can take less than a day, or it can take years. The plan from the previous preparation step is put into action so that clients and customers experience the program (see the box on page 74 for an example). The programmer must pay attention to the details of conducting the program according to the plan.

For example, program resources such as budgets, staffing, and facilities are recruited (see chapter 10).

Perhaps more than ever before, programmers must develop revenue sources for and from organized recreation. Bill Mullins of the U.S. Navy's MWR operation writes:

> To increase the revenue-production potential of bowling programs, military services expanded their bowling operations to include attractive and well-maintained game rooms, quality fast-food operations, and an appealing resale area. As a result, services have improved and so have the profits. In fact, in fiscal year 1990, Navy bowling center profits increased 35.7 percent over the previous year. (1991, p. 40)

Program operation also invariably requires selecting activities, arranging schedules, developing program policies, preparing cancellation plans, and even naming programs (see chapter 10). Once the program is up and running, programmers and leaders must monitor them (see chapters 11 and 12). This is vital for a smooth operation. **Program monitoring** essentially means the programmer works carefully to see that the program is accomplishing what is intended and customers are satisfied. This might include developing strategies for program progression and offering special events to keep up the program's vitality. Monitoring may also require working with registration and reservation strategies. Many leisure service organizations now conduct programs, such as classes, leagues, and workshops, that require the initial payment of fees during a preliminary sign-up period. Furthermore, registration procedures have become increasingly efficient through the use of phone-in or Web-based registration systems.

Monitoring a program may involve participant orientation as well as publicity and public relations.

In particular, the program must be promoted often to sustain customer interest and support. As well, public relations efforts may be needed to inform and influence a supervisor or governing body, such as city officials or hospital administrators, to keep the program running. Such **formative evaluation** efforts are necessary to keep programs dynamic.

Program implementation also requires careful **risk management** and the enforcement of sound safety and accident-prevention practices (see chapter 13). Risk management involves loss prevention and control as well as handling all incident reports, claims, and other insurance- and litigation-related tasks. For the programmer, this means preparing contingency plans, developing emergency procedures, and complying with standards and regulations. Depending on the size and scope of the program, risk management may also include managing crowd control, security, and plans for dealing with demonstrations or terrorism. The point here is participant and public safety.

Implementation on Wheels

Many recreation programs sponsored by city and county governments are implemented "on the move." These mobile recreation programs bring varied activities and events directly to neighborhoods, urban streets, and small towns. Over the years, mobile recreation has brought portable swimming pools, in-line skating, theaters, sports tournaments, nature discovery, planetariums, libraries, arts and crafts, parties, and picnics to areas without permanent parks or community centers. Using vans, buses, trailers, trucks, and even motor homes, recreation leaders bring programs to constituents not typically served by the agency's other program services. Every year, for example, Oakland County Parks and Recreation in Michigan makes more than 160 mobile program visits to communities and neighborhoods around the county, bringing rock climbing, puppetry, hockey, in-line skating, parties, shows, and other programs to constituents (Oakland County Parks and Recreation, 2002-2006).

Mobile recreation programs are an important component of the recreation programming sponsored by the Oakland County Parks and Recreation Department.

The Programming Process: Program Planning

In 2004, the City of Westerville Parks and Recreation Department applied for and won a grant to help their citizens become healthier. Because of the Westerville Health Initiative, many new programs and activities promoting physical activity, healthy eating, and other healthful actions are now being put in place. The sponsors of the grant were the National Recreation and Park Association and the National Heart, Lung, and Blood Institute. Why was Westerville selected? Quite simply, the city succeeded because of creative and thorough adherence to the program planning process.

The grant application contained all the important considerations and decisions. Beginning with the preparation step, Westerville programmers assessed obesity and other lifestyle-related health problems of both children and adults community wide. This effort included conducting a citizen health survey and a market analysis that categorized residents into lifestyle types according to primary and secondary program targets. The Westerville programmers also established program goals and objectives, including becoming a leader in advocating the principles and values of public health and fitness in the state of Ohio. These objectives were followed up with the determination of measurable outcomes from the program, such as decreased heart rate and reduced blood pressure.

In the implementation step of program planning, Westerville programmers developed strategies such as an incentive program that included a trip for two to Hawaii for participants who excel in the healthy activities of the program. Specific activities were identified for inclusion in the initiative, corporations were solicited to support employee participation, special events such as health fairs were developed to keep the program vital and further motivate participation, and a schedule was determined for the initial launching of the program and specific events. Also, a marketing plan detailing promotions, advertising, direct mail, and Web site development was prepared. All this was slated into a budget of fiscal, facility, and staff resources.

Finally, in the evaluation step, the Westerville Health Initiative grant application specified how the goals and objectives for the program would be assessed. For example, the programmers wanted to determine if heart rates and blood pressures of participants actually did decrease as a result of the program, so they developed a plan to assess samples of participants in various fitness measurements. The evaluation strategy also included determination of how satisfied participants were with the program, as well as how efficiently the program was managed.

Westerville's bid for the health initiative grant was successful because of thorough use of the preparation, implementation, and evaluation steps of program planning.

All these implementation actions require data, and today's programmer must be able to work with databases (see chapter 12). Supported by various technologies, programmers create and interpret facilities inventories, reservation and attendance records, staff performance files, financial ledgers, program segmentation information, maintenance work orders, and accident and incident reports. Having comprehensive data on all program components is critical for effective program implementation.

To illustrate, for programmers in therapeutic recreation services, client documentation—a special kind of database—is useful. **Client documentation** involves written records of the actions taken for, with, and by each patient or client (Stumbo & Peterson, 2004). One such client documentation database is the Therapeutic Recreation Accountability Model (TRAM), which emphasizes four components about patients: assessment results, treatment plans, progress notes, and discharge or referral summaries. For programmers in therapeutic settings, as well as in other programming situations, such client documentation databases directly connect the needs assessment and program plan with the measurement of program and client outcomes in the next step: evaluation.

Evaluation

The third and final step in the recreation program planning process is evaluation. Bringing full circle the formative evaluation efforts in the previous implementation step, a **summative evaluation** is conducted at the close of the program. Summative evaluations provide information that can be used to compare programs with one another or with previous program offerings. Programmers measure efficiency and effectiveness outcomes to determine if the program achieved what was projected and in the correct way. This means you are interested in knowing the impact of the program and the efficiency of delivering the program. Did the program provide the benefits intended? Was the program implemented well? This final phase is extremely important because it instructs the next round of planning, thus maintaining the cyclical nature of the programming process (see figure 5.2 on page 71).

Programmers have available to them a menu of approaches for evaluation (see chapter 14). You might measure success by comparing your program against accreditation or other professional standards. A balanced scorecard, benchmarking, cost-effectiveness, or cost–benefit procedure might be employed. You may employ one or several of these approaches, depending on the nature of the success being measured.

As with other aspects of programming, there are important guidelines to follow in program evaluation (see chapter 14). In particular, these include integrity and ethics, professionalism, timing, funding, and staffing.

Finally, since evaluation itself is a process, programmers follow systematic steps in carrying out comprehensive assessments of program outcomes (see chapter 15). These include evaluation design decisions, sampling, data collection, data analysis, and recommendations. Further, the evaluation is not complete until you prepare a report so that evaluation findings can become the basis of decision making about new or modified programs.

The three steps of preparation, implementation, and evaluation that make up the recreation program planning process can be valued as professional tools. They guide you in the creation of successful program services. By following these steps, you'll be able to offer programs that achieve their desired ends. The recreation program planning process helps you to rely on sound knowledge, develop rational choices, be both visionary and practical, make appropriate decisions, work effectively with others, and learn from mistakes. For more information on this topic, see worksheet 5.3 in chapter 5 of the CD-ROM.

Summary

This chapter reviews the philosophical models and planning steps of the recreation program planning process. You should understand the following key points:

- Programs based on social advocacy, social planning, marketing, or community development models specify a continuum of involvement by planners.

- Regardless of program model, professionally offered recreation program services follow a three-step procedure: preparation, implementation, and evaluation.

- In the first step—preparation—the programmer initially seeks to understand the sponsoring organization and community as well as to understand and garner support from the program's intended clients. Preparation also includes assessing program needs, developing the program's goals and objectives, and writing a specific program plan.

- The second step in the program planning process is implementation—potentially a large and complex phase that brings together various program operation components, program resources, program monitoring, risk management, and databases.

- The third step in the program planning process is evaluation—an assessment of the program's ability to achieve the desired benefits and efficiency outcomes. Evaluation approaches, steps, and guidelines not only make for more accountable programming but also serve as the basis for repeating the program planning process to make adjustments to programs or establish new ones.

For more information on this topic, see "More Options for Individual Programing Practice," option 3, and "Group Discussion Ideas," option 3, in chapter 5 of the CD-ROM.

Glossary

program model—A philosophically based overall structure for a program.

social advocacy model—Programs that actively promote a cause.

social planning model—Programs that distribute resources according to need.

marketing model—Programs that meet the expressed desires of customers.

community development model—Programs that are used to stimulate local initiative.

program planning process—Cyclical step-by-step procedure for designing programs.

needs assessment—A formal collection and analysis of information to identify the needs, interests, and problems of program constituents.

interagency partnerships—Multiple community organizations combining resources for joint sponsorship of a program or event.

goals—Broad statements of purpose.

objectives—Concrete, short-term, measurable statements of specific intentions.

program monitoring—Seeing that the program is accomplishing what is intended and customers are satisfied.

formative evaluation—Ongoing assessment of the program's success while the program is in progress so that changes or corrections can be made during program implementation.

risk management—The identification, analysis, and then elimination or reduction of risks to program clients and staff.

client documentation—Written record of the actions taken for, with, and by each client.

summative evaluation—Conducted at the end of the program to provide useful information for determining the program's success.

References

Boys and Girls Clubs of Metro Atlanta. (2004). Retrieved January 7, 2005, from www.bgcma.org.

Kraus, R. (1997). *Recreation programming: A benefits-driven approach.* Boston: Allyn & Bacon.

Mullins, B. (1991). Managing fiscal transition. *Parks and Recreation, 26*(10), 32-33.

Oakland County Parks and Recreation. (2002-2006). Retrieved March 6, 2007, from www.oakgov.com/parksrec.

Russell, R.V. (1982). *Planning programs in recreation.* St. Louis: Mosby.

Searle, M.S., & Brayley, R.E. (2000). *Leisure services in Canada: An introduction.* State College, PA: Venture.

Special Olympics. (n.d.). About us. Retrieved July 24, 2006, from www.specialolympics.org/Special+Olympics+Public+Website/English/About_Us/default.htm.

Stumbo, N.J., & Peterson, C.A. (2004). *Therapeutic recreation program design: Principles and procedures.* San Francisco: Pearson/Cummings.

Travel Reservations Center. (2006). In-depth Princess Cruises information. Retrieved July 24, 2006, from http://cruises.res99.com/c/cruiseline.asp?lineid=40&vw=2.

PART

Planning Preparations

Step 1 in the program planning process is preparation. The task is to understand all the elements necessary for satisfying leisure experiences. That is, you make preparations to get the mix of people, places, objects, rules, relationships, and actions just right. In this part of the book, we consider the following:

- Chapter 6 initiates the preparations in the planning process by explaining the importance of understanding your organization and community. What are the visions, values, and policies that serve as a context for the recreation programs you plan? This chapter also includes an overview of the importance of getting constituent support for and involvement in the planning process itself. How can the general public, politicians, and other community organizations support the program preparations?

- Chapter 7 continues with the preparations by suggesting ways of understanding your clients and customers. What is the nature of these clients, and how might they best be served by programmed leisure? Answering these questions requires systematically assessing program needs. What needs should the recreation program strive to meet?

- Chapter 8 summarizes the planning process up to this point of the establishment of program goals and objectives. As a result of understanding your organization, community, and clients, what is the rationale for the program, and what specifically do you hope it will accomplish?

- Chapter 9 discusses the final act of preparation—deciding on a program plan. What will be the program design for achieving the goals and objectives?

CHAPTER 6

Understanding Your Organization and Community

In this chapter, you can look forward to the following:

- Discovering the role of an organization's philosophy and vision
- Employing existing databases to plan for the provision of community leisure services
- Understanding what an existing conditions analysis and environmental scanning consists of
- Analyzing trends in a community
- Identifying and understanding the many types of constituents that may be gathered to support recreation planning
- Understanding the important role of personnel who contribute to the advisory or policy-making aspect of a leisure service delivery system

Texas Instruments, located in Dallas, Texas, began its extensive employee service and recreation program with an annual Christmas party. Shortly after that, in 1953, the Texins Association constitution and bylaws were adopted, and the 50th anniversary of what is now known as Texins Activity Centers—consisting of three facilities in Dallas, Plano, and Sherman, Texas—was celebrated in 2003. The Dallas Texins Activity Center, which is used by the Texins Association Clubs but professionally managed by Health Fitness Corporation, consists of a 68,000-square-foot (6,300 square meter) facility featuring a natatorium, indoor and outdoor jogging tracks, a gymnasium, two sand volleyball courts, three softball fields, two tennis courts, fitness rooms, and many other amenities (ESM, 2001). Texas Instruments' Live Healthy Initiative, which the Texins Activity Center is part of, is a program designed to help employees better maintain health and wellness, as well as the employee services and recreation arm of the corporation, which drives numerous health-oriented activities, including incentive programs, educational seminars, healthy options in vending machines, regular communications and much more to reach employees globally. A great deal of planning based on company philosophical and societal trends occurred to make Texins what it is today (Texas Instruments, 1995-2006). All this demonstrates the key nature of laying a preliminary foundation for program planning by way of understanding your organization and community, which is the focus of this chapter.

The Texins' karate classes are a Texins Activity Center program.

Being a recreation programmer for an organization in a community is an exciting position. What awaits is a tremendous amount of responsibility invested in organizing needed programs and services that provide for community quality of life – that is, what benefits the individual benefits the community as a whole, including your organization. In this chapter, you will learn how an organization's structure and purpose, as well as a community's character, shape programming. This requires a sound approach toward developing data and documents that provide a framework for decision making, with the ultimate goal of planning sound programs and services.

Philosophy and Values

What constitutes organizational philosophy and values? Organizations operate within a collection of employee beliefs. Sometimes, differing employee beliefs cause clashes that affect the ability of staff to deliver services. For example, some employees may be more oriented toward a philosophy of selling goods and services to the public, while others may be more apt to promote the delivery of services to those who need them most, regardless of ability to pay. Although both perspectives are common and desirable in organizations, neither is effective if there is no overall organizational philosophy to guide everyone engaging in the delivery and consumption of the services. This is why organizational philosophy and values are articulated in the planning process so that they will be reflected in the structuring of leisure experiences. When this occurs, your personal philosophy is absorbed into the organizational philosophy.

When an organizational philosophy is put into words, it becomes a planning tool. It becomes a great mobilizer of efforts to gain funding, garner resources, and plan future facilities and programs. The organizational philosophy and accompanying value statements provide the framework within which the planning process may begin.

What do organizations value? Some examples follow from a collection of value statements evident in many recreation program brochures:

- We value the quality of life of all citizens.
- Our company believes in a healthy employee and a healthy work environment.
- We want to encourage the healthy lifestyles of all tourists.
- We like our guests to have the experience of a lifetime.
- We stand for happiness.
- We believe in the power of one. The benefits are endless.

These are just a few statements that identify the value an organization places on the delivery of a positive leisure experience for all who participate. These statements, while somewhat simplistic, provide a background from which to plan programs that deliver on those values.

Vision

The vision of an organization is a statement that identifies its desired overall direction. Organizations usually undergo a discussion process that helps develop an overall **vision statement**. In conceiving a vision statement, an organization may facilitate several forms of discussions (described later in this chapter), involving both staff and community members. In one method, the people involved in the programming process participate in guided meetings designed to determine the overall approach that needs to be taken. This approach is then reflected in a constructed vision statement. From that vision statement, more specific statements arise that eventually result in decisions to build, operate, extend, and offer services (see the box on page 85 for an example). For more information on this topic, see worksheet 6.1 in chapter 6 of the CD-ROM.

The vision statement of the Westerville Parks and Recreation Department identifies several directions

---

PROS 2000 Vision

The Parks, Recreation and Open Space 2000 (PROS 2000) plan, a vision of the Westerville Parks and Recreation Department to become a first-class system, involves the following:

- Building a community center
- Creating a sports complex
- Expanding partnerships
- Renovating existing park sites
- Preserving the city's greenways and open spaces
- Developing a bikeway and leisure path system
- Achieving a balance of active and passive facilities and programs
- Creating year-round indoor and outdoor recreation facilities and opportunities for all ages and abilities

City of Westerville Parks and Recreation Department, 2000.
Parks Recreation Open Space (PROS) 2000.

In Westerville, attention to the vision statement provided support for a waterpark development.

---

for the agency, guiding the organization through many initiatives that brought greater facilities and services to the city. From this statement, shown in the box on page 83, the entire planning process was shaped by the kind of vision that develops through focused discussion. The goals that were ultimately established include an extensive list.

Several approaches can be used to establish a clear picture of the organization's vision. These approaches, which may be modified according to the service delivery setting, are important methods to secure background information to guide the direction that should be taken in a recreation program plan.

Environmental Scanning

Organizational planning requires identifying trends and realities and understanding the existing conditions. These are reflected in the demand for leisure services. An **environmental scan** is the process of studying the trends and circumstances around which an agency needs to operate. In studying this environment, it is possible to reflect the unique aspects of programs that are ultimately offered. Scanning may be very analytical or may be the result of observation of circumstances that occur frequently enough

to be considered important. For more information on this topic, see worksheet 6.2 in chapter 6 of the CD-ROM.

Existing Information Bases

How can professionals determine the direction their organizations should take? Another approach to determining your organization's vision is to begin with existing information about the culture, the population served, the economy, the business climate, and so on. Through the review of such secondary data, a consistent picture may emerge about many features of the organizational climate in a community. For example, if a chamber of commerce has developed a profile of the business community using information pulled from census data, and this shows an increase in the Latino population, a programmer may benefit from this data by planning new recreation programs and services tailored to Latino customs and traditions. From this secondary data, gaps may also be identified that require further study; then primary data collection may be planned more strategically.

The following list contains existing sources of secondary data, or information bases, that may be useful to you:

- *The census.* Taken every 10 years in the United States, census data show the demographic characteristics of a population, particularly age, race, ethnicity, educational level, occupations, and socioeconomic status. The census may be compared with past censuses to analyze longer-term shifts in the demographic composition of an area and the changes in the nature of services that may be anticipated and further examined based on this information. For more information on this topic, see "Can You Solve This Programming Issue?" in chapter 6 of the CD-ROM.

It is important to know the existing condition of facilities and equipment as a starting point for understanding what to offer patrons.

Automated Batting Cages, Inc.

INFORMATION

ABC is Automated Batting Cages, Inc. We manufacture baseball and softball batting range equipment for commercial-use batting range installations.

Our products include baseball and softball "wheel-style" pitching machines, coin/token boxes, conveyor/ball-feeding and -sorting systems, sign packages, light boxes, control panels, main mast slide collars, complete netting systems, design consultation, and more.

Our systems also come with accessories to complete your project, including helmets, baseballs and softballs, netting repair accessories, bats, and more.

ABC doesn't stop there. We lead the competition in customer satisfaction with our technical support program. Our service technicians are available seven days a week and can help you with any problem that may arise.

ABC also leads the industry in safety operations. Our operating manuals, safety bulletins, safety program, and our periodical *The Fun Times* publication will keep you up to date with the latest information and safety procedures.

ABC's pitching machines are state of the art, the most accurate and most reliable machines on the market.

SERVICES

Automated Batting Cages is fully prepared to help you with any aspect of your new business venture!

Right from the start, ABC will help you to determine what size batting range is feasible in your area and the size of your property. From there, if needed, ABC will custom draw a set of construction blueprints for your facility. (Yes, this is a full set of construction drawings.) ABC also provides consulting services for upgrading existing batting range systems. Operations, safety, and management materials are also available. ABC provides an extensive customer service program, including same-day shipping and a service technician available seven days a week! ABC's exclusive one-year limited warranty on equipment systems [is a positive feature of our equipment]. Also included are technical construction assistance and turnkey construction services.

HISTORY

Batting cages have been in operation for approximately 35 years. The first cages had baseball pitching machines only as no softball machines had yet been developed. The early batting cages were typically erected using an "open field" approach, with balls being hit into an open field (much like the current-day golf driving ranges). Cages which were enclosed were built using asphalt, telephone poles as vertical posts, and golf-type netting systems. Most cages of this era were developed and designed by the owner, and no standard dimensions were available throughout the industry.

The equipment available during this time consisted of "arm-style" machines. Balls were either not retrieved and needed to be gathered in and around the entire area and fed back to each machine, or the floor was sloped back to the machine area. From this point, the balls were lifted by hand and fed to each machine hopper. This was a very time-consuming process and required considerable downtime to gather these balls. Obviously, this was not a very economical method. The equipment of this time was developed primarily for team use, and they required considerable maintenance and upkeep for commercial duty.

In 1978, the owners of ABC developed the first automatic retrieval/conveyor system to lift and sort both baseballs and softballs from a sump area in the batting cage and to feed all machines within the batting range. This development revolutionized the industry. Combined with complete building plans, developed by the manufacturer, developing and building batting cages became a much easier venture.

The owners of early batting ranges included golf driving range owners, miniature golf owners, and stand-alone batting range operations. Many of these operations closed during the 1960s and early 1970s. The reasons for these closures varied. Some operations were just too troublesome for the operator. Others were unprofitable due to the excessive labor required, and still others were closed as a result of the property values rising to a "higher and better use."

With the advent of automatic feeding systems, better and more reliable pitching machine equipment and related equipment, supplies designed for commercial use, and more detailed construction blueprints, new operators are entering the industry. Estimates of operators prior to 1980 would range from 100 to 200 total batting ranges. Today, that total number would be in the 1,200 to 1,500 neighborhood. We believe that these figures will increase four- or fivefold in the next several years.

Automated Batting Cages, Inc.
8811 Huff Ave. NE
Salem, Oregon
United States 97303
Phone: 503-390-5714
Toll free phone: 800-578-2243
Fax: 503-390-4974
info@battingcages.com
www.battingcages.com

Aims International. 2005.

- *Long-range planning documents.* These documents, often developed by other entities, are valuable for identifying trends, potential conflicts, and potential competitive directions that need to be taken into consideration when planning programs. For example, the Westerville PROS 2000 recreation plan examined the plans for the local school system, nearby state parks, and other city park and recreation departments. Also, regional long-range planning elicits 30- to 40-year plans that may directly affect the direction taken by your organization.

- *Industry profiles.* Often, a subsegment of the leisure industry (e.g., water parks or hospitality) will identify trends through studies conducted to improve facility development. These industry profiles are helpful when integrating plans for new facilities that will house new programs. They also identify new trends that should be taken into account when adapting existing facilities. An example of an industry profile is shown in the box on page 85. Part of understanding an organization from a programming point of view includes clearly understanding the vision and mission of the organization and what facilities, areas, and spaces are available for use.

Census, long-range planning, and industry profile documents are secondary data sources that complement primary research, which also must take place within the organization. When both primary and secondary research data are reviewed, the information provides a compelling picture for planning and managing programs. For more information on this topic, see "More Options for Individual Programming Practice," option 4, in chapter 6 of the CD-ROM.

In reflecting your organization's vision in program planning through primary research, such approaches as existing conditions analysis, trend analysis, and determination of social and political atmospheres can be conducted. The next section identifies these.

Existing Conditions Analysis

One way to primarily identify directions in program planning is to conduct an existing conditions analysis. An **existing conditions analysis** is the step-by-step process of analyzing the inventory of areas, facilities, and programs to determine what is in need of review, repair, or reorganization.

Often, an organization already keeps detailed documentation of many of the items needed for an existing conditions analysis so that the documentation only needs to be reviewed and studied further. This documentation may be available in ongoing record keeping of maintenance, supplies ordered, accidents, program participation statistics, and so on. The documents are consistently reviewed for any gaps or pressing needs, and the results form the basis for examining what exists currently and what is still needed. For more information on this topic, see worksheet 6.3 in chapter 6 of the CD-ROM.

In Westerville, the existing conditions analysis consisted of the following documentation:

- The city's population trends
- The community's existing natural and cultural fixtures and facilities
- The existing park and public school facilities

Figure 6.1 illustrates this analysis for park facilities. The ultimate goal was "to create a unified plan for park and recreation and open space facilities which will encourage optimum utilization of the community's assets to realize a greater return of the public's investment" (City of Westerville Parks and Recreation Department, 2000, p. 15).

Westerville carried out an existing conditions analysis for cultural and natural facilities as well. The "Natural Features Analysis" on page 88 shows examples of an existing conditions analysis that gave direction to the planning process of the PROS 2000 plan. The "Cultural Features Analysis" on page 88 demonstrates this even more.

Trend Analysis

Once the existing conditions are reviewed, it is time to take a look at trends to determine the directions programmatic planning may take. One point of comparison is trends that are occurring in leisure pursuits within the region, the nation, and other areas. Through analysis of programmatic trends, it is possible to develop programs that can be easily adapted to major and unexpected shifts in trends. For example, one unanticipated shift in program need in Westerville has occurred with the significant migration of Latino families to the Midwest. Many departments have significantly changed their program directions to accommodate the increasing populations of people who have different program needs.

Available sources for reviewing trends include the following:

Existing facilities: Westerville parks	Alum Creek Park North	Alum Creek Park South	Astronaut Grove	Bicentennial Park	Boyer Nature Preserve	Brooksedge Park	Ernest Cherrington Preserve	Community Tennis Courts	Electric Avenue and ET State Street
Indoor									
Outdoor	•	•	•	•	•	•	•	•	•
Classification (1)	C	H	A	A	G	H	G	E	A
Land area (acres)	11.3	30	2.6	0.1	11.4	3.9	12.5	1.6	0.2
Parking	•		•		•			•	
Court games									
Badminton/Volleyball	1								
Basketball	1								
Horseshoes									
Shuffleboard									
Tennis								5	
Field games									
Baseball	1								
Football									
Soccer									
Softball									
Picnicking									
Grills	•		•						
Picnic tables	•		•			•			

Figure 6.1 An existing conditions analysis of Westerville, Ohio, parks.

Reprinted, by permission, from Westerville Parks and Recreation Department.

- Futurists who predict global trends in weather, resources, the economy, food and energy scarcity and plenty, and other long-term projections
- Educational enrollment by age cohort, which predicts the number of school children; analysis of employee sectors; and other long-term projections
- Business trends and directions that might predict the establishment of new forms of manufacturing and light business in communities
- Written works that focus on general trends that can predict key changes in many directions
- Other indicators that might result from crises and unexpected events, such as 9/11 and its effects on people's thoughts about terrorism and world security

Natural Features Analysis

As a community develops rapidly, the identification and preservation of that city's natural features are essential. Such natural features include waterways, topographic features (including ravines), and outstanding vegetation masses. Through such an analysis, areas may better be identified for preservation (limited use), passive recreation (moderate use), and active recreation (intensive use). The result is a more unified plan for parks and recreation, which will encourage the optimum utilization of community assets and thus realize a better return of the public investments. The most significant river corridors within the city are

- Alum Creek
- Big Walnut Creek

Cultural Features Analysis

The development of the city's street system has been the most significant factor of influence in Westerville's physical development. The city's existing arterials include the following:

- Sunbury Road
- Cleveland Avenue
- East and West Schrock Road
- North and South Spring Road
- North and South State Street
- West Main Street (between 1-71 and South State Street)
- Maxtown Road (between Sunbury Road and North State Street)
- East Walnut Street (between South State Street and Sunbury Road)
- County Line Road (between North State Street and Sunbury Road)

With the annexation of the nine hundred forty-one (941) acres to the north, proposed arterial street improvements include improvements to Hanawalt Road and Maxtown Road (between Worthington-Galena Road and North State Street). The city's neighborhoods are currently served by the following primary existing collector streets:

- East College Avenue (between South State Street and Sunbury Road)
- Huber Village Boulevard (between South State Street and South Spring Street)
- Dempsey Road (actually outside of Westerville, between Westerville Road and Sunbury Road)

Next to a city's street system, major land use patterns related to primary commercial, office, and industrial uses influence park and recreation patterns. This is particularly true as alternative modes of transportation are examined, such as bikeway systems. The most significant commercial use is Uptown Westerville, centered at South State Street and Main Street/College Avenue. Other primary commercial centers are focused along West Schrock Road at Cleveland Avenue and South State Street, Maxtown Road at North State Street, County Line Road, and Central College Road at Sunbury Road. Primary office and industrial uses are found along West Schrock Road and in the newly annexed nine hundred forty-one (941) acreage to the north.

City of Westerville Parks and Recreation Department, n.d.

For more information on this topic, see "More Options for Individual Programming Practice," option 1, in chapter 6 of the CD-ROM.

Of course a large part of developing effective programs is responding to what is indicated in primary research. This means that the social and political realities also need to be taken into consideration. The following section provides a background for reading the social landmarks in preplanning for community need.

Social and Political Atmospheres

Many of the most prominent trends occur within the social and political systems. When economies change and new leaders emerge in government, key changes are often made that affect the way leisure service delivery takes place. The most recent change in social and political systems has occurred around the threat of terrorism and crime, which has altered how many leisure service delivery systems operate. What is key to the program planner is sensitivity to such political and social trends that might mitigate or expand programmatic directions within an organization. For this reason, it is important that programmers cultivate effective partnerships, with the intent of forming **collaborative ventures** to deliver programs to constituents.

For example, in Westerville, many partnerships have been developed to assist in the delivery of programs and services to residents and visitors. Here are but a few of the many significant partners that work with the Westerville Parks and Recreation Department:

Westerville has focused on youth programming to address an area of demand.

Photo courtesy of Westerville Parks and Recreation Department, Westerville, Ohio.

- Community partnership with schools enables hundreds of programs to be offered at times when schools are not in use.

- Parks and recreation employees work with government agencies in other communities to link into the Ohio River and Lake Erie bike trail system.

- The police and fire departments have worked with the Westerville Parks and Recreation Department to establish "safe escape" and "home alone" programs for children and adults.

- The department secured a healthy living grant in conjunction with the American Cancer Society.

Other partnerships include more than 50 agencies, businesses, non-profit agencies, and schools.

Much of the information in the remaining sections of this chapter falls under program management. You may or may not be required to perform these tasks, depending on the size of your organization. In smaller park districts, the manager may serve as the programmer and the program coordinator; be in charge of volunteers, partnerships, and task forces; attend public meetings and forums; and perform other duties. In other words, the smaller the organization, the more management tasks you may have to do.

Network of Individual Constituents

Perhaps now more than ever, understanding your community requires the availability and wise use of constituents in voluntary, advisory, and policy-making capacities. In a recent World Leisure Congress, a network of volunteers was noted as one of the most important aspects of running a leisure service system. This network forms a strong advisory and advocacy process that is tapped into when assessing needs and writing program plans. For more information on this topic, see "More Options for Individual Programming Practice," option 2, in chapter 6 of the CD-ROM.

People volunteer in many ways, and their reasons for volunteering are both personal and altruistic. When we take a look at the many ways departments use volunteers, it is truly amazing how many advisors and workers contribute to the operation of an

A typical volunteer serves many functions.

providing a specific service (e.g., a local hospital may offer blood pressure screenings at a community center).

- *Endowed support of long-term projects.* Usually as a result of a development campaign, people or companies may provide full financial support to establish a program, build a park, or fund an individual staff member.

- *Dedication of land and facilities.* People often deed their land and facilities to a leisure service organization. This is often a tremendously significant endeavor that can add great value to the opportunities available.

- *Support of recreation activity participants.* Individuals and organizations often provide program support to participants in the form of scholarships and supplies.

- *Support of businesses.* Incentives can help businesses support programs and facilities. For example, a hotel operator builds an office complex near a local community center for businesses to operate. This develops a synergy that allows those businesses to support the center, and vice versa.

- *Discounted goods and services.* Many businesses provide extensive discounts to leisure service organizations as a part of philanthropic support in a community.

- *Revenue from taxpayers.* The willingness of the residents to be taxed for certain local endeavors provides a great deal of support for a public leisure service enterprise.

organization. Yet too often, the value of volunteers is diminished and ignored. If we look at the full network of constituents who serve in several capacities, the degree of support given to the system is incredible. A broad view of this type of assistance is in order.

Figure 6.2 shows the network of people who may singly or jointly assist a leisure service delivery system. Volunteers may lend one or more forms of support to the organization as follows:

- *Direct financial support.* People may donate funds through individual commitment or solicitation. Gifts of outright cash are often extremely valuable to an organization.

- *Indirect financial support.* People may also donate time or money that indirectly benefits the operation of a program. By sponsoring a team, for example, program costs may be kept to a minimum, and the program is therefore more affordable to a wider range of participants who otherwise could not afford entry fees.

- *Donation of goods.* Often it is easier to provide a contribution of supplies and equipment rather than outright cash gifts. Many organizations use the gifts catalog, which presents pictures and descriptions of equipment and supplies needed by a community.

- *Donation of services.* Many businesses or individuals can supply program support by

In short, leisure service delivery systems, regardless of whether they are public, private, or commercial, have clients and interested parties at their disposal to bring about programmatic change and development. Very often this constituent support can yield millions of dollars in financial aid that would otherwise be unavailable to the organization. The key goal is to determine ways to manage, sustain, and recognize these many contributions. It is also important to identify where support may be garnered and how

© Human Kinetics.

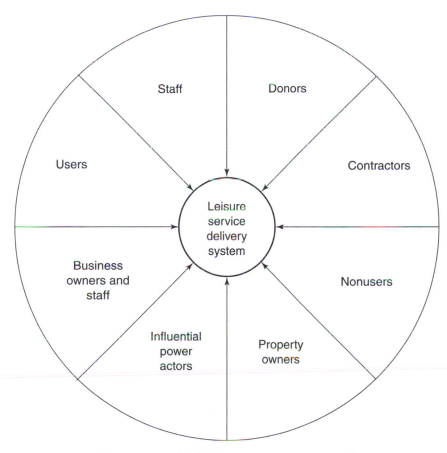

The diagram shows a large circle divided into eight segments, each pointing toward a central circle labeled "Leisure service delivery system." The eight outer segments are labeled: Staff, Donors, Contractors, Nonusers, Property owners, Influential power actors, Business owners and staff, Users.

Figure 6.2 An incredible network of individuals supports leisure service delivery systems.

The dedication of the new Westerville Community Center was a momentous occasion that included the honoring of the many residents who volunteered to help with its planning.

to use that support to best articulate the needs of the agency.

As a start, it is important to treat any individual or group associated with your leisure service organization as a volunteer. Regardless of whether the contribution is time, money, or goods, it is worth an amount of funding that is saved or that enables expansion. We can calculate a monetary value for every type of volunteering as follows:

- Donation of time: number of hours multiplied by the hourly rate of a person who does comparable work
- Donation of money: actual cash value of donated cash
- Donation of goods: market value of the goods at the time of donation

The second point is that all those connected with the organization should be managed in much the same way as staff is managed. Specific roles should be assigned, such as a particular job (with relevant duties) or a contributor or a partner, and the duties associated with each role should be identified. Those accepted as volunteers, contributors, or partners need to be trained (oriented) and evaluated (stewarded). Finally, all should be recognized and rewarded regularly through informal and formal mechanisms.

Network of Group Constituents

Although many individuals donate goods, services, and funds to leisure service organizations, countless groups also directly or indirectly support the leisure service delivery system, and are, thus, vital contributors to your efforts to understand your organization and community. This section discusses the many ways these groups provide support and direction.

• *Task forces.* A **task force** draws together people with common concerns and abilities in order to solve problems. Once an issue is resolved, the task force is usually disbanded. Task forces may be formed for periodic master planning, handling crisis issues, or brainstorming ideas for programmatic directions. Whatever the purpose, citizens and constituents who are most familiar with the problems and are effective when working in small groups are the most likely to be tapped to participate in a task force.

• *Public meetings and forums.* Another format is the meeting process. **Public meetings** are often held to discuss and generate ideas about plans for development. Programmatic and facility plans may be discussed and issues noted. These meetings are usually required by law in governmental settings or made as a requirement for private developments. Normally, the public meeting format is time restricted, usually not more

than two hours in length, and time limits are provided for those who wish to present or speak.

Public forums are slightly different in that they are organized by the group developing the program plan. Forums are often a part of design development or priority setting, and they may involve brainstorming or the nominal group process (used to help the group arrive at some consensus). For more information on this topic, see "Group Discussion Ideas," option 3, in chapter 6 of the CD-ROM.

• *Service and philanthropic organizations.* These groups meet regularly for specific purposes and may be tapped to assist with many aspects of programs and services. Some groups may provide a service in exchange for use of facilities, and others may identify a program for an annual service project.

A task force may be very effective in securing support from other interested parties.

© PhotoDisc.

• *Citizens advisory boards.* **Citizens advisory boards** and commissions are formed via enabling legislation, nonprofit organizational structure, or business start-ups. These bodies have either advisory or policy-making capacity and in many ways exert great power regarding the direction of a leisure service delivery system. Persons serve specific roles in appointed or elected staggered terms, meeting on a regular and often public basis to provide feedback and decision making on policies and issues affecting the system. People who serve in these capacities often spend countless hours learning about the department, and they continue to be supporters even after they complete their terms. Cultivating positive relationships with boards and commissions is essential for success. For more information on this topic, see "More Options for Individual Programming Practice," option 3, in chapter 6 of the CD-ROM.

• *Advocacy groups.* In every community, there are groups that provide continued support for issues that affect individual quality of life. Often, these **advocacy groups** are active in changing policies and approaches to how organizations operate or the way development occurs. Advocacy groups may be very useful in addressing issues concerning the well-being of children, the environment, the availability and accessibility of services, or the needs of a particular group of constituents. Leisure service delivery systems often house meeting space and programming for advocacy groups who often support the programmatic needs of an organization as long as their particular advocacy issues are addressed. For more information on this topic, see "Group Discussion Ideas," option 2, in chapter 6 of the CD-ROM.

• *Political parties.* Any leisure service delivery system, whether it is public, private, or commercial, is affected by the political environment in which it operates. In communities where a strong mayoral presence exists, the quality of life in a community might shift every time a new mayor is elected. Through sound planning, programmers can solidify positive relationships with the political systems in the community.

• *Existing community agencies.* A community's leisure service delivery system includes many agencies that offer recreation services. Therefore, it is increasingly important that a governmental agency serve as the overarching coordinator of services and that the coordinating function allows for all those involved in leisure service delivery to play a part in providing programs. This means working with agencies and businesses to decrease duplication of services, coordinate facility use, and reduce costs through bulk purchase and other joint ventures. Such **interagency partnerships** with these agencies may avoid gaps in service that typically occur without adequate comprehensive planning. In many areas, interagency partnerships are also formed to extend program delivery.

Many special events are made possible through the collaboration of several groups.

The Programming Process: Reading Palms

The Westerville Parks and Recreation Department seeks to achieve specific accomplishments through its program services. Programming staff spend lots of time "taking the pulse" of their constituents as well as analyzing themselves, never assuming they know everything about who is serving whom. An elaborate web of need and interest analysis takes place throughout the year.

One example is an analysis to determine the need for volunteer staff in the department. A series of task forces and advisory groups was developed, and hours of volunteer involvement were documented. Department staff learned that approximately 1,100 volunteers work almost 14,000 hours per year doing such department tasks as clerical duties, computer work, reception, surveys, tree planting, and operating recreation activities and neighborhood projects. This free labor represents about $113,000 per year in saved costs.

This surprising commitment from volunteers prompted the department to develop special programs and services for just the volunteer staff. The VISION (Volunteers in Service in Our Neighborhoods) program features volunteer recruitment brochures, time sheets, job descriptions, tracking systems, and recognition programs.

The VISION program is an important element within Westerville's comprehensive plan, PROS 2000 (introduced earlier in the chapter), which provides the entire city of Westerville with a parks, recreation, and outdoor space blueprint for the development of state-of-the-art recreation programs, facilities, and areas.

This vision-driven study resulted in priority setting and planning for future directions for the entire department. It affects hiring patterns, qualifications of personnel, work programs, budgets, targeted populations of people served, and new service directions. The PROS 2000 plan represents the culmination of all the planning decisions, tasks, and perspectives we've considered so far; and because of its nature and breadth, it affects the entire quality of life in the community. For more information on this topic, see "Group Discussion Ideas," options 1 and 4, in chapter 6 of the CD-ROM.

Summary

This chapter is an overview of the early stages of the program planning process. You should understand the following key points:

- An organization should plan recreation programs according to a strong vision statement.
- Use existing standards, data bases, and industry profiles as points for comparison.
- Assess the existing areas and facilities for gaps in service.
- Ask participants to become involved in the planning process.
- Use a network of constituents to meet organizational goals.
- Consider strategic partnerships to deliver programs.

Glossary

vision statement—A creed that expresses the direction of an organization.

environmental scan—A system for reviewing what is going on within a community and the trends that may affect the community.

existing conditions analysis—A system for determining what programs and facilities exist within an organization.

collaborative ventures—The outgrowth of partnerships between public, private, and commercial leisure service delivery.

task force—A group formed primarily to complete a specifically assigned problem.

public meeting—An open meeting designed by law to allow citizens access to governmental decision making.

public forum—A structured meeting developed to enlist feedback on a variety of leisure service delivery issues and priorities.

citizens advisory board—A publicly recognized group of people formed, in this case, to deliberate over directions established by a public, private, or commercial leisure service delivery system.

advocacy group—A group that strongly supports a cause.

interagency partnerships— Multiple community organizations combining resources for joint sponsorship of a program or event.

References

Aims International. (2005). Batting cages. Retrieved January 8, 2005, from www.aimsintl.org

City of Westerville Parks and Recreation Department. (n.d.). Parks Recreation Open Space (PROS) 2000. Retrieved January 5, 2005, from www.ci.westerville.oh.us.

City of Westerville Parks and Recreation Department. (2000). *Parks Recreation Open Space (PROS) 2000*. Westerville, OH: City of Westerville.

ESM. (2001). Internships. Retrieved January 28, 2006, from www.esmassn.org/internships/esminterntexasinstruments.htm.

Texas Instruments. (1995-2006). Health. Retrieved January 28, 2006, from www.ti.com/corp/docs/company/citizen/health/wellnessprograms.shtml.

CHAPTER 7

Assessing Patrons' Program Needs

In this chapter, you can look forward to the following:

- Understanding the nature and purpose of a needs assessment
- Identifying the values and uses of the results of a needs assessment
- Comprehending how needs assessments fit into the overall program planning scheme for an organization
- Understanding how to study clientele needs and services
- Recognizing the variables that identify characteristics of the patrons
- Developing a marketing plan that addresses individual differences and targets within the programmatic environment

With a mission to "keep Gainesville the healthiest community in America one person at a time, one business at a time," the Gainesville Health and Fitness Center (GHFC), a commercial recreational sport and fitness firm, uses cutting-edge approaches to fitness and wellness programming. The core purpose of GHFC is "to create a fitness experience that helps people get the most out of life" (GHFC, n.d.a). By offering a needs-based programming experience that will directly affect all residents of Gainesville, Florida, the program directly links critical health issues in the community with programming services that address all fitness concerns—from optimizing daily health to restoring wellness once debilitating health problems are encountered. GHFC was voted business of the year by the Gainesville Area Chamber of Commerce; and in 2003, Gainesville itself was noted as the healthiest community in America by the Wellness Councils of America (GHFC, n.d.b). This firm represents the positive ways needs assessments help communities plan appropriate leisure program services.

At GHFC, assessing patron needs led to the health of the community as a key service goal.

A **needs assessment** is the formalized process of determining the needs, wants, desires, and preferences of **patrons** and prospective patrons. By learning what the community needs, the programmer gathers information about the excesses and shortfalls in leisure service delivery. The assessment forms the basis for developing a program plan, marketing plans, master planning documents, grants, contracts, and many other planning materials. For more information on this topic, see "Group Discussion Ideas," option 3, in chapter 7 of the CD-ROM.

According to Management Learning Laboratories (MLL, 2002), a needs assessment serves the following purposes:

- To gather information that the organization may utilize to gain a better understanding of its constituency

- To investigate how citizens of the community wish to use their discretionary time and how the organization may coordinate its efforts in these areas

- To explore and suggest efficient methods for the provision of leisure opportunities in meeting time and availability constraints of the members of the community

- To evaluate current and ongoing recreation opportunities in terms of peoples' desires to participate

- To explore the most effective methods of disseminating information to the public about recreation programs, facilities, and opportunities

- To ascertain the community's attitudes and opinions about the organization's programs, facilities, policies, and services

- To give community residents the opportunity to offer suggestions, comments, and concerns about the leisure opportunities provided for them by the organization

- To provide information about the feasibility of and need for new developments, both in programs and facilities

Just how much information is needed to assess recreation and park needs within a leisure service delivery system? How much is enough, and what is the most effective way of ensuring that dollars are being spent wisely for services that are used maximally? A needs assessment involves a detailed data-collection process. Such an assessment identifies key demographic aspects of the organization, leisure use, leisure programs, and priorities. For more information on this topic, see worksheet 7.1 in chapter 7 of the CD-ROM.

Perhaps the most important aspect of data gathering in a leisure service delivery system is keeping excellent records of use patterns in all **facilities, areas,** and programs. This chapter identifies how to use available information and gain additional information about patron needs within a leisure service organization. From the baseline data available throughout the operation of a department to the data secured through surveys, the establishment of need is an important component of the planning process. We identify these key components and show programmers how to gather and use this information so that their programs reflect the needs, wants, and desires of the patrons.

Methods of Needs Assessments

Patrons' needs can be identified through several sources, including organizational literature, surveys, interviews and observations, and focus groups. This section outlines these different methods.

Organizational Literature

What is **organizational literature?** Simply stated, it is information used in the operation of a department. In addition, it is information gathered intentionally for the purpose of analyzing needs and future plans. Organizational literature can consist of regularly kept records and reports. These materials can provide an accurate picture of the use patterns and demands for service that typically affect a successful operation. It also helps to review this material to identify patterns of reduced participation and use, then to make plans to accommodate other needs and to change or extend programs that are affected by the program life cycle.

The following documents are examples of organizational literature that may be reviewed when preparing a needs assessment:

- *Monthly reports.* These reports reflect budgetary information; attendance (in classes, special events, and so on); incidents (such as accidents) that occur during the course of a program; and other data considered essential for sound record keeping. Frequently, staff and policy boards use this information to address immediate operational concerns. "Project and Program Highlights" on page 100 shows a monthly report submitted in Westerville, Ohio, regarding services.

- *Annual reports.* These are an aggregated form of yearly or biannual information that are formally prepared and distributed. They are often compiled by combining monthly reports, and they contain weekly information that may be useful to a wider audience. An annual report shows the financial health and progress of an organization.

- *Planning documents.* These are published as the planning process is completed. It is the result of an existing plan, and this information may be compared with ongoing planning processes. (Chapter 9 identifies and expands on each type of planning report used in an organization.)

- *News items.* Media reports often uncover information that has not been gathered. This information may be valuable in addressing problems identified in the course of day-to-day operation.

- *Budget documents.* These are yearly or biannual comparisons of budget funding sources and expenditures that may be analyzed for future planning.

- *Program evaluations.* Regularly conducted formative and summative evaluations are valuable for determining other ways in which data need to be gathered. (Chapters 14 and 15 detail the program evaluation process and outcome.)

Once all these organizational materials are collected, they may be studied for trends, patterns, concerns, problems, and needs.

In addition to studying existing literature that is readily available, you can also collect new information for a comprehensive needs assessment.

Project and Program Highlights

- Adult softball leagues began April 19. There are 139 teams in 15 leagues, playing at two locations: Highlands Park and Hoff Woods Park.
- Adult volleyball leagues are progressing toward playoffs.
- Spring sport classes started. Classes offered include midget and peewee basketball, floor hockey, indoor soccer, and two instructional volleyball classes.
- Special needs group attended *Vaudvillities*, Central Ohio's largest Broadway show.
- Two new jewelry classes began at 64 Walnut, with 12 people enrolled.
- Conducted VISION volunteer dinner on April 25, with approximately 150 people in attendance.
- Volunteer awards were given out at dinner on the 25th using the new awards format.
- Participated in fourth Friday event uptown on April 23, distributing department information.
- Big Band Bash on Friday, April 30; approximately 100 attended. The featured band was the Classics.
- The AARP tax preparation program at the senior center concluded, with 378 returns completed. Compliments go to Maury Cook and his four volunteers.
- A chair massage program has begun at the senior center. April and May sessions will be given free as a demonstration. Informational signs have been posted promoting the benefits of massage. The fees will be $15 and $10 for 15 and 10 minutes, respectively.
- The senior center's 55 Alive driving class was attended by the maximum (20).

- The Agawa train trip (Mackinac Island) presentation had very good attendance, with 31 already registered.
- 107 men attended the annual breakfast meeting for the golf league; 28 attended the ladies golf luncheon.
- Faith Bible Church has terminated its weekly rental of the senior center.
- Great Time Getaways (formerly Oliver's Excellent Adventures) took place April 5th to April 9th. Participants traveled to several new locations this year, getting to experience the Newport Aquarium and Boonshoft Museum of Discovery. Each day participants traveled somewhere different and had a lot of fun.
- The citywide Easter Egg Hunt was conducted on April 10 and went off great, with approximately 2,000 attending. Perfect weather and great compliments for the event.
- Group fitness classes kicked off the spring session. This session had 45 classes, with 1,374 people registered for the programs.
- What's in the Night? is a class that lets participants explore the outdoors at night and learn about nocturnal animals. Eight children were enrolled.
- First Annual Underwater Easter Egg hunt was conducted on Thursday April 8 at the Community Center leisure pool. There were approximately 600 children and their parents attending the event. The event was successful and will be continued for the upcoming years.
- Baby Bargain was held on April 24; 38 vendors tables were sold, and approximately 800 to 1,000 shoppers were in attendance during the day.

Westerville Parks and Recreation, 2004.

Surveys

A needs assessment can take the form of a questionnaire that is distributed to a random sample of constituents to gather information about the following:

- *Leisure patterns.* Data from the questionnaire are analyzed to determine how patrons currently engage in activities according to type, frequency, and consistency.
- *Leisure priorities.* Patrons are asked to rank or share the level of importance attributed to

leisure activities. Data from all respondents may show what activities are considered most needed.

- *Leisure needs and gaps.* Respondents are asked to identify programs and facilities they would like to see. These may be programs and facilities that do not exist as well as an expansion of current offerings.

- *Suggestions for future growth and development.* An open comment area on the questionnaire allows the respondent to identify any concern or idea that may be important to the patron or patron group.

- *Willingness to pay and support new initiatives.* The level of funding opportunities is explored by determining pay patterns for existing programs, anticipated spending for future programs, or support for tax levies that may provide bonds for programs.

- *Evaluation of existing programs and services.* Program users are encouraged to rank or rate existing services.

The survey technique is often the basis for mass distribution of a questionnaire to a population of respondents who may or may not currently access leisure services. When developing a questionnaire, it is important that you avoid the pitfalls of poorly constructed questions. Many standard questionnaires can be adapted for an organization, according to the investigated population. Questionnaire distribution needs to be handled so that everyone has an equal chance of being selected to respond. This is accomplished through a random process such as that noted in chapter 15.

Remember to safeguard the anonymity and confidentiality of the questionnaire respondents. This means choosing a method that ensures no one else has access to the questionnaires and making sure data used in analysis make no reference to any specific individual's remarks or responses. Finally, analyze data according to acceptable statistical procedures so that results are trustworthy; weak analysis may result in lost credibility.

Interviews and Observations

Techniques for interviewing and observing should follow prescribed standard procedures used by field researchers. Be as consistent as possible when asking questions and viewing subjects. A preestablished set of questions to guide the process is essential. These questions are developed with the agency vision in mind and can vary considerably from program to program. In addition, take extensive notes for either form of research. For example, in an interview, a tape recorder backup will provide more complete transcripts, and your field notes may focus on a wider range of observations to provide context for the interview. When observing facilities and programs, you may keep notes and also record observations as they occur.

When analyzing transcripts that result from interviews, use a system of either manual or electronic coding to identify response categories and themes. This systematic method of organizing field notes allows you to highlight key themes and common references.

A charrette often results in the development of key priorities.

Focus Groups

From the data gathered in the survey process, excesses and gaps are identified. It is important to verify the nature of these findings, often by formally discussing the information in organized meetings known as focus groups, also often called charrettes. A representative group of constituents meets to discuss the needs as expressed in the survey or as identified through the group's experience with the services. From the findings inherent within this process, formalized quantitative findings may be compared with those articulated in the focus group process format. In a focus group, a representative group of people is invited to participate in a discussion that utilizes group process techniques.

This means that focus groups employ a group interview system to gather as much input as possible in a 90- to 120-minute period. Potential group members are identified and invited to attend. A facilitator guides the group through a multistep brainstorming process to determine priorities of needs or to generate responses to a particular problem. A group is composed of six to twelve members in order to secure the greatest amount of information in a short time.

A **charrette** is usually a more focused work session where invitees (key representatives or stakeholders) are divided into groups to work on a specific project. Such a project usually involves a more concrete work objective such as a specific program.

In Westerville, the formal needs assessment consisted of a multifaceted approach to gain community input about future programs, facilities, and services (City of Westerville Parks and Recreation Department, 2000). The planning process involved interviews, a youth survey, town meetings, planning charrettes, and a comprehensive citizen questionnaire. Stakeholders involved in the interview process included more than 40 groups. The youth survey distributed to more than 200 students yielded information on favorite parks and top-ranked facility needs. Town meetings, open to the public and broadcast on the city's cable television channel, allowed for candid feedback from all who wished to attend. Two charrettes were then formed to provide specific strategic input. Finally, a recreation preference questionnaire was distributed to a random sample of Westerville citizens. This questionnaire yielded a multitude of preferences for future facilities and programs. Results from the survey were used to form the PROS 2000 plan (mentioned in chapter 6), which determined expansion of facilities and programs in Westerville.

Identification, Interpretation, and Utilization of Data

Once the survey results and the focus group's findings are reviewed, demand for programs and services may be compared with standards in the field, with existing conditions that reveal gaps, and with trends that have been identified through census or industry profiles.

Standards are minimum guidelines for operation established by recognized authorities. In 1983 and 1995, the National Recreation and Park Association published guidelines for parks, recreation, and open spaces. These guidelines are often used to compare facilities and areas needed per 1,000 people in a population.

Standards are not readily available for all facilities, however. If you do consult standards, remember they are only guidelines for developing leisure program services. It is essential that any comparison with standards take into account the unique characteristics of an organization and community. For more information on this topic, see "More Options for Individual Programming Practice," option 1, in chapter 7 of the CD-ROM.

The existing conditions assessment discussed in chapter 6 is also a source for determining the size of and demand for program services when compared with the dynamics of growth and change in the population. Finally, trends that have developed over the past 10 years can be analyzed to determine changes that need to be made in program development over the next 10 years.

Once programmatic needs are identified and a comparison is made with standards, the next step is to begin formulating priorities for planning over the next 10 years. The information gathered so far provides the basics for a planning document. (Chapter 9 identifies this in more detail.) The needs assessment process is completed as a precursor to any planning considerations, and it is valuable in providing baseline information that may justify support. Because the needs assessment is a form of organizational research, it is important to identify which research techniques are useful in conducting the assessment. In addition, if organizational personnel wish to conduct a needs assessment, how do they go about it? Stakeholders (those who will benefit from the program) are asked to provide feedback through various phases of a needs assessment.

Conducting a Needs Assessment

As noted earlier in the chapter, a needs assessment is part of the process of gaining insight into the priorities for leisure program service delivery. Using organizational literature as an ongoing source of evaluation may be helpful to a certain degree in determining program priorities. It is important, however, to provide information in a formal, unbiased manner so that the information gathered stands alone in its usefulness to the organization.

Many data-gathering techniques are used in a needs assessment. All techniques must follow strict research protocol to be viewed as credible to stakeholders, funding sources, and critics. The processes described in this section are typical parts of a needs assessment, and all are viewed as essential in some way; however, budget constraints or scope of an organization may preclude use of all methods. For more information on this topic, see "More Options for Individual Programming Practice," option 2, in chapter 7 of the CD-ROM.

The goals of a needs assessment are met through state-of-the-art methods of **qualitative** and **quantitative** modes of data collection. For example, in a typical needs assessment, the key tasks conducted by MLL consulting firm include, but are not restricted to, the following (MLL, 2002):

- Extensive in-depth interviews of decision makers in the organization
- Extensive in-depth interviews of members of special interest groups in the community
- Focus group discussions with decision makers in the organization
- Focus group discussions with members of the community, including user groups and special interest groups

- Content analysis of printed materials produced by the organization
- Development of a questionnaire suitable for the needs of the organization and the community it serves
- Administration of the questionnaire by first-class mail
- Data coding
- Data analysis
- Production of a final report
- Presentation of an exhaustive set of recommendations
- Development and installation of a computerized data-based query tool

Using focus group methodologies, advanced questionnaire designs, and computerized data analysis, MLL delivers the following to the organization (MLL, 2002):

- Final questionnaire that can be used in future surveys
- Executive summary of findings
- Detailed report of the results of the survey
- Recommendations for future planning
- Oral presentation of results and recommendations
- Computerized data-based query tool called CompuRec

Using a consultant, such as MLL, is a common way to garner support for what is viewed as a fair, unbiased process. Many agencies and organizations use consultants, educational institutions, or in-house experts.

Regardless of the method used for needs assessment data gathering, steps must be taken to ensure reliability and validity of the instruments and methods. A research method is valid if it yields accurate and correct results. Questions should be specific and presented in such a way that there is no confusion that might affect the data analysis. For example, when asking a survey respondent to list her favorite facilities in priority order of 1 to 5, be sure to note if 1 is the highest or lowest ranking. When instructing an interview respondent to identify issues about meeting program demands, make sure he knows which program is being referred to.

A research method is reliable when it yields the same form of results over repeated measuring (e.g., a citizens' survey that yields consistent results when administered from year to year or across wider populations). It is imperative to determine if a survey instrument can get consistent results over repeated administrations. Often, organizations seek a consultant to provide a reliable instrument (i.e., the instrument is consistently used in other organizations, so results are comparable over time).

Uses of a Needs Assessment

Once a needs assessment is conducted, the results can be used in many ways. The most specific application is the completion of a master plan that includes strategies for funding needed programs. The results are also valuable in many other ways.

- *Marketing plan.* A needs assessment forms a basis for identifying target markets and reflecting the characteristics of groups who may be attracted to program services. A **marketing plan** is a written document that identifies the segments of the population that will consume the services; it must be flexible enough to adapt program services to an identifiable group of patrons who have similar characteristics. (We address this use later in this chapter.) You can approach the market with a **concentrated strategy** that focuses on one or two key markets or a **diffused strategy,** which permeates several markets equally.

- *Evaluation.* Once a needs assessment is conducted, results may be used to make changes in ongoing program services. Problems may be identified and addressed during the current operation of a program. (See chapters 14 and 15 for more information on evaluation.)

- *Grants.* A needs assessment can often provide the required background research to show the significance of a proposed grant.

- *Partnerships.* Needs assessment data may provide insight into new and expanding partnerships with other organizations to meet needs identified in the results. For more information on this topic, see "Group Discussion Ideas," option 1, in chapter 7 of the CD-ROM.

Aside from their many uses, regularly upgraded needs assessments may form the backbone for continual improvement of programs. In developing programs for constituents, the programmer must review needs assessment results in order to plan an array of services that appeal to the widest range of patrons. Developing programs that attract people is a challenging task. Based on needs assessment results, several basic characteristics should be reflected in a program plan. That is, when programming leisure services, you need to be especially aware of the needs and expectations of the clientele, or patrons.

Characteristics of Clientele

With an understanding of your clientele and community, you can begin targeting subsegments of the population for programs. A grouping of patrons with similar identifying characteristics is referred to as a **target market.** Once a market is identified, you can develop programs that attract this market by reflecting their needs and desires. The following target markets, or segments of the population, are typically considered when developing program services.

- *Ability.* One of the first and foremost variations in programming takes into account the various physical, social, emotional, and developmental abilities of patrons. The ability to learn new skills is varied according to factors such as developmental level and the presence of injury. For more information on this topic, see worksheet 7.3 in chapter 7 of the CD-ROM.

- *Gender considerations.* Interest levels sometimes vary according to gender. You must take an objective look at your schedule and attempt to offer programs that have universal appeal to everyone. Another aspect is identifying those areas that may be perceived as gaps and developing programs for both genders. Programming with gender in mind requires openness to new requests and the changing needs of men, women, boys, and girls. It also involves removing stereotypical program offerings in order to encourage participation in a wide array of activities, even those not traditionally popular with men or with women.

- *Age.* Skill development and enjoyment of leisure activities vary by age; however, many changes are being made in the way people of all ages participate. Of particular concern is the establishment of ages when participation should start, such as in sport programs. Equally important is offering programs that challenge and involve those of advancing age. People today are active participants into their 90s. Today's older participants engage in active leisure, unique travel programs, and exciting special events, as well as Bingo and pot luck dinners. Snowflake Castle, as described in the box on this page, is an example of an intergenerational activity involving both youth and adults. For more information on this topic, see "Can You Solve This Programming Issue?" in chapter 7 of the CD-ROM.

• *Race and ethnicity.* Inequities according to racial and ethnic stereotyping have long been documented. It is your responsibility to develop programs that are sensitive to the needs and interests of those with varying origins. Participation must be encouraged and cultivated through the program planning process. Often, people of color and those from different ethnic backgrounds will be attracted to a programming approach that reflects the cultural characteristics of their particular group. Programs sensitive to holidays and events are often very popular, such as Martin Luther King Day and Cinco de Mayo celebrations.

• *Lifestyle.* A study of the typical lifestyles prevalent in a community is an important way to understand how people operate and what they value. For example, Stanford Research Institute has been studying the lifestyles of Americans for years and has developed the VALS (Values, Attitudes, and Lifestyles Survey) typology. Through VALS, segments of the American population are divided according to economic categories and how these individuals use recreation and leisure. For more information on this topic, see worksheet 7.4 and "Group Discussion Ideas," option 2, in chapter 7 of the CD-ROM.

• *Residential situation.* Understanding the varying needs of a particular **residential situation,** such as neighborhood districts, planned communities, and mobile communities, is often an important consideration in program planning. A residential community often has a personality of its own, and those who reside there are proud of that identity. If there is little identity, then it is your responsibility

A key target market, such as youth, can be a major focus for an agency or business.

Snowflake Castle

For the 18th year, the Westerville Senior Center is holding the Snowflake Castle, a special Christmas event for children in preschool and kindergarten. And the seniors of Westerville are the ones who run this event and make it special for the kids.

The Snowflake Castle runs from Monday, December 2, to Friday, December 6, at the Westerville Senior Center at 310 W. Main Street. The hours are Monday through Friday from 10:00 a.m. to noon and 1:00 p.m. to 4:00 p.m.

At this event, kids can enjoy a Christmas movie, puppet show, toy trains, and face painting; visit the gift shop; become one of Santa's favorite reindeer; and, of course, visit with Santa Claus.

The admission for this event is only $1 per child, and a picture with Santa is $2. The tour through the Snowflake Castle will take approximately one hour. No reservations are required except for groups of five or more.

Westerville Parks and Recreation, 2005.

to find those programming elements that generate pride and satisfaction in living in a particular residential situation.

The following list describes various residential situations that affect the way programmers describe and understand clientele:

- *Urban:* a lifestyle oriented toward high-density living in and among city businesses and services
- *Suburban:* more decentralized residential living associated with more open space, yards, and separation from city or corporate life
- *Rural:* vast open space with great distance between homes and from business centers
- *Multifamily dwelling:* shared open facilities and close living quarters
- *Single-family dwelling:* a home that sits on property that is a part of the individual home
- *Condominium:* houselike but shared living situation with defined common areas to be used by all
- *Planned urban development:* planned communities with common areas as part of urban planning, which is the process of creating a built environment that has essential services, businesses, and residences
- *Apartment:* private or public building with certain shared access to recreation outlets

Multifamily residential situations may differ from single-family residential situations.

© Patrick Bennett/CORBIS.

- *Subsidized housing:* housing for low-income residents; usually small with minimal recreation facilities

For more information on this topic, see worksheet 7.2 in chapter 7 of the CD-ROM.

Pleasing the Patrons

Programmed leisure requires extensive study of and focus on the needs and expectations of clientele, residents, employees, tourists, and customers. Once you identify these patrons, you can examine their values, beliefs, needs, desires, stage in life, constraints, generation, and motivation in order to provide a program that is accessible, attractive, and affordable. These three "As" are described further as follows:

1. *Accessible:* Where and how are programs offered? Are all patrons who desire them able to get to locations and participate fully? The idea of access is increasingly important to the patrons you serve. People may desire a program opportunity but are prevented from participating because of lack of transportation or because a disability prevents them from meeting the programmatic requirements.

2. *Attractive:* Does the program appeal to the patrons' interests, values, needs, desires, or sense of tradition? The characteristics of your patrons determine how you shape a program of leisure services. The VALS typology study from Stanford Research Institute (mentioned on page 105) represents a cross section of American people defined according to lifestyles. By understanding how people live, what they chose to do with their time, and what they desire, programmers using the VALS typology can create approaches that attract patrons. Regardless of how patrons are studied, through values typology or other means, tapping into their processes allows for creative and attractive programs. The resulting strategy is more sensitive to a group of prospective patron because it reflects more in-depth wants, needs, and habits.

3. *Affordable:* What is the economic capacity of individual patrons? A marketing plan considers a patron group's ability and willingness to pay for a program or service and establishes an affordable pricing system. Programs that are too expensive may be poorly attended or may fail to serve the target audience.

From Needs Assessment to Marketing Plan

One of the uses, then, of assessing patrons is a marketing plan. The marketing plan is a written document prepared after extensive study of the patron, the environment, and the product. Market plans consider four key factors that affect the patron, known as "the four Ps" of marketing—product, place, price, and promotion. The end result is a plan or approach that reflects a typical patron or patron group known as the target. This information is then incorporated into a marketing plan that drives how programs are introduced to users.

Product

Crossley, Jamieson, and Brayley (2001) view products as "bundles of benefits that meet consumer needs" (p. 215). Examples of benefits, according to Crossley and colleagues, include such items as the following:

- Escape from daily routine
- Improved health
- Improved personal appearance
- Social interaction
- Skill development
- Stress relief
- Education
- Ego enhancement
- Aggression release
- Authentication

The benefits movement of the National Recreation and Park Association has identified many of the advantages available to patrons. Its campaign, "The Benefits Are Endless," provides a foundation for offering program products that have met and continue to meet patron, community, and organization needs.

Products—in this case, leisure programs—are developed according to an understanding of the benefits to and needs of the patron. According to Crossley and colleagues (2001, p. 217), "the satisfaction of consumer needs should be the primary motivation for product modification or new product development." For example, alternative sports are on the rise in the United States and Canada. Many alternative sport enthusiasts use areas and facilities such as streets, guardrails, steps, roads, sidewalks, and pristine mountain trails to engage in their sports. Public and private organizations have responded in various ways by setting ordinances to restrict such usage and engaging youth in the development of alternative facilities and programs. One such response to this need occurred in Columbus, Indiana. Chuck Wilt, executive director of Columbus Parks and Recreation, developed a youth task force that provided input and raised funds for the development of a skate park suitable for in-line, skateboard, and bike sports. This park now meets the needs of a large number of area youth.

Program and service products are developed, extended, and extinguished as a result of patron needs, desires, and expectations. The updated and ongoing study of those needs results in a proactive marketing plan.

Place

Referred to by Crossley and colleagues (2001, p. 227) as "distribution and allocation," place is an important aspect of matching the patron with the best way to reach the intended program or service. When studying patron groupings or target markets, a marketing plan targets key groups for which programs are developed. In Westerville, an example is the Orange Study, which identified the millennial cycle of the population and divided the citizens into generational subsegments, described in the box on page 108. In this section, various market segments are identified in terms of name, characteristic, birth, and life span. Therefore, if a target market is a generational group such as "Silent," programs can be planned for people categorized into that group.

Of course target markets may also be identified within broad groupings such as parental stages, youth subcategories, gender, and so on. In considering place, or distribution, of programs and services, the goal is to attract the widest range or number of target markets. For example, many companies offer programs right in the workplace, where most employees can easily access the services before, during, and after the workday.

Price

Price sensitivity and the patron is an issue marketing plans must address. Patrons will pay for what they perceive as affordable and the best value for their investment, all things being equal. Where is the best aerobics class, swimming program, or art lesson? Am I willing to pay more for added value—better social experience, child care, longer meeting time, extra services? The marketing plan must determine the best starting price to set according to clients' needs.

For example, the 2004 Westerville Community Center marketing plan offers a package of services that allows flexibility and choice for patrons as well as affordability. The PASSport program involves a variety of passes from which patrons may choose. There are seven unique PASSports, including trial and three-month passes. An added family discount is applied to two PASSport categories, offering a 10 percent discount to families of two or three, up to a 20 percent discount to families of six or more.

The database generated by PASSport sales reflects the **demographics,** or characteristics of the popu- lation, to assist with updating pricing and program needs. The box on this page shows age demographics and descriptions that assisted in the development of the PASSport Program.

Promotion

Finally, promotion results from the outcome of the study of patrons with respect to product devel- opment, distribution of programs, and pricing of services. The resultant package reflects new under- standings of how to reach the intended market or patron. In learning about the market, Westerville, for example, identified market characteristics that were worked into the promotional plan. Objectives were as follows (City of Westerville Parks and Recreation Department, 2000):

- To increase total resident sales of the Commu- nity Center PASSports to 5,445, representing a 5 percent increase
- To effectively manage PASSport renewals during 2004 to renew 75 percent of current PASSport holders
- To create awareness and encourage use of the Westerville Community Center

Orange Study

The Orange Study used a lifestyle typology to introduce the type of promotions needed to attract target mar- kets. In 2004, through the use of PASSports, it was possible to gauge the type of user attracted to Westerville programs. The following table shows the lifestyle dimensions identified as typical users and how they may influence and demand services over the millennial cycle.

Generation name	Characteristic	Birth year	Possible life span
Silent	Adaptive	1925-1942	1925-2022
Boomers	Idealistic	1943-1960	1943-2040
Gen X	Reactive	1961-1981	1961-2061
Millennial	Civic	1982-2003	1982-2083
Cycle	Adaptive	2004-2025	2004-2115

From Westerville Parks and Recreation Department, Westerville, Ohio.

The Programming Process: Give 'em What They Want

As we've already noted, the Westerville Parks and Recreation Department is a good example of the usefulness of studying patron needs. How does such information translate to programming?

A few years ago, a citizens' questionnaire was administered to the residents. The demand and support for additional recreation programs for older adults in the city resulted in additional funding and program staff for the senior center.

Adding these new resources has meant a huge increase in programs available to Westerville elders. For example, the Westerville Senior Center now manages an extensive transportation program that takes participants to medical appointments, two different grocery stores, the local beauty school, the public library, uptown shops and banks, a local mall, and four different discount stores. Center buses typically travel more than 50,000 miles (80,000 kilometers) annually, providing free transportation services to more than 6,000 people. Such wellness services as mammograms, flu and pneumonia vaccines, and health-related seminars are also now available. Monthly support groups include Alzheimer's, arthritis, and Parkinson's, and the Kind Call program offers daily computer-generated safety telephone calls to residents who are housebound.

Assessing the needs and interests of patrons has also resulted in some outstanding just-for-fun programs at the senior center. For example, there's Girls' Night In, a program that gives the lady participants at the senior center a special night of pampering. The evening begins with a pizza party. Then the "girls" spread out to other parts of the center for a chair massage, foot spa, pedicure, manicure, and other relaxing activities. The evening concludes by picking up the pace with some karaoke.

Thanks to continual assessment of client needs, Westerville's older adults now have expanded programs.

Photo courtesy of Westerville Parks and Recreation Department, Westerville, Ohio.

- To increase the number of PASSport holder upgrades from a trial pass to an annual pass

Assessment of patron needs, in other words, not only provides information upon which program services can be targeted, but also reveals data about patrons that is useful in attracting them to these services. Think of it as needs assessment providing the "flashlight" that guides both program planners and program participants alike.

Summary

This chapter identifies the value of conducting a needs assessment—and planning marketing that reflects these needs—before developing the program plan. You should understand the following key points:

- Organizational literature provides a valuable initial source of review to determine programmatic needs.
- Formalized research in the form of quantitative and qualitative assessments is an important component to objectively analyze needs and determine accuracy and priority of programs.
- Data gathered through the process of needs identification are the basis for review, priority setting, and initial program planning processes.
- A needs assessment provides the framework for a marketing plan as a basis for planning the promotional aspects of programs.
- Varying demographic characteristics gathered through needs assessments must be taken into consideration when planning programs.

Glossary

needs assessment— A formal collection and analysis of information to identify the needs, interests, and problems of program constituents.

patrons—Those who use and consume leisure services.

facilities—Constructed buildings and grounds designed to serve recreation users.

areas—Park land and open spaces designed for recreational and passive users.

organizational literature—Information used in the operation of a department.

charrette—A designated group that actively engages in an assigned task.

quantitative—An approach to research that uses numerical information as data.

standards—Minimum guidelines for operation established by recognized authorities.

qualitative—An approach to research that uses words and symbols as data.

marketing plan—A written document that outlines the strategies to attract participants into a program.

concentrated strategy—The strategy for marketing that identifies key targets of clientele to program for.

diffused strategy—A strategy for marketing that takes into account several different targets.

target market—A segment of the population that programs are aimed at.

residential situation—The locale of clientele that affects the way people access leisure services.

demographics—Characteristics that identify a population and differentiate it from others.

References

City of Westerville Parks and Recreation Department. (2000). *Parks Recreation Open Space (PROS) 2000.* Westerville, OH: City of Westerville.

City of Westerville Parks and Recreation Department. (2004a). *Parks and Recreation sports festival/sportstown marketing plan.* Westerville, OH: City of Westerville.

City of Westerville Parks and Recreation Department. (2004b). *The Pool at Highlands Park 2004 marketing plan.* Westerville, OH: City of Westerville.

City of Westerville Parks and Recreation Department. (2004c). *Westerville Community Center 2004 marketing plan.* Westerville, OH: City of Westerville.

Crossley, J.C., Jamieson, L.M., & Brayley, R. (2001). *Introduction to commercial recreation and tourism.* Champaign, IL: Sagamore.

Gainesville Health and Fitness Center. (n.d.a). Our mission. Retrieved March 3, 2006, from www.ghfc.com/about_mission.cfm.

Gainesville Health and Fitness Center. (n.d.b). Why us? Retrieved March 3, 2006, from www.ghfc.com/about_whyus.cfm.

Lancaster, R.A. (Ed.). (1983). *Recreation, park, and open space standards and guidelines.* Alexandria, VA: National Recreation and Park Association.

MLL. (2002). MLL's services. Retrieved March 2, 2006, from www.m-l-l.com/service.html.

Westerville Parks and Recreation. (2004). *April monthly report.* Westerville, OH: Recreation Division.

Westerville Parks and Recreation. (2005). Senior Center. Retrieved January 2005, from www.ci.westerville.oh.us/Default.aspx?tabid=134.

CHAPTER 8

Program Goals and Objectives

In this chapter, you can look forward to the following:

- Summarizing the program preparations up to this point with the establishment of program goals and objectives
- Understanding how goals and objectives specify what the program wants to accomplish
- Appreciating the context of formulating goals and objectives
- Developing the ability to prepare goals and objectives for recreation programs

RVing Women is an international support network organized by and for women who are interested in RVing. In fact, the only requirement for membership is that you are a woman interested in sharing knowledge about and building friendships through RV travel. Owning a motor home, van, fifth wheel, travel trailer, tent trailer, or camper is not a prerequisite.

Through programs such as camping rallies in different locations, RVing Women seeks to meet its goal of helping members enjoy the RV lifestyle.

Education and training are shared within the network of more than 2,500 members through programs such as camping rallies in different locations, a monthly magazine, an Internet message forum, and rig technical assistance. How does the organization know these programs are the most appropriate? Because of their ability to help achieve the organization's goals as follows:

- To identify the needs of women RVers
- To provide national recognition of women RVers through marketing the organization
- To provide members with educational opportunities for their information, growth, and enjoyment
- To provide technical support to members
- To facilitate networking for members

Adapted from RVing Women, 2005, www.rvingwomen.org/goals_objectives.html.

Often, leisure service organizations are created to offer specific types of programs in order to achieve specific purposes. For example, the program purpose of Walt Disney World in Orlando, Florida, is to provide hospitable entertainment for families, while the programs of Recreation Integration Victoria (RIV), located in British Columbia, focus on enabling people with disabilities to pursue active lifestyles. Elderhostel provides courses, classes, and trips around the world for older adults; and Play for Peace brings together children from conflicting cultures to get to know each other through play. Programmers in these and many other leisure service organizations work with a programming purpose that is specific to the reason the organization was originally established.

On the other hand, some organizations that provide leisure program services seek to meet wider purposes. A local YMCA, for example, provides social, health and fitness, craft, travel, camping, adventure, voluntary service, and many other programs for people of all ages, lifestyles, interests, and abilities. Its purpose is broad and comprehensive, with a menu of different programs focusing on different specific purposes.

For all programmers, regardless of the breadth of their agency's purpose, organized leisure is the means for achieving that purpose. Each organization has specific or broad ends that it promotes through participation in recreation activities. This means agencies use a recreation program as a tool for obtaining their goals and objectives (Tillman, 1973). Let's delve into this a bit more.

Program Rationale

What is the reason for the recreation program? There is at least one reason for every program you prepare! Indeed, this is the whole point of establishing program goals and objectives—to articulate the program's rationale. As with many things, preparing goals and objectives for your programs is not as simple as just sitting down and writing out a list. In addition to the preparations we've already discussed—such as understanding the culture of your organization and community, understanding and involving your clientele, and assessing needs—developing programming rationale through goals and objectives requires attention to some other issues. Program goals and objectives must directly reflect your organization's mission and policies, your profession's philosophy, and other factors such as laws. To review what we've discussed in previous chapters, think of these things as "filters" for your program's rationale (see figure 8.1).

Professional Philosophies

Recreation program goals and objectives mirror professional philosophies. For example, if you are a programmer for sport and fitness services on a university campus, you will likely abide by the framework of values established by such professional societies as the National Intramural-Recreational Sports Association (NIRSA).

As another example, according to the Commission for Accreditation of Park and Recreation Agencies (2003, p. 47), recreation program services "shall be based on

- conceptual foundations of play, recreation, and leisure;
- constituent needs;
- community opportunities;
- agency philosophy and goals; and
- experiences desirable for clientele."

This professional philosophy firmly establishes the patron as the starting place for planning program services. As further confirmation of this professional stance, the accreditation manual also states that programs should be delivered to a wide range of participant backgrounds and that participants should be involved in their planning.

Professions, by their very nature, have such philosophical mandates. For the leisure professions,

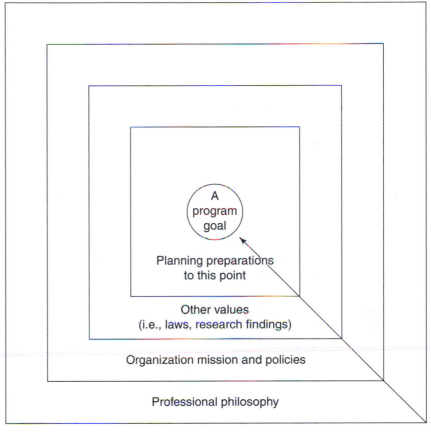

Figure 8.1 Program goals and objectives reflect your organization, profession, and other "filters."

this mandate is grounded in meeting the needs of society—positively contributing to its well-being and the quality of life of its people. Recreation professionals have viewed their work as providing a **human service**. That is, organized leisure has the power to accomplish social goals. As we've made clear in chapter 1, leisure contributes to the physical, emotional, and social benefit of people. It strengthens communities, promotes economic health, and enriches cultural life. This is our professional human service mandate.

Yet, over time, professional philosophies change. In the leisure professions this can be reflected in the increasing importance of a marketing mandate. Today we share a human service philosophy with a more entrepreneurial mandate. More than ever, park and recreation agencies at all levels place increasing reliance on revenue sources to support their facilities and programs. The philosophies of the world of business have adjusted our orientation so that many professionals now see leisure as an industry, and program participants are seen as customers.

Basically, this marketing approach seeks to attract and serve those who can pay. The economic attraction of a recreation activity or event, and the purchasing power of its potential participants, steers programming decisions. This is counter to the human service approach because it lowers the priority given to those groups of people who have less market value, such as the unemployed worker, welfare-dependent family, at-risk teenager, or economically disadvantaged elderly person.

Whether we like it or not, marketing principles now share priority with human service values in shaping the mandate of professionals who program leisure. Programs must contribute to personal and community development while at the same time increase the fiscal resources that support them. Both philosophical stances are so interwoven throughout this book that you may not have noticed the distinction. For more information on this topic, see "Can You Solve This Programming Issue?" in chapter 8 of the CD-ROM.

Mission

Leisure service organizations must be able to clearly articulate who they are providing services for, what they are trying to accomplish, and to what extent they have been successful. Usually all this is captured in the organization's **mission statement**. A mission statement—basically a summary of an organization's purpose—defines the organization's function in the community. This statement is customarily formulated by administrators, sometimes with staff and patron input. Once approved by policy boards, it becomes an important part of the organization's official documents.

Mission statements can take the form of bylaws, preambles to constitutions, charters, authorizing legislation, or strategic and long-range plans. They may be found in annual reports, on Web sites, and even in promotional brochures. See "A Sampling of Mission Statements" for an assortment of mission statements from various leisure service organiza-

---

A Sampling of Mission Statements

Parks Canada: "On behalf of the people of Canada, we protect and present nationally significant examples of Canada's natural and cultural heritage and foster public understanding, appreciation and enjoyment in ways that ensure their ecological and commemorative integrity for present and future generations." (Parks Canada, 2006; reproduced with the permision of the Minister of Public Works and Government Services Canada, 2007)

The Cheer Guild Volunteers at Indiana University Medical Center: "With a careful tradition since the first gift of flowers was presented to a child more than 65 years ago, about 6000 men and women today through individual memberships or statewide chapters donate time, talent and treasure to help patients feel more at home . . . adding the special touch that only caring hands can bring." (Riley Childrens Hospital, 2000-2006)

Holland America Line: "During our 134 years, we have extended hospitality and world-class service to more than 10 million guests. We make it our goal to create an excellent work environment for all our staff. At Holland America Line, we know that it is our more than 14,000 employees who have made us one of

the most respected cruise lines in the world. It is their effort, loyalty, dedication and talent that are vital to our success and our future." (Reprinted, by permission, from Holland America Cruiseline, 2001-2006)

Denver, Colorado, Parks and Recreation Department: "As stewards of Denver's legacy, the Department of Parks and Recreation is dedicated to customer satisfaction and enhancing lives by providing innovative programs and safe, beautiful, sustainable places." (City and County of Denver, n.d.)

Polynesian Cultural Center: "The Polynesian Cultural Center is a unique treasure created to share with the world the culture, diversity and spirit of the nations of Polynesia." (Reprinted, by permission, from Polynesian Cultural Center, 2007).

Northern Berkshire (Massachusetts) YMCA: "To put Christian principles and character development into practice through programs and services that build healthy spirit, mind and body for all. The YMCA does not feature any particular program or serve any group. The YMCA deliberately remains flexible so it can offer programs that are in each community's best interest." (Northern Berkshire YMCA, n.d.)

tions. For more information on this topic, see "More Options for Individual Programming Practice," option 2, in chapter 8 of the CD-ROM.

In preparing goals and objectives for recreation programs, the programmer works from the mission statement because programs must make a direct contribution to the purpose of the sponsoring organization. If the mission is broad and all-encompassing, such as that for the Denver Parks and Recreation Department, you will have a great deal of latitude in regard to matching programmed services. If the organization's mission statement is specific and narrow, such as that for the Cheer Guild Volunteers at Indiana University Medical Center, the programs you prepare will likewise be more closely focused.

Mission statements often reflect important social values and professional "best practices." For example, Little League baseball publishes a 135-page manual that deals with all aspects of programming, from national administration to coaching procedures. One stipulation refers to sexual harassment:

> No individual shall be subjected to verbal or physical sexual behavior. Sexual harassment will be treated as misconduct, and may result in the application of appropriate corrective action up to and including dismissal. (*Operations Manual*, 1994, p. 19)

Other Values

Recreation program goals and objectives also reproduce other values. When incorporating the agency's mission and a professional philosophical mandate, you will be influenced by such other important factors as laws, risk management considerations, research findings, and even what you learned in your college leisure services course work!

For example, as a programmer, you may legally be bound to uphold agency charter requirements, city ordinances, state enabling legislation, and judicial precedents (Kraus, 1997). These "laws" affect all aspects of the operation of a park and recreation

organization, especially its programs. These regulations include such requirements as not restricting participation based on race, ethnicity, gender, or age, as well as the need to adhere to constitutional rights of free speech and assembly.

Concern about possible negligence and resulting lawsuits is also paramount for agencies providing leisure services. How well can and should the risk be managed in programmed leisure? When establishing program goals and objectives, professionals consider the degree of risk for a particular activity or event and the availability of insurance coverage in case of injury or death. So forceful is this factor that, unfortunately, some activities have been eliminated by their sponsoring organizations because they represent too great a lawsuit risk. (More detailed information about risk management appears in chapter 13.)

Programmers need to retain their professional relevancy by reflecting research-produced "state of the art" in their program goals and objectives, too. In North America, scholars and professionals annually report on hundreds of research studies. *Journal of Leisure Research, Annals of Tourism Research, Therapeutic Recreation Journal, Journal of Sport Management, Research File, Leisure Sciences,* and *Journal of Leisurability* are just a few examples of publications that present the findings

Your professional preparation is also a useful value to reflect in program goals and objectives.

The Programming Process: Program Goals and Objectives

Among the many outstanding programs offered by the City of Westerville Parks and Recreation Department, there is one that may just be for you! The department includes an internship program in its services. This program serves many purposes. First, it furthers college students' professional education by helping them apply theory to actual situations. Additionally, the experience provides for intensive self-evaluation as students develop a professional attitude toward their chosen career and improve their ability to successfully handle a wide variety of people and situations. Finally, the internship program provides the department with quality personnel to supplement its regular staff.

How are these purposes for the internship program converted into the actual program? The establishment of program goals and objectives helps translate "a good idea" to real-life experiences for students. For example, here are two goals for the program, along with their corresponding objectives (Westerville Parks and Recreation Department, Internship Handbook, 2004):

1. *The internship should expand the student's acquaintance with recreation and allow him or her to learn firsthand what it means to be a full-time recreation professional.*

   • During the eight-week internship period, the student intern will attend at least two state or national professional association meetings.

   • Internship responsibilities are scheduled based on a 40-hour, five-day workweek.

   • The student will exhibit professional work behaviors by being on time for meetings and programs 100 percent of the time.

   • Within one week of the completion of the internship, the student submits to the university supervisor a three-page document outlining what was learned about the full-time management of recreation programs and facilities.

2. *Students should engage in intensive self-evaluation by looking at strengths and limitations in light of practical work situations.*

   • As judged by their departmental supervisor, student interns will maintain a professional appearance and manner at all times.

   • Student interns will complete both a midpoint and final self-evaluation questionnaire.

   • Student interns will complete both a midpoint and final evaluation of their departmental supervisor using a questionnaire.

Reprinted, by permission, from Westerville Parks and Recreation Department, 2004, *Internship Handbook*. (Westerville, OH: Westerville Parks and Recreation Department).

For more information on this topic, see worksheet 8.1 in chapter 8 of the CD-ROM.

Photo courtesy of Westerville Parks and Recreation Department, Westerville, Ohio.

The college-student internship program at Westerville's Parks and Recreation Department has several goals and objectives to achieve.

of original investigations about leisure behavior and its management.

Finally, we are serious in stating that the rationale you develop for your program services will reflect what you learned in your professional training, beginning with this course. And, since education is a lifelong and career-long undertaking, your program goals and objectives, as well as decisions you make about program implementation and evaluation, will constantly be influenced by the classes, workshops, institutes, certifications, and other learning opportunities you take advantage of.

Formulating Goals

Leisure service organizations operate according to a wide variety of goals. There are performance goals for employees and volunteers, planning goals for facility construction, fiscal goals, goals for information technology, and, of course, program goals.

As a reminder, goals for a program you are planning do not get "thought up" in a vacuum. All the preparations we have presented so far in this first step of the program planning process are instrumental to the goals you establish. By assembling informa-tion about your organization (chapter 6), community (chapter 6), and clientele (chapter 7), you are able to craft your program goals.

Program goals are abstract, idealized state-ments of desired outcomes from the organized recreation service. They are a statement of purpose of, reason for, or intent of the program. Program goals are brief but comprehensive, and they are not directly measurable. Usually goals are idealistic, yet they are capable of being put into operation through corresponding objectives. In table 8.1, examples of program goals for a fitness class are provided in the first column.

The content of goals can be varied, but they always refer to desired outcomes. For example, emotional, cognitive, physical, and social changes or improve-ments are common desired outcomes for program participants. Goals can also reflect desired outcomes for the sponsoring organization, community, or broader society. Goals to reduce or eliminate a social problem, enhance the image of an agency, or heal a wounded community spirit are also frequently found in program preparations. The goals illustrated in table 8.1 concern the organization's efficiency and reputa-tion in the community and the physical, mental, and social health of program participants.

TABLE 8.1

Sample Goals and Objectives for a Fitness Class

Program goals for a fitness class	Corresponding objectives
Our organization will do the following:	At the end of the 6-week fitness class, our agency will have done the following:
1. Be efficient	1. Generated a 10% profit from program fees that can be reapplied to enhancing the program for the next session
2. Improve exposure within the community	2. Attracted 25% more participant registrations for the next session
Participants will experience improvements in the following:	At the end of the 6-week fitness class, participants will do the following:
1. Physical health	1. Record a 5% decrease in their 1-minute resting heart rate
2. Mental health	2. Report higher positive body image on a questionnaire
3. Social health	3. Continue interaction with at least one other class participant not previously known outside the class sessions

Adapted, by permission, from C.C. Riddick & R.V. Russell, 1999, *Evaluative research in recreation, park, and sport settings: Searching for useful information* (Champaign, IL: Sagamore Press), p. 288.

In other words, goals carry forward the statement of purpose contained in your agency's mission statement by determining program direction. Accordingly, goals are critically important in program evaluation, the third step in the planning process. That is, in determining the program's ultimate success, you compare what happened with what you hoped would happen. (You'll read about this process later in chapters 14 and 15.) For more information on this topic, see "More Options for Individual Programming Practice," option 3, and "Group Discussion Ideas," option 1, in chapter 8 of the CD-ROM.

Even though it can be challenging to identify program goals, numerous goals are possible for recreation programs. How do you decide which ones to accept? Weiss (1972) makes three important points in selecting and crafting goals:

1. *Practicality.* Goals must be appropriate and feasible for the constituents, sponsoring organization, and community. They must also be feasible within time, budget, and staffing resources. For example, can a Saturday afternoon craft program reasonably accomplish an improvement in participants' self-esteem within the time frame of only several hours?

2. *Relative importance.* Deciding relative importance of competing goals requires value judgments. Programmers and other staff need to decide what is vital to their mission and what is secondary. Although you may have intuitive reasons for offering a program, the choice of goals must often be made through collaboration with other staff, supervisors, and policy makers. For example, what is of highest priority for a program's sponsor: for participants in a wilderness challenge program to make new friends, achieve personal milestones, or appreciate nature? How is this determined?

3. *Incompatibilities.* Because many programs are multifaceted, attempting to satisfy a number of needs, programs typically have more than one goal. Therefore, choosing just one goal is shortsighted. Yet, what if there are incompatibilities among goals for a program? Celebrating an agency's 50th anniversary may be incompatible with the goal of keeping costs down. For the program to be successful, goal contradictions must be negotiated and resolved if both can't be achieved.

For more information on this topic, see worksheet 8.2 in chapter 8 of the CD-ROM.

How do you write goals for programs? There are no strict rules as long as the goal statements are general, clear, and brief and target the program intention. One "recipe" for writing goals follows:

1. Review your organization's mission in order to reflect it in the goal statements.

2. Review the results of the needs assessment in order to reflect potential patron interests and abilities in the goal statements.

3. Review your organization's fiscal, staffing, and facility resources so that goals are within these capacities.

4. Brainstorm all possible goals.

5. Determine the usefulness and appropriateness of each brainstormed goal.

6. Select the best goals and develop first-draft goal statements.

7. With help from staff and patrons, reevaluate the drafted goal statements.

8. Revise and finalize the goal statements.

This process will lead to better goals and, in turn, better and more vital programs.

Preparing Objectives

Once program goals have been determined, programmers next develop program objectives. **Program objectives** are the measurement points of goals. Like the program goals they refer to, program objectives are statements of purpose or intent, but unlike goals they are much more specific. Program objectives describe in concise terms the actions an organization intends to carry out and the outcomes expected for participants as a result of the program. Objectives are a refinement of how the goals become realized through programs.

There are basically two types of program objectives: those that specify the intentions for implementing the program and those that describe the desired outcomes or results from the program. The first, **implementation objectives**, often involve such intentions as new and expanded services, personnel performance and assignments, fiscal arrangements, public relations, and other actions intended to promote the organization's efficiency. For example, an agency may want a program to extend positive news coverage, generate new funds, increase membership, or serve a minimum number of participants. In table 8.1 on page 117, the first set of objectives in the second column shows examples of implementation objectives.

The second type of objectives, **outcome objectives**, is what the organization desires for participants, the community, and even the broader society. Outcome objectives are intended to promote the organization's effectiveness. For example, programmers may intend that a program reduce the high level of vandalism at the community center, establish an antilittering ethic at the resident camp, or even lengthen the life span of members of the older adult center. Such community and societal outcome-focused objectives often focus on solving social problems in the community or among a social group. Participant-centered objectives refer to the changes in program users' knowledge, skills, behaviors, attitudes, or values. Participants learn to swim, understand weather, or appreciate risk as a result of the program. In table 8.1 on page 117, the second set of objectives shows examples of outcome objectives. For more information on this topic, see "Group Discussion Ideas," option 2, in chapter 8 of the CD-ROM.

In some leisure service organizations, such as the clinical settings of hospitals and rehabilitation centers where recreation programs are part of a patient treatment plan, outcome objectives focused on participants are often called **behavioral objectives**. These refer to the specific actions clients will perform in the program, such as making eye contact, listening without interruption, identifying their own options for transportation, or increasing range of motion in the legs.

In some cases, implementation and outcome program objectives are ready-made for programmers by professional or legal authorities. As first presented in chapter 7 and labeled "**standards**", these are approved guidelines of practice formulated by authorities in the field or developed by professional organizations. Indeed, standards established for the agency accreditation program sponsored by the Commission for Accreditation of Park and Recreation Agencies include a standard (Standard 6.3) for program objectives that specifies, "There shall be written and specific objectives established for each program or service" (2003, p. 49).

Standards are available to programmers from a variety of professional authorities, such as those pro-

A ladies luncheon might have the program objective of increasing socialization opportunities for the club.

vided by the National Youth Sports Camp (administered by the National Collegiate Athletic Association). Professional standards have also been developed and published by the American Therapeutic Recreation Association (ATRA) and the National Therapeutic Recreation Society (NTRS). As well, the U.S. Armed Forces publish manuals containing standards for operating recreation programs on military bases. In Canada, the National Fitness Leadership Advisory Council (NFLAC) is dedicated to developing and promoting standards for fitness leadership. Keep in mind, however, that standards such as these are usually considered statements of minimal levels of quality or performance, rather than optimal or best levels. For more information on this topic, see "More Options for Individual Programming Practice," option 4, in chapter 8 of the CD-ROM.

Objectives for this square dance program must be written as specifically and as measurably as possible.

In most recreation program situations, however, agency programmers write their own objectives, with help from other staff and patrons. Identifying and writing objectives that are useful is a difficult task. Program objectives must be clear, specific, and observable so that their achievement can be documented and evaluated. Our advice is that good implementation and outcome objectives should have four characteristics: specificity, measurability, criteria, and a delineated constituency (Riddick & Russell, 1999).

1. *Specificity.* Program objectives must be written as specifically as possible. To accomplish this, use an action verb that can be observed or self-reported. For example, an outcome objective that states "Participants will improve their skill in square dancing" is not specific because it is not clear which square dancing skill is to be improved, nor how exactly you'll know when the skill has been improved. Vague words that are open to multiple interpretations should not be used as part of an objective statement. These include *improve*, *learn*, *know*, *understand*, and *appreciate*. Instead, such specific words as *demon-*

strate, *identify*, and *perform* more clearly delineate the outcome expected from the program. The previous example can be rewritten as "Participants will demonstrate their skill in square dance steps and patterns."

2. *Measurability.* But we're not yet finished. Program objectives also must be clear about their documentation—how is the outcome measured? The action in the statement must be put into operation. This becomes particularly critical for the third evaluation step of the program planning process. To do this, a measurable quality is matched with the action verb. For example, "Participants will demonstrate their skill in square dance steps and patterns by dancing without caller prompts." Notice, "by dancing without caller prompts" is observable and thus measurable.

3. *Criteria.* Objectives are even more useful if they contain criteria, or yardsticks, that indicate how much progress toward an objective marks success. Suppose that in our fitness class sample in table 8.1 on page 117, the objective for physical health stipulated only a decrease in the one-minute heart rate. Would a 1 percent, 2 percent, or 3 percent decrease mean the program was a success? Without the criterion of "5 percent," we cannot truly know if the objective has been achieved.

4. *Constituents.* Finally, program objectives should delineate the specific patron group to be affected by the program. Again, in our example of the fitness class, it is the class participants who are the target population of the outcome objectives, not their children, who are in a day-care program while the class is in session. Also in the example, the sponsoring organization is the target population of the implementation objectives.

For more information on this topic, see "More Options for Individual Programming Practice," option 1, and "Group Discussion Ideas," option 3, in chapter 8 of the CD-ROM.

Summary

This chapter suggests that in making recreation program preparations, an important requirement is specifying goals and objectives to achieve over the course of the program. You should understand the following key points:

- Program goals are crafted by assembling the information you have acquired through your preparations up to this point in the planning process.

- Program goals directly reflect your profession's philosophy, your organization's mission, and such other factors as laws.

- Program goals are abstract, comprehensive, idealized statements of desired outcomes. They are a statement of purpose, reason, or intent for the program.

- Once program goals have been determined, programmers next develop program objectives.

- There are basically two types of program objectives:

    1. Implementation, which specify the intentions for implementing the program

    2. Outcome, which describe the desired outcomes or results from the program

- In some cases, implementation and outcome objectives are ready-made for programmers by professional or legal authorities. These are labeled *standards.*

- When writing implementation and outcome objectives, make sure they include four characteristics: specificity, measurability, criteria, and a delineated constituency.

Glossary

human service—A professional philosophical approach holding that the purpose of recreation programs is to improve the human condition.

mission statement—A summary of an organization's purpose.

program goals—Idealized statements of desired outcomes from an organized recreation service.

program objectives—The measurement points of goals.

implementation objectives—Specify the intentions for implementing the program.

outcome objectives—Specify the desired results from the program.

behavioral objectives—Outcome objectives for the specific actions patrons will perform in the program.

standards—Approved guidelines for professional practice formulated by authorities in the field.

References

City and County of Denver. (n.d.). Parks and Recreation Department. Retrieved August 22, 2006, from www.denvergov.org/Parks_Recreation/template324743.asp.

Commission for Accreditation of Park and Recreation Agencies. (2003). *Self-assessment manual for quality operation of park and recreation agencies.* Ashburn, VA: National Recreation and Park Association.

Holland America Cruiseline. (2001-2006). Employment. Retrieved March 6, 2007, from www.hollandamerica.com/about/employment.do.

Kraus, R. (1997). *Recreation programming: A benefits-driven approach.* Boston: Allyn & Bacon.

Northern Berkshire YMCA. (n.d.). Mission statement. Retrieved August 22, 2006, from http://northernberkshireymca.org/ipw-web/portal/cms/modules.php?name=Content&pa=showpage&pid=2.

Operations manual. (1994). Williamsport, PA: Little League Baseball.

Parks Canada Agency. (2006). Parks Canada's mandate. Retrieved August 22, 2006, from www.pc.gc.ca/agen/index_E.asp.

Polynesian Cultural Center. (2007). Mission statement. Retrieved January 5, 2007, from www.polynesia.com/purpose/mission.html.

Riddick, C.C., & Russell, R.V. (1999). *Evaluative research in recreation, park, and sport settings: Searching for useful information.* Champaign, IL: Sagamore.

Riley Childrens Hospital. (2000-2006). Cheer Guild Volunteers. Retrieved August 22, 2006, from http://rileychildrenshospital.com/document.jsp?locid=259.

RVing Women. (2005). RVW goals and objectives 2005. Retrieved August 22, 2006, from www.rvingwomen.org/goals_objectives.html.

Tillman, A. (1973). *The program book for recreation professionals.* Palo Alto, CA: Mayfield.

Weiss, C. (1972). *Evaluation research: Methods of assessing program effectiveness.* Englewood Cliffs, NJ: Prentice Hall.

Westerville Parks and Recreation Department. (2004). *Internship handbook.* Westerville, OH: City of Westerville.

The Program Plan

To be able to implement such an elaborate program event, Mercy Health System's programmers needed a plan. In architecture, a scale drawing in diagrammatic form showing the basic layout of the interior and exterior spaces of a building is called a *plan*. It instructs the carpenters, concrete layers, electricians, plumbers, and many others how to proceed. And so it is with leisure program planning. All your decisions about the values and visions of your organization and community, as well as your assessment of the needs of potential program patrons and the accompanying program goals and objectives, are recorded in a plan. The **program plan** is a design—a blueprint of sorts—for the delivery of the program. From this plan, recreation leaders, facility maintenance supervisors, outside contractors, and others know how to proceed.

Purposes of a Program Plan

There are many different types of program plans. Depending on the breadth and duration of the program service or event, for example, the blueprint might be a single page in length or a spiral-bound booklet covering a long-range program of five years or more. We'll discuss the types and components of program plans in later sections of the chapter, but first let's focus on their purpose.

In addition to providing a document to guide the actions of others involved in the implementation of a program service, program plans have many other uses that make them worth the effort. For example, program plans translate the goals and objectives for patrons, the community, and the organization into operational terms. Details such as activities, location, staffing, safety precautions, and budgeting are worked out through the program plan. It provides the particulars for the program's implementation. What procedures should be followed? What logistics should be taken care of first? Because writing program plans is demanding, particularly for large programs, some leisure programmers mistakenly see preparation of this document as the entire scope of planning (Russell, 1982).

Program plans are also necessary from the perspective of accountability. Without a written statement of a program's intended design, it is more difficult to adequately evaluate how well the program was implemented. We'll discuss program evaluation in the last two chapters of the book, but for now it is important to appreciate the role of the program plan in establishing a "bullseye," not only to guide the program's implementation but also, upon periodic review, to determine how accurately the bullseye was achieved. For more information on this topic, see worksheet 9.3 in chapter 9 of the CD-ROM.

Overall, two important skills are necessary to prepare program plans. You must be able to make sound decisions and think creatively.

Decision Making

All professionals in leisure services are decision makers, but when it comes to programming, decision making determines the exact program to be implemented (see the box on page 125 for an example). For a programmer of outdoor experiences, for example, the choice between two different hiking routes will make a difference in the quality of the program. If a particularly challenging route is chosen without

The Federal Safe Routes to School Program

Less than 35 years ago, when your parents were going to school perhaps, walking or bicycling to school was a part of everyday life. For example, in the United States in 1969, about half of all students walked or bicycled to school (Federal Highway Administration, 1972). Today, however, less than 15 percent of all school trips are made by walking or bicycling, 25 percent are made on a school bus, and more than 50 percent of all children arrive at school in private automobiles (Federal Highway Administration, n.d.). "This decline in walking and bicycling has had an adverse effect on traffic congestion and air quality around schools, as well as pedestrian and bicycle safety. In addition, a growing body of evidence has shown that children who lead sedentary lifestyles are at risk for a variety of health problems such as obesity, diabetes, and cardiovascular disease" (U.S. Centers for Disease Control and Prevention, 2004). The purpose of the federal Safe Routes to School (SRTS) program is to address these issues. At its heart, SRTS empowers communities to make walking and bicycling to school safe and routine activities once again. The program makes funding available for a wide variety of projects, from building safer street crossings to establishing programs that encourage children and their parents to walk and bicycle safely to school. The Web site for SRTS provides details of how to implement these programs in local communities. This plan offers specific guidance to be carried out in the administration of SRTS funds.

Federal Highway Administration, n.d., http://safety.fhwa.dot.gov/saferoutes.

A program plan outlines the specific details needed to successfully implement a program, such as one that encourages children to walk or ride to school.

consideration for the terrain, elevation, predicted weather, and energy and skill levels of the hikers, the result could be much more problematic than a late return to camp.

Although programmers make choices in every step of the program planning process, the decisions made at the program design phase are particularly crucial. As decision maker, you must apply all the expertise and information available to decide exactly how to accomplish the program's intention. Of course, any program plan will be a compromise between what you would like to achieve and what is possible to achieve. Perhaps your senior citizen achievement awards banquet would be wonderfully enhanced if Elvis Presley served as master of ceremonies, but that's just not possible.

What is decision making? For one, it is rational thought. The common phrase "make up your mind" aptly suggests that decision making is the deliberate act of selection—by the mind—among alternative ways to accomplish certain goals (Russell, 1982). A great deal of good advice is available about making good decisions. However, at the core of good decisions is rational thinking. **Rationality** is being able to think soundly and logically. As a programming decision maker, rationality means that you do the following (Russell, 2005):

- Set high standards for the decisions
- Search as broadly as possible for alternatives from which to choose
- Thoroughly investigate alternatives in order to have control over the outcome of choosing them

For more information on this topic, see "More Options for Individual Programming Practice," option 2, in chapter 9 of the CD-ROM.

This means, for example, that in deciding where to locate a new "lunch with the arts" program in the community, you strive to select not only the most convenient location but also the best place for aesthetics, safety, and easy setup for musicians and artists. The previous list of what it means to think rationally also suggests that you not restrict yourself to the more usual locations, such as city parks, but extend your consideration to more unusual possibilities, such as the local botanical garden, a downtown intersection, or the lobby of a large corporation headquarters. Finally, following these guidelines means that you thoroughly check out the downtown intersection to determine if blocking off the access streets would be too disruptive to the downtown economy. For more information on this topic, see "Group Discussion Ideas," option 2, in chapter 9 of the CD-ROM.

An interesting question about the decision making required to prepare a program plan is whether individuals or groups make better decisions. Group decision making offers both advantages and disadvantages. Table 9.1 summarizes these. For more information on this topic, see "Group Discussion Ideas," option 3, in chapter 9 of the CD-ROM.

Notice that one of the disadvantages of group decision making is groupthink. What is this? **Groupthink** is what happens in a group decision-making situation when group members overemphasize achieving agreement in the decision. Groupthink occurs when people choose not to disagree with each other because they don't want to spoil a positive and cohesive group. With such reluctance, however, choosing the best program design can be greatly compromised. For more information on this topic, see worksheet 9.2 in chapter 9 of the CD-ROM.

Exactly how are program design decisions made, either individually or in groups? Basically, they are accomplished through two opposing efforts—generation and reduction (Russell, 1982). First, the process of generating as many potential choices as possible provides an optimal way to start. One technique for accomplishing this is brainstorming.

Brainstorming is a way of producing many ideas to choose from in deciding the best design for a program. The technique requires you to expand the horizon of your mind and generate both apparently practical as well as impractical program elements. It asks the brain to "storm" for ideas, with no limitations (Russell, 1982, p. 125).

Let's suppose that a goal you've designated for a new teen program on your company's cruise ships is to provide opportunities to learn about future career possibilities in the cruise industry. You and other staff could brainstorm all the possible program designs (e.g., activities, schedules, promotions) for carrying out the program. You might have on your list of options these activities: shadow the crew day,

TABLE 9.1

Advantages and Disadvantages of Group Decision Making

Advantages	Disadvantages
1. A group's knowledge should be greater than that of any one group member.	1. Some groups may lack the maturity needed to make good decisions.
2. A group's motivation for better decisions is higher.	2. Individual group members bring a variety of motives to the decision.
3. There is a perceived safety in numbers for making a decision.	3. Poor communication makes group decision making ineffective.
4. Group-made decisions usually mean wider acceptance of the decision.	4. Group decision making is more time consuming.
5. Greater quantity and diversity of alternatives for choice are available in groups.	5. Disagreements may delay decisions.
	6. Groupthink may develop.

Based on Russell, 2005; Bartol & Martin, 1998; Johnson & Johnson, 1994; and Bateman & Snell, 2002.

a crew-in-training program, an Internet cafe evening devoted to exploring cruise careers, an illustrated talk by the ship's captain, a behind-the-scenes tour of everything from the engine room to the kitchen, and a cruise crew and teen buddy system.

Russell (1982) outlines the important principles to keep in mind for effective brainstorming:

- *Deferred judgment.* Critical evaluation of ideas is postponed to allow for the flow of creativity.

- *Quantity produces quality.* Many ideas ultimately result in better ideas.

- *Multiplying effect.* One idea stimulates another by changing it, improving it, or "hitchhiking" on it.

After you've generated as wide and diverse a list of program design options as possible, decision making next requires the opposite focus—reduction. Now you reduce your options by screening out those alternatives that are less valuable. The critical judgment you suppressed during the generation of program alternatives is now applied. You must be critical and ask which ideas are the most valuable.

How do you carry out this screening? Most planners usually agree that the best programs should involve the least cost, have the least undesirable consequences, and provide the most desirable outcomes (Russell, 1982). The criteria you use will depend on the specific goal of the program you're planning, but here are some typical decision criteria:

- Is there adequate staff, money, and facilities for this idea?

- Does the broader community and our agency support this idea?

- Is the program idea as safe and healthy as possible, or are there risks our agency is unwilling to assume?

- Is the ability level suitable for patrons?

- Is the idea likely to lead to the accomplishment of program goals and objectives (i.e., accomplish what is intended)?

- Is it easy to implement?

When groups make decisions, brainstorming is a useful strategy for generating ideas to choose from.

- Is it timely?

- Does it fit well with other program services already offered?

Creativity

Let's go back to considering Elvis Presley. Although it may be impossible to invite him to the senior citizens achievement awards banquet, it certainly might be possible to arrange for an Elvis Presley impersonator to serve as master of ceremonies. This is where the second important skill in preparing a program plan comes in—creativity. As you were probably already guessing from the discussion of brainstorming, developing a program plan requires not only rational thinking but also creative thinking.

Creative thinking requires an attitude that allows you to use your knowledge and experience as stepping-stones to new ideas. Creative thinking involves playing with ideas so that the ordinary might become the extraordinary. It is a discovery process—looking at the same thing as everyone

The National Sports Center for the Disabled (NSCD)

The National Sports Center for the Disabled (NSCD) is a therapeutic recreation program based in Colorado. For more than 30 years, the NSCD has planned and implemented a variety of summer and winter sports for children and adults with almost any mental or physical disability. People involved in its programs "take to the ski slopes, rivers, trails and cliffs to learn more about mountain sports and themselves" (NSCD, 2004b). Through NSCD's outdoor therapeutic recreation programs, more than 48,000 individuals have discovered their abilities. With specially trained instructors and its own adaptive equipment lab, the NSCD can accommodate patrons with blindness, paraplegia, amputations, stroke complications, cancer, cerebral palsy, hearing impairments, and spina bifida (NSCD, 2004a). For more information on this topic, see worksheet 9.1 in chapter 9 of the CD-ROM.

A program of the National Sports Center for the Disabled (NSCD) of Colorado.

else and thinking something different. Creativity in developing the program plan means assembling new ideas from old, familiar, unrelated ones. Creative programming starts with not only understanding the patrons but also trying to view their needs and interests in unique ways (see the box on this page). For example, you might go to a video game store and ask what teens are buying (or are interested in buying) as a way of developing a plan for game playing in an after-school program. Or why not hold a Christmas tree decorating competition at the local art museum? In both of these examples, familiar ideas are turned into something new.

Creativity is important because programmers face the dual challenge of offering programs that meet the needs and interests of their patrons, community, and organization as well as establishing new and invigorating trends that further the profession.

How do you enhance your capacity for creativity? Creative thinking requires practice; it's something you need to work at. To increase your creativity in leisure programming, try these activities (Russell, 1982):

- *Read.* Read a wide variety of books, magazines, newspapers, and Web sites on a wide range of topics.
- *File.* Develop a way to file the array of interesting ideas your reading uncovers.
- *Watch.* Pay attention to what is going on around you. Be a student of popular culture; look at what others overlook—under, behind, above, and below the obvious.
- *Listen.* Listen to what is going on around you; ask questions and focus on the responses.
- *Meet people.* Talk to others and mimic their originality; what interesting things are they doing?

For more information on this topic, see "More Options for Individual Programming Practice," option 3, in chapter 9 of the CD-ROM.

Types of Program Plans

There are many types of program plans. Indeed, in your leisure service organization, strategic plans, tactical plans, and operational plans may guide you. These plan types differ according to the level of the organization that uses them. For example, strategic plans are usually used by those in the top management level, tactical plans are typically the design of middle management, and operational plans refer to the efforts of individuals or first-level units in the organization (Bartol & Martin, 1998).

Program services and event plans are most often categorized according to the length of time the plan covers or the breadth of the program service. For example, **long-range plans** detail programming design for an extended period of time, such as five years. These plans typically focus on the programmatic achievement of future goals for an organization's patrons. A **comprehensive plan**, on the other hand, establishes the design for all programming responsibilities of the organization. Its reach is wide, unifying all program areas and facilities. In some leisure programming situations, such as therapeutic recreation, plans are also prepared for individual patrons. These **individual participant plans** usually set forth daily, weekly, or monthly programmatic approaches for using leisure to achieve therapeutic goals. For more information on this topic, see "More Options for Individual Programming Practice," option 1, and "Group Discussion Ideas," option 1, in chapter 9 of the CD-ROM.

As you initially move into your professional programming career, you are more likely to prepare plans for specific programs or events. We'll simply refer to this type of plan as the program plan. A program plan outlines how a single program service should be carried out. It refers to the design of, for example, a horseback riding therapy program, summer swimming instruction at the pool, a Halloween party for residents of the assisted living facility, a community cleanup program, a speedskating festival at the ice rink, a lecture series at the senior center, or a biking tour of Nova Scotia. The following case from Westerville Parks and Recreation Department demonstrates what a program plan might look like.

Elements of a Program Plan

The leisure service organization you work for is likely to stipulate precisely what a program plan should contain. Further, since a plan is needed for the delivery of every program you prepare, the exact elements of the written document may be somewhat different from program to program. Although the example of the plan for the Half-Pint Hullabaloo program presented in the Westerville case box gives a clue as to some of the elements possible for a program plan document, it is not intended as a universal model. What follows is a more comprehensive list of the basic details most often expected in a program plan:

- Program title
- Goals and objectives for the program
- Activities and events
- Marketing details
- Pricing of the program
- Budget for the program, including direct and indirect costs and income sources
- Facilities needed and their setup
- Materials and supplies required
- Safety and risk management procedures
- Staffing: the number and types of employees and volunteers needed
- Registration procedures
- Policies
- Cancellation strategies
- Required reports
- Program evaluation plan

For more information on this topic, see "Can You Solve This Programming Issue?" in chapter 9 of the CD-ROM.

Another important element of a written program plan is the structure of the program experience itself. What are the specific components of the program, and in what order will they be presented to participants? Figure 9.1 suggests the structure for a leisure education program. Developed by Dattilo and Murphy (1991), these components and their order are recommended for programs that teach people ways to enhance the role of leisure in their lives.

In this example, the recommended elements of the single program session include an orientation activity; an introduction of the participants, the session's topic, and the objectives; a formal presentation about the topic; a group discussion about the topic; a learning activity to experience the topic; a debriefing; and a conclusion. As another example of this level of program plan, an evening campfire session at a Girl

The Programming Process: Get the Plan in Writing

The Westerville Parks and Recreation Department is a national gold medal winner in large part because of its excellence in program plans. Staff operate program services from a wide array of program plans, ranging from the extensive master plan called PROS 2000, presented earlier in the book, to small specific event plans, such as for Half-Pint Hullabaloo. What follows is an abridged version of the plan for Half-Pint Hullabaloo.

Event: Half-Pint Hullabaloo

Date: Friday, March 14, 2003
Time: 9:30 a.m. to 12:00 noon
Location: Westerville Community Center
Target population: children aged one and up and their parents
Preschool and day-care classes from area agencies
500-plus expected
Cost: children aged one and up = $3.00
Adults = free
Cosponsors: Westerville North and South High Schools' Work and Family Life Departments

Staff

Lynn Kiger, recreation program supervisor (coordinating overall events including publicity, entertainment, concessions, training and supervising of volunteers, procurement of materials and supplies)

Carole Stephenson, accounting assistant (typing thank-you letters and helping in admission ticket area)

Recreational leaders (five) (helping to gather supplies, set up and tear down, supervise parking, and lead activity stations)

Jason Fallon, administrative assistant (designing publicity brochure, event layout map, and publicity fliers and signs and writing news release)

Volunteers and Contributors

Westerville Fire Department
Hometown Buffet (mascot Hometown Bee)
Westerville Public Library
Wal-Mart
Westerville Senior Center
Columbus Clippers (mascot Lucille the Seal)

Marketing

Write-ups in winter and spring department program brochures
Word of mouth
Fliers to preschool classes and Westerville Public Library
News releases to local newspapers

Entertainment

Sunshine & Friends (clowns) ($180.00 for two 20-minute shows and roving between performances)

Facility setup

Tables and chairs on stage area
Activity stations in multipurpose room
Supply boxes at each station
Trash boxes put together and placed around
Story tent in the Maple Room
Mascots and drinks in Buckeye B Room
Information station in lobby
Sound system throughout

Activities

Cruisin' Station
Tunnel of fun
Story time
Crafts area
Snacks
Clown entertainment
Balloon sculptures
Water play
Tumbling
Hula bubble play
Roving sport mascots

Timing

Publicize four weeks before
Set up Thursday evening, March 13
Set up refreshments one hour before
Staff arrive one hour before

Courtesy of Westerville Parks and Recreation Department, 2003.

The Half-Pint Hullabaloo program sponsored by the Westerville Parks and Recreation Department.

Photo courtesy of Westerville Parks and Recreation Department, Westerville, Ohio.

Objective 1

Demonstrate knowledge of the meaning of gardening

Session Length

90 minutes

Orientation Activity

Play "gardening word scramble."

Introduction

Outline the many forms and locations of gardening, as well as its popularity worldwide.

Presentation

Conduct a PowerPoint presentation illustrating such characteristics of gardening as plots, soil, seeds, landscape features, and production manipulation.

Discussion

Encourage all participants to discuss their attitudes about gardening and how they hope this program might change their attitudes.

Learning Activity

Make collages of garden designs using poster paper, scissors, paste, and several gardening magazines.

Debriefing

Participants share their garden collages and discuss why their collages reflect their attitudes about gardening.

Conclusion

Summarize what was covered in this session, and indicate what's in store for the next session.

Figure 9.1   The structure of a leisure education gardening program.

Adapted from J. Datillo & W.D. Murphy, 1991, p. 324-328.

Scout camp might have the following elements in this order: solemn filing in of campers to seats around a dark campfire; dramatic lighting of the fire while singing a call-to-the fire song; two or three more songs; a dramatic event such as a skit or acted-out story; two or three more songs; snacks; informal conversation; and taps played on a trumpet.

The Role of Program Life Cycles

The **program life cycle**, or the natural process of a program's duration, is a concept adapted from the life cycle of a product, which suggests that everything has a "shelf life." In other words, not all programs last forever. Many factors result in the need to eliminate, revitalize, rethink, or refresh programs from time to time. Often programs simply become obsolete and unimportant to the patrons who originally were interested. Other times lifestyle and societal changes demand a program change. Program plans must account for this and indicate either how changes will be made or how and when programs will be eliminated and replaced.

According to Russell (1982) and Crompton (1979), the life cycle of a recreation program has five stages. This is shown in figure 9.2, where the vertical scale represents the interest and participation of patrons, and the horizontal scale represents time. This illustration is meant only as a generalization of the life cycle concept. The actual time span of each stage is subject to the complex realities of the situation. For example, the life cycle for tennis instruction at a summer children's camp may be quite different from tennis instruction at a private tennis center.

The first stage in a program's life cycle begins when the program is implemented. It is initially introduced, promoted, and offered, and participants begin to attend. As the program is discovered in this first stage, participant acceptance is often positive yet light and slow. At this stage it is important that program quality be in place because the program's ultimate success depends on making a good first impression.

Second is the stage of rapid growth of the program. In this takeoff phase in the cycle, participation

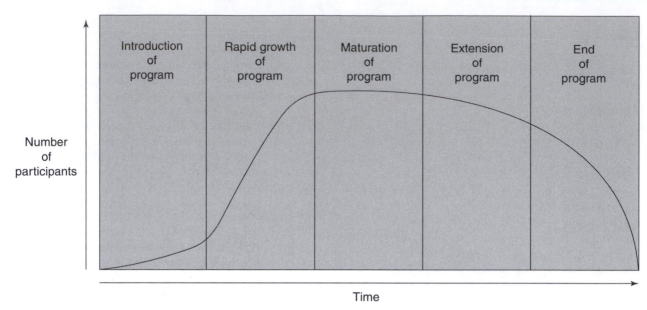

| Introduction of program | Rapid growth of program | Maturation of program | Extension of program | End of program |

Number of participants

Time

Figure 9.2 Stages of a program's life cycle.

grows without much effort needed to promote it. Third is the saturation, or maturation, stage. Participant interest in and loyalty to the program have reached their highest plateaus. This stage can be as short as one hour for a Saturday afternoon Drool in the Pool event for dogs and their owners at the municipal swimming pool or as long as decades for the stamp collecting club at the community center.

Fourth is the extension stage. This is the point at which interest begins to decline, when programmers make an effort to reinvigorate the program and reflect changed interests. From here the program's end is ultimately imminent, but planners may be able to keep it going a while longer by mounting a new promotional campaign, changing the type or format of the activities in the program, infusing new budgetary, leadership, or facility resources, and so on.

In the final, or decline, stage the point is reached when it is no longer feasible to continue offering the program. The decision to eliminate a program must be taken seriously by planners. Sometimes an alternative to program termination is offering the program less frequently or on a smaller scale. Any decision to eliminate a program should be carefully planned, with consideration given to those participants remaining in the program (Russell, 1982). But ultimately, the decision to cancel a program must be made in order to liberate staffing, facility, and fiscal resources for new programs.

What is important to appreciate about program life cycles is that they are a program management tool. It

is necessary to understand the current stages of the various programs you are responsible for in order to anticipate the potential changes needed. You'll need a plan for addressing the saturation, extension, and elimination stages of each program. This can be aided through program evaluation—a topic we take up in later chapters.

Summary

This chapter advocates the development of a written program plan. You should understand the following key points:

- A program plan is a scheme or design for the delivery of a program. From this plan, recreation leaders, facility maintenance supervisors, outside contractors, and others know how to proceed in implementing the program.

- There are many reasons why a written program plan is a good idea. For example, plan documents are able to translate the goals and objectives for patrons, the community, and the organization into operational terms. Also, plan documents make planners accountable for accomplishing through the program what is intended.

- Program plans require the two important skills of decision making and creativity—both ultimately necessary reasons for successful programming.

- There are many types of plans, but the form most used by programmers outlines how a single program service should be carried out.
- Program plans include such components as goals and objectives, implementation logistics, and the structure for the program experience itself.
- Programs have natural life cycles, and the program plan should also include a strategy for managing a program's rise, saturation, and decline.

Glossary

program plan—Detailed outline of the resources needed to carry out a specific program service or event.

rationality—Being able to reason soundly and logically.

groupthink—What happens in a group decision-making situation when group members overemphasize achieving agreement in the decision.

brainstorming—A way of producing many ideas to choose from in deciding the best design for a program.

long-range program plan—Outline of the resources needed to meet long-term organizational goals for programs.

comprehensive program plan—Outline of the resources needed for implementing programming across a wide diversity of program areas and facilities.

individual participant program plan—Outline of the resources needed for implementing a program intervention for a single patron.

program life cycle—The natural rise, saturation, and decline of a program event or service.

References

Bartol, K.M., & Martin, D.C. (1998). *Management* (3rd ed.). Boston: McGraw-Hill.

Bateman, T.S., & Snell, S.A. (2002). *Management: Competing in the new era.* New York: McGraw-Hill.

Crompton, J.L. (1979). Recreation programs have life cycles, too. *Parks & Recreation, 14*(10), 52-57, 69.

Dattilo, J., & Murphy, W.D. (1991). *Leisure education program planning: A systematic approach.* State College, PA: Venture.

Employee Services Management Association. (2005). Mercy Health System's children's holiday party earns Employee Services Management Association's Innovative Program Award. Retrieved June 19, 2006, from www.esmassn.org/Mercyrelease.pdf.

Federal Highway Administration. (1972). *Transportation characteristics of school children, report no. 4: Nationwide personal transportation study.* Washington, DC: Author.

Federal Highway Administration. (n.d.). Safe Routes to School. Retrieved September 18, 2006, from http://safety.fhwa.dot.gov/saferoutes.

Johnson, D.W., & Johnson, F.P. (1994). *Joining together: Group theory and group skills* (5th ed.). Boston: Allyn & Bacon.

National Sports Center for the Disabled. (2004a). Nordic skiing & snowshoeing. Retrieved September 15, 2006, from www.nscd.org/programs/winter_nordic.htm.

National Sports Center for the Disabled. (2004b). Winter program. Retrieved September 15, 2006, from www.nscd.org/programs/winterbrochure.htm.

Russell, R.V. (1982). *Planning programs in recreation.* St. Louis: Mosby.

Russell, R.V. (2005). *Leadership in recreation.* Boston: McGraw-Hill.

U.S. Centers for Disease Control and Prevention. (2004). *Physical activity and the health of young people.* Atlanta: Author.

Westerville Parks and Recreation Department. (2003). *Half-pint hullabaloo flyer.* Westerville, OH: City of Westerville.

PART III

Program Implementation

Step 2 in the program planning process is implementation, when programmers "turn out" the program they've planned. After as thorough a preparation as possible in step 1, focus now on putting your preparations into action. To implement a program means to deliver it to customers and clients. This entails running the program efficiently and effectively so that it produces the operational and participant outcomes desired. You have reached the managerial aspect of programming, and your focus is on seeing that everything runs according to plan.

- Chapter 10 discusses recruiting and managing program resources. What are the fiscal, marketing, and facility requirements for your planned programs? As well, what scheduling and policy decisions do you need to make in order to implement the program?

- Chapter 11 presents operational decisions relative to staffing programs. How should programs be supervised and led?

- Chapter 12 discusses the activities of program monitoring. How do you keep programs operating at their best? As well, what must be documented about the program and its delivery?

- Chapter 13 presents advice on keeping programs as safe as possible. How is risk managed in a leisure services program?

CHAPTER 10

Making Operational Decisions

In this chapter, you can look forward to the following:

- Creating a program budget that includes decisions about cost allocation, cost tracking, pricing, and other ways to increase program fiscal resources
- Choosing and assigning programs to facilities
- Understanding the importance to program communication of naming, scheduling, and promoting events
- Developing program operational policies

Every year since its founding in 1919, the Los Angeles Philharmonic orchestra has been lauded as southern California's leading performing arts institution. Today, under the baton of Esa-Pekka Salonen, the Philharmonic is world renowned for its performance brilliance and innovative programming (Los Angeles Philharmonic Association, 2006). Although the orchestra and its organization are commercial leisure service enterprises, they provide a wide array of programs that include free concerts and instruction (e.g., the School Partners program and the Teaching Artist Faculty program, in which orchestra musicians teach in the schools). The orchestra gives free school-day concerts for students and teachers and performs many community and neighborhood concerts. A family concert series is offered, and Summer Sounds is held each year for kids at the Hollywood Bowl. The Browislaw Kaper Awards provide instrumental competition for young musicians, and preconcert talks and events are also scheduled for venues throughout the L.A. area.

Adding to all this, the Philharmonic's crowning achievements are perhaps its critically acclaimed international tours. In August 1992, the Philharmonic became the first American orchestra in residence for both operas and concerts at the Salzburg Festival. The Philharmonic's distinguished touring history began in 1956 with a 10-week, 58-concert "goodwill journey" through Asia, under the direction of Alfred Wallenstein. The tour was sponsored by the U.S. State Department. Eleven years later, Zubin Mehta led the Philharmonic on its second State Department tour, playing 39 concerts in 23 cities around the world.

As one of America's leading orchestras, the Los Angeles Philharmonic is constantly in demand at home as well as abroad, and every season it performs a series of concerts in New York and other cities on the U.S. east coast. Finally, at home, the orchestra association presents guest artists of classical, jazz, and world music at two of the most extraordinary places anywhere to experience music—the new Walt Disney Concert Hall and the world-famous Hollywood Bowl.

© Carlo Allegri/Getty Images.

The Los Angeles Philharmonic orchestra's wide array of programs requires an extraordinary coordination of facilities, schedules, and budgets.

You are now ready to embark on an important key to programming success—deciding, developing, and managing the resources for the programs you've planned. No matter how thorough and creative your preparations to this point, if you drop the ball now, your plans will not produce programs that achieve their intent. Indeed, this illustration of the Los Angeles Philharmonic orchestra is impressive in the amount of coordination of operational decisions needed for the program. This chapter presents an overview of the most critical of these operational programming decisions: budgeting, facility choices, communication, and policies. For more information on this topic, see "More Options for Individual Programming Practice," option 3, in chapter 10 of the CD-ROM.

Budgeting

Programs must be budgeted. Many systems are available for preparing budgets, and each organization typically has its own guidelines for budget planning. The **line-item budget** is common in leisure service agencies operated by governments. This system allocates specific amounts of money to each expenditure item listed in the budget. That is, funds are assigned to such categories as staff salaries, supplies, and repair and maintenance of equipment (Brayley & McLean, 1999). Other leisure service organizations operate according to a **zero-based budget**. Here, each subunit of the organization is required to build its budget beginning with zero amounts each year—justifying every expenditure estimate and developing every source of income from the beginning rather than relying on past expenditures and revenues (Brayley & McLean, 1999). Another common budgeting system is the **program budget**. In this budget, money is allocated for expenditures according to major program areas, such as golf, fitness, aquatics, or outdoor recreation. For more information on this topic, see worksheet 10.1 and "Group Discussion Ideas," option 1, in chapter 10 of the CD-ROM.

In its simplest form, a **budget** is defined as an estimated plan for keeping expenses in line with income. Budgeting can be considered as planning in financial terms—the basic idea is to balance costs and revenues. First, let's consider the costs side of the ledger.

Direct and Indirect Costs

Programs cost money, of course, and determining what a program requires in monetary support entails a process called cost allocation. **Cost allocation** means determining the costs, or expenditure estimates, for various details of program implementation. How much will it likely cost to hire the part-time staff needed for the program? Do you want to purchase new equipment for the program this year? How much will it cost? How much should you purchase? Are there printing costs for promoting the program? How much?

The goal of all these cost allocation questions is to determine as accurately as possible the amount of money required to provide the program. This requires considering two types of costs: direct and indirect. **Direct costs** are those specifically assigned to a particular program. This means if the program is not offered, the cost does not occur. For example, in a beginners' class in indoor wall climbing, direct costs might include salaries for the instructors, safety equipment such as helmets, and the rental fee for the indoor climbing wall. These are considered direct costs because if the wall climbing class is not offered, your agency does not need to hire instructors, purchase helmets, or rent a facility.

Indirect costs, sometimes referred to as overhead costs, are those the organization incurs regardless of whether a specific program is offered. For example, a salary for the agency director and

In preparing a budget for a beginners' class in indoor wall climbing, direct costs and indirect costs need to be considered as expenditures.

funding to upgrade agency computers are incurred costs even when indoor wall climbing classes are not offered. Even so, all the programs and services must share in absorbing the costs of the director's salary and new computers.

The total cost of a program, then, is the sum of its direct costs and its share of the indirect costs. How are direct costs and indirect costs determined? Direct costs are more easily derived. The cost of paying wall climbing instructors could be the going rate for this type of employee in your area multiplied by the number of class sessions. Contacting your agency's sport equipment wholesaler could provide a cost estimate for the purchase of helmets, and checking the wall climbing facility's Web site may provide information about rental charges.

Another obvious way to determine direct costs for a continuing program is to consult the most recent evaluation report for expenditures the last time the program was offered. This can be extended into cost tracking. **Cost tracking** involves paying attention to the cost and use of a budget item over time. Data for even a series of similar programs, accumulated over time, can be used as a guideline for the direct costs portion of a specific program budget. Figure 10.1 provides a sample budget containing direct costs for an indoor wall climbing class for beginners.

Figure 10.1 also provides a sample of indirect expenditures in a budget, in this case labeled as general administration. Budgeting for indirect costs requires decisions that are more philosophically based. There are different strategies for determining the indirect costs a particular program is to share, if any. In fact, this is one of the strategies—certain programs are exempt from contributing to the overhead costs of the agency. This may be the policy

Sample Budget for an Indoor Climbing Wall Beginners' Class

Anticipated Expenditures

1. Leadership $360
   a. Number of leaders required: 1 instructor and 1 general spotter
   b. Salary for each: $12 per hour for instructor; $8 per hour for spotter
   c. Hours per week: 3
   d. Weeks of program: 6

2. Facility $2,475
   a. Rental cost of commercial climbing wall: $100 per hour
   b. Special rider for liability insurance policy: $675 per year

3. Materials and Equipment $565
   a. Extra ropes, harnesses, carabiners, and so on: $400
   b. First aid supplies: $50
   c. Copies of instructional handout: $20
   d. Copies of assumption of risk form: $20
   e. T-shirts at $5 each: $75

4. Publicity $250
   a. Radio spots: $150
   b. Fliers: $100

5. General Administration $100
   a. Proportion of overhead costs for agency (indirect costs): 1%

Total expenditures $3,750

Anticipated Revenue

1. Registration $1,200
   a. Participant fee: $75
   b. Number of participants: 16

2. Rebate of rental cost by climbing wall agency for every program participant who joins the facility after the program: $360
   a. 10% based on 2 joining participants

3. Grant from the Climbing Gym Association (CGA) $1,300

4. Sale of T-shirts: $15 each for 15 participants (assuming 1 participant doesn't buy a T-shirt) $225

5. Donation of climbing materials by commercial outfitters store $400

Total revenues $3,485

Summary

Total expenditures = $3,750

Total revenues = $3,485

Balance = $265

Figure 10.1   A sample budget for a beginners' class in indoor wall climbing.

for programs that need to be more inexpensive for participants. Otherwise, the methods for determining the indirect costs of a program include equal share and percentage of budget.

An equal share of indirect costs means that each program is equally responsible for the indirect expenses of the agency. The agency director's salary and the computer replacement costs are therefore equally shared. With this method, there is no consideration of the indirect costs consumed by each program, as the assumption is that all programs equally contribute to the overall success of the agency, whether or not this is perfectly accurate. Sometimes leisure services professionals want to ignore the possible inequity of this approach because determining the proportion of indirect costs according to each program's usage requires considerable time and money.

Another method of determining the indirect costs of a program is according to its percentage of the budget. Here, each program is assigned a percentage of indirect costs that equals its percentage of the agency's overall budget. To demonstrate, let's assume the director's salary is $75,000 a year, and the overall agency budget for the year is $500,000. Further, let's assume the total budget for the youth sports portion of the agency's services is $150,000. To determine the amount of the director's salary that the youth sports program is responsible for,

first determine the percentage of the overall agency budget represented by the youth sports budget: 30 percent. Thus, according to this method, 30 percent (or $22,500) is the proportion of the director's salary that comes out of the youth sports program budget (see figure 10.2).

Revenues

Now that we've considered the expenditures side of the program budget, let's turn to the income, or revenues, side (see anticipated revenue in figure 10.1). Where does the money come from to cover the costs of providing the program?

One common source of revenue is the fee charged to program participants. As such, another budgeting task is to set the price for participation in the program. This is called **pricing**.

Fees charged for any recreation program are usually based on two factors (Kraus, 1997):

1. The actual costs of a program, including staff, materials, equipment, facility usage, transportation, and so on

2. Non-cost-related factors, such as the fee levels prevailing for similar activities provided by other agencies, as well as the extent or intensity of consumer demand, along with the social benefit of the program

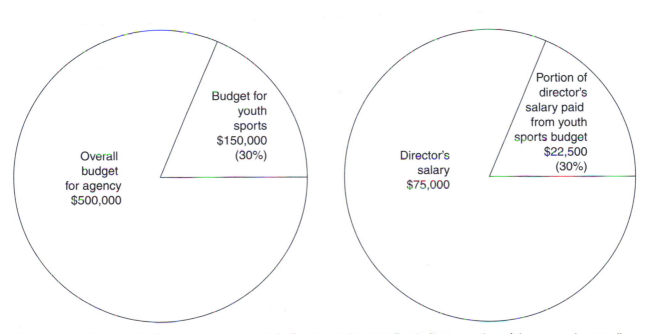

Figure 10.2 One way to determine a program's indirect costs is according to its proportion of the agency's overall budget.

Choosing among—and balancing—these two kinds of factors can be tricky because sometimes both cannot be achieved simultaneously. For example, the social benefit of a midnight basketball program might not cover its actual costs. The program may need to be free to participants and thus account for none of the cost of providing staff, equipment, and the facility. Wading through such pricing dilemmas requires pricing strategies. For more information on this topic, see "More Options for Individual Programming Practice," option 1, in chapter 10 of the CD-ROM. ◉

There are three basic pricing strategies for recreation programs. Although each pursues different goals and produces different results, each can be used simultaneously across the array of programs an organization offers (McCarville, 2002). These three strategies are penetration pricing, neutral pricing, and skim pricing.

First, **penetration pricing** keeps prices low in order to encourage participation. This strategy attempts to entice participants to begin, continue, or increase their patterns of involvement in the program. The goal is one of appealing to, then retaining, participants. Penetration pricing is appropriate for those who either have limited financial resources or are unsure whether the program is of interest to them.

Penetration pricing is the typical strategy for public leisure service organizations. City, county, provincial, state, and federal sponsors of organized leisure services are often able to use tax-based subsidies to keep participant-paid fees to a minimum.

There are many more ways to keep program fees to a minimum. As typically seen in museums, particular days or times can be set aside when no fees are charged. Program "scholarships" are also possible for economically disadvantaged participants—preferably using confidential procedures to protect their privacy. Work exchange programs can also enable participation at a low cost. For example, in the United States and Canada, a "workamper" program uses the assistance of campers to operate campgrounds in exchange for free RV campsites and utilities. Alternatively, RVers can work and be paid small salaries by the campground (Workamper.com, 1996-2006). Another strategy for reducing participation fees is a variable fee policy, which requires user permits in some areas or neighborhoods but not in others.

The second pricing option is to use a neutral pricing strategy. **Neutral pricing** avoids both high prices and low prices. The price is set for a program so that it seems to customers to be neither "pricey" nor a "bargain." With neutral pricing, the fee is low enough

that clients are not discouraged from participating. As well, the fee is high enough that they are not tempted to be suspicious about the program's quality. Neutral pricing is also useful when programs must generate revenue for their own support because the price is typically set at the break-even mark—the costs of the program are exactly covered by the fees paid by participants.

The neutral pricing strategy can be tricky, however, because what is considered "pricey" and a "bargain" differs across patrons. For example, a $100 fee for a weekend camping trip may be pricey for a low-wage single working parent of four, but a high-wage single working adult with no children may see it as a bargain. Indeed, by using this pricing scheme, specific clientele will be either attracted or not attracted to the program, which may be a goal of the program.

Finally, in **skim pricing** the focus of charging a participation fee is on making money. Prices for programs are based not on the cost of the service, or on extending participation, but on "what the market will bear." Essentially, the programmer offers a service that is in high demand and charges prices that exceed the cost of providing it (McCarville, 2002). To use skim pricing effectively, program clients must be price insensitive—their interest in the program does not vary as the price increases. This means the patron wants the program badly enough that price isn't an issue, or the program is not available at a lower price elsewhere. For more information on this topic, see "Group Discussion Ideas," option 2, in chapter 10 of the CD-ROM. ◉

Indeed, one of the most powerful ways to create price insensitivity is through scarcity. Have you ever observed that when there is only one item and many interested buyers at an auction, buyers become willing to pay prices they had considered unacceptable even hours before? In recreation programs, price insensitivity can happen when new concepts are first introduced or when highly customized programs require a great deal of time and energy to deliver (see the box on page 143 for an example).

Which pricing strategy should you use for a particular program? Well, it depends. Foremost, it depends on adherence to important guiding principles. Then, it depends on what is called the pricing triangle. Let's look at each of these in turn.

According to McCarville (2002), there are three guiding principles of pricing. If you ignore fairness, choice, and communication, major pricing mistakes can be made. The principle of fairness, of course,

GrandLuxe Rail Journeys

Return to the days of deluxe rail travel on board North America's premier private train. In a once-in-a-lifetime journey to national parks in the west, Copper Canyon in Mexico, and trans-Canada, you'll experience comfort, classic service, fine dining, and spectacular scenery. On our graciously preplanned land cruises, you'll be accompanied by professional guides, naturalists, and tour managers who will enrich your experience.

A trip on board the *GrandLuxe* train is costly. Such a specialized program must be priced according to the extensive and unique railroad equipment (modernized vintage Pullman cars), staff (renowned chefs), and services (evening bed turndown). For example, an eight-day trip in the American Southwest (from Los Angeles to San Antonio) costs up to $5,290 per passenger.

Tourists choosing a luxury trip are willing to pay high fees for the experience. Passengers enjoy the nostalgia of the Seattle Lounge car aboard the GrandLuxe Express, North America's premier private train.

Photo courtesy of GrandLuxe Rail Journeys. © Walter Hodges.

Adapted from GrandLuxe Rail Journeys, www.americanorientexpress.com/Index.html.

---

refers to what is right. Prices thought by patrons to be inappropriate will be considered unfair, and patrons will not pay to participate in these programs. Such feelings of unfairness are most likely to appear when a program price is introduced for the first time or when prices are increased significantly.

Once the program client feels a price is fair, concern moves on to the principle of choice. Everyone seeks choices when making participation decisions, so programmers should make multiple fee options available. Imagine the success of a graduated duration series of programs for new golfers. That is, participants could select from a one-day golf workshop, a weekend golf camp, or classes meeting for two hours every Friday for three months. Pricing would be lower or higher accordingly.

Finally, the pricing principle of communication requires programmers to continually inform participants about pricing rationale. Tell patrons if fees are being used to improve services or that a particular program component is expensive. Program participants are more likely to support fees, and even fee increases, if they consider it important for the quality of the program.

So how exactly do you establish the price for participating in a program? Many programmers rely on

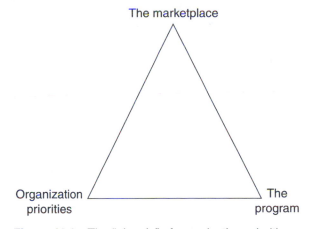

Figure 10.3 The "triangle" of organization priorities, program requirements, and the marketplace helps programmers set program prices.

Adapted from R.E. McCarville, 2002, *Improving leisure services through marketing action*, p. 171.

what is called the **pricing triangle** (see figure 10.3). The pricing triangle includes three criteria for setting prices: organization priorities, program requirements, and the marketplace (McCarville, 2002). First, organization priorities include its mission, philosophy, and program objectives. (Review chapter 8 for more information.) If you are a programmer for a theme park, your agency's priority is more likely to be on skim pricing; whereas if you are a programmer for a Girl Scout council, your agency's priority is likely to be closer to at least neutral pricing.

Next, price decisions are based on the characteristics of the program itself. Such factors as level of service and program costs are directly instructive of what price to charge. For example, a basic program scheduled at an inconvenient time can be offered at a reduced price. Also, if the expense of staff salaries, facility maintenance, and equipment purchases is high, a higher fee for the program is likely to cover at least some of these costs. Programmers frequently decide to price a program below or above its cost, depending on the first criterion of organization priority.

Finally, the marketplace is perhaps the most important pricing criterion. The marketplace for recreation programs is usually the participant. As you know from the preparations in the first step of the program planning process, clients differ in interests, needs, and socioeconomic characteristics. They also bring to programs their own expectations for the price. Programmers need to pay careful attention to this.

If fees charged for programs do not cover the costs—because of pricing policies or social benefit priorities—there are additional methods for generating revenues. In fact, this may be the most important lesson to learn about developing program resources. Lack of money has always been an easy rationalization for not attempting program expansion, program improvement, or program creativity. Finding a programmer with unlimited resources is rare. Yet must you just give up your good ideas? Doing without program essentials or even program frills is not always the best way to overcome a limited budget (Russell, 1982).

A recreation program that is based on clearly identified needs and thorough planning can find financing from various alternatives, including taxes, grants, contract programming, joint sponsorship, and special interest associations. Of course, these alternatives must be compatible with the philosophy and mission of the organization.

As a public agency, the Westerville Parks and Recreation Department, for example, partially derives its funding for recreation programs from local tax collections—on average, **taxes** contribute about 63 percent to the revenues budget. On the other hand, private membership leisure service organizations, such as a Girl Scout council, and commercial leisure service organizations, such as a theme park, typically do not have taxes as a source of revenue. Therefore, many recreation program sponsors must rely on revenue sources in addition to taxes and participation fees.

Additional revenue sources include **grants**. Requests for financial assistance for programs can be made to both governmental (municipal, state or provincial, federal) and private granting agencies. Private funding is usually channeled through philanthropic foundations. Private foundations are nongovernmental, nonprofit organizations that are established to give financial assistance to social, charitable, educational, and religious activities that serve the common welfare. These contributions serve, in turn, as tax deductions for the foundation. Foundations can be sponsored by corporations, communities, or families.

Careful preparation when applying to governmental granting agencies and private foundations may mean the difference between obtaining substantial awards and receiving none. Bradford Woods Outdoor Recreation and Education Center in Indiana has been very successful over the years in funding its programs through grants because of the detailed attention it pays to preparing grant applications. Even though no two grant seekers use the same approach, there are some basic guidelines to follow. Successful grant seekers seem to agree on these steps (Russell, 1982):

1. *Understand your goal.* Locate granting sources whose goals match those of your program. A well-defined goal is thus the necessary first step. (See chapter 8 for more information.)

2. *Weigh your chances.* Early in the effort, you need to realistically assess your chances for successfully obtaining the grant funding. Chances for success depend on many things, including your agency's track record in securing grants.

3. *Gather your resources.* Appoint a grant coordinator, create effective internal agency communications, know the other organizations with similar projects that are also competing for funds, and start building contacts with influential people.

4. *Locate your prospects.* Identify those governmental agencies or private foundations that have previously funded projects similar to your programs. Web and library references are available to help you research the most promising matches.

5. *Research your prospects in depth.* This should lead to a set of priorities that identifies which agency or foundation to approach first with your funding assistance request.

6. *Make the first contact.* Now you are ready to arrange an exploratory meeting or telephone or e-mail communication with appropriate representatives from the agency or foundation. Although face-to-face meetings are usually more productive, if this is not possible, ask if a letter of inquiry would be welcomed. The point is to learn their interest in your program.

7. *Write the proposal.* Proposals written for private foundations and those written for governmental agencies usually differ markedly in their final form. The granter usually provides the proposal outline.

8. *Submit the proposal.* When submitting the formal proposal, also include a submittal letter and an addendum, if necessary, and always send the original copy. The proposal should be neatly and clearly prepared and proofread. After mailing or delivering the proposal, seeking verification that it was received is justifiable, but checking on its progress is not.

9. *Wait.* Relax and be patient. The results will be made known to you as soon as they are determined. If the response is "yes," write a thank-you letter immediately, and continue to maintain a good report system with the agency or foundation about your program's progress. If the answer is "no," write a letter thanking them for their consideration and request approval to keep in touch. Exit gracefully.

Many of the programs available to participants at Bradford Woods Outdoor Recreation and Education Center in Indiana have been made possible through grants, in particular from the Riley Foundation.

Photo courtesy of Bradford Woods/Indiana University.

Another alternative for program funding is **contract programming**. This option entails a legally sanctioned contract between a recreation agency and a commercial business firm. The firm has a service it specializes in performing, and the recreation organization signs a contract to purchase it. The most prevalent examples are the contracts signed for such concession services as park restaurants, boat marinas, and park bus lines. Some ice skating, snow skiing, golf, preschool day care, and outdoor adventure programs are also becoming more common examples of contract programming. Contracts are given to usually profit-motivated business firms that bid on opportunities to conduct the program services for you. When handled wisely, contract programming can bring in revenue above the cost of the contract in addition to providing the service.

Joint sponsorship is another way to fund programs. Indeed, it is becoming rare for programs to be exclusively sponsored by a single recreation agency. Programmers are increasingly tapping the resources of other agencies and citizen groups within the

The Programming Process: Operational Decisions

Youth sports in Westerville have been bursting at the seams! The city's two major youth sports organizations, the Westerville Youth Baseball and Softball League (WYBSL) and the Westerville Amateur Soccer Association (WASA), for which the department facilitates field usage, are extremely short of fields. The WYBSL has grown to more than 2,700 youth participating in summer leagues and an additional 1,500 involved in a new fall league. In fact, in the summer, youth are turned away because of the lack of playing fields. The soccer craze also hit Westerville hard, with more than 2,200 youth involved in WASA's spring program and an additional 2,200 youth in the fall program. The leagues play on every piece of open space available in parks and on school grounds, but still the demand is not met. Simply put, there are not enough baseball, softball, and soccer fields to meet the sports interests of the youth in the community.

Youth sports are very popular in Westerville, Ohio, thus requiring creative thinking for additional facilities and funding.

In addition, indoor programming space is very limited. In 1997, a small amount of space was acquired, allowing daytime, evening, and weekend programs to expand for preschoolers, youth, teens, and adults. Quickly, however, the demand for indoor programs far exceeded the space. Citizens of all ages and abilities jumped at the new program opportunities and requested more, especially expanded fitness and wellness opportunities and indoor aquatics. Waiting lists have become longer and available space more scarce. The department relies heavily on schools for indoor sports leagues and summer day camps, but this resource is being squeezed too as the schools' demand for gym space increases.

What can be done to meet this challenge and secure more space? The Westerville City Council decided to leave the decision up to its citizens and placed a quarter of 1 percent (.25 percent) income tax increase on the ballot. Because of a groundswell of interest for the already established new programs, as well as the promise of even more programs, Westerville citizens voted "yes" to the initiative. Thanks to the resulting $3 million–plus in new annual funding, construction of new fields and an indoor center was quickly underway. WYBSL kicked off its 2000 baseball season on new fields; the Sports Complex, home of WASA's new soccer fields, was ready for the spring 2001 season; and the new Community Center, housing a gymnasium, swimming pool, climbing wall, youth and teen game room, preschool room, and other programming space, was completed in 2002 (Westerville Parks and Recreation Department, 2004).

community to cooperatively offer programs. In the Westerville Parks and Recreation Department case earlier, for example, youth baseball and softball programs are jointly sponsored by the department and the Westerville Youth Baseball and Softball League. The league provides the coaching and referee staff, as well as administrative program preparations, and the Westerville Parks and Recreation Department provides the facilities.

In addition to expansion of the budget, advantages of joint sponsorships include more and better staff, additional facilities and equipment, and more

creative ways of meeting client needs. In other words, joint sponsorship can greatly extend the programming capability of an agency. Perhaps the greatest advantage of a cosponsored program is the opportunity to develop favorable community support and understanding. To be successful, however, programs sponsored by multiple organizations must reflect a joint philosophical base so that each sponsor feels equally represented in program planning and program policy setting.

Finally, **special interest associations** provide a source of program funding. Cultural arts associations, such as the Los Angeles Philharmonic orchestra, are typical examples. Many mutual benefits are derived from such an arrangement between a recreation agency and a special interest association. First, the constituency is served by an organization that is administratively and financially independent. Because the clients often constitute the association membership, attention is better focused on the needs of that constituency. Second, the agency's responsibility for the provision of special interest programming is minimized, thus liberating department resources for other programming areas.

Facility Usage and Coordination

Budgeting is just one of the many implementation decisions that need to be made in program implementation. Another is deciding what facility or facilities to use for the program. Preschool programs require playgrounds; aquatic programs need beaches and pools; outdoor concert programs could benefit from band shells; equestrian programs involve stables, riding rings, and trails (and, of course, horses); skating programs take place at rinks; baseball requires fields; dancers need smooth floors; drama programs are located in theaters; and nature programs require nature.

Many organizations offer a wide variety of recreation facilities. For example, fitness centers are increasingly needed; and public, private, and commercial agencies alike are equipped with weight and exercise rooms, tracks, courts, gyms, lap pools, locker rooms, saunas, and whirlpools. Cities as well as hotels have invested considerably in these facilities.

Also, water-play parks, family recreation centers, amusement and theme destinations, lake and river marinas, indoor multigame arcades, environmental centers, and bikeways are becoming more plentiful, elaborate, and innovatively designed for leisure experiences.

Although some leisure service organizations sponsor a wide array of different facilities, other organizations operate a single facility. As well, some recreation program sponsors do not manage any facilities of their own at all, relying on borrowing or renting those of others. A travel organization is a good example—the transportation equipment, hotels, and tourist destinations are all owned by other organizations.

Regardless, an important task in program implementation is assigning events and activities to spe-

cific facilities. In which park should the day-camp program be held, and in which section of the park? What hotels should the tour use? Should the swimming lessons be offered at the outdoor or indoor pool, or both? Should the dance be held in the community center's multipurpose room or outside in the parking lot? Which sections of the Appalachian Trail should the adventure program use for the backpacking trip?

In selecting facilities for programs, follow these guidelines to ensure that facilities are used to their maximum capability:

1. *Assign facilities equitably.* Program elements should be assigned to facilities or locations in a way that ensures a fair balance of leisure opportunities throughout a community or region and that reflects special needs according to age, socioeconomic status, ability level, or other characteristics.

2. *Assign facilities efficiently.* Coordinate program placement and scheduling so that programs are offered at optimal times and locations for participants as well as for maximal usage of the facility.

3. *Coordinate with other agencies.* To the degree possible, publicly owned facilities should be made available for use by private groups, such as when community athletic fields are scheduled by youth sports leagues that operate the actual programming.

4. *Use sound environmental practices.* In all programs, enforce caring and wise ecological principles to prevent environmental damage, pollution, or other harmful consequences.

5. *Use sound maintenance practices.* Efficiently plan and apply maintenance programs to reduce vandalism, graffiti, and other forms of abuse that degrade facilities and make them unattractive.

For more information on this topic, see "More Options for Individual Programming Practice," option 4, in chapter 10 of the CD-ROM.

Recreation areas and buildings are sometimes not optimally designed for programs. As well, programmers are not normally encouraged by their agencies to request costly areas and facilities to better suit their program goals. More likely they need to make do with what is available. Often at this step, then, you must make the proposed program fit the available facility resources.

This can sometimes be a challenge because all programmed activities have minimum requirements for area, facility, and equipment resources. Racquetball tournaments cannot be held in church basements, and white-water kayak programs are not as feasible when the nearest stream rapids are 500 miles (800 kilometers) away. So, you must assess not only the appropriateness of existing facilities but also whether these facilities can be adapted to better fit the planned program. To make proposed programs fit available facilities, you may need to apply your creativity; many facilities used primarily for certain purposes can be creatively used for others. For example, a college recreational sports program can use little-used squash courts for stationary cycling classes, such as Spinning. For more information on this topic, see "Can You Solve This Programming Issue?" in chapter 10 of the CD-ROM.

By and large, assigning programs to facilities is a matter of scheduling—generally one of the easiest tasks for programmers. Yet, if incorrectly done, facility scheduling can also be one of the most nightmarish programming tasks. An ineffective facility scheduling system leads to double booking, with lots of user displeasure and a poor image for the organization.

Perhaps worse, poor scheduling can also result in underutilized facilities.

Competently scheduling programs into facilities requires a good scheduling system. The most foolproof system, perhaps, is to create a **matrix** that displays each facility and each day and hour that may potentially be scheduled in the facility (see figure 10.4). To draw up a schedule, enter the name of the program or group that will occupy the facility according to each day and hour in every matrix space. This yields a picture of the schedule so you can see that each space (day and hour) can be scheduled only once. All methods of facility scheduling, including computer software, use this simple, basic procedure.

How, then, can facility scheduling go wrong? Not paying attention to detail is the most common error. A busy staff member may give out a reservation for the senior center dining room but fail to record it on the master matrix schedule. As well, remember to schedule time for facility maintenance, custodial care, setup and teardown of program equipment, and so on. No matter how stellar the program, a dirty, poorly maintained facility can produce lots of participant dissatisfaction.

Time	Monday	Tuesday	Wednesday	Thursday	Friday
9:00 a.m.					
10:00 a.m.					
11:00 a.m.					
Noon					
1:00 p.m.					
2:00 p.m.					
3:00 p.m.					
4:00 p.m.					
5:00 p.m.					
6:00 p.m.					
7:00 p.m.					

Figure 10.4 Example of a facility scheduling matrix.

Program Communication

Obviously, patron communication is a vitally important operational task when implementing programs. Without a plan for "getting the word out" you'll have no program, no matter how thorough the planning. Although you'll certainly incorporate such typical communication tools as advertising, publicity, and promotions, program communication also depends on effectively naming and scheduling programs.

Naming

You may be tempted to think selecting a title or label for a program is easy and of no real significance. Yet stop and think about your own behavior when you glance through a recreation program brochure, skim an advertisement, or scan a Web site. Most people allocate only a few seconds when looking for program information. They are searching for things of interest to them. If a title catches their attention, they'll read more thoroughly (McCarville, 2002). So, your task in naming programs is to select titles that not only describe the program but also catch interest and attention (see the box on this page for an example).

Names represent dominant cues to customers. Thus, a program's name may be one of the most important pieces of information you can offer to prospective patrons. Names represent "the hook that hangs the brand on the product" (Ries & Trout, 1986, p. 71). Consider the name Exercise Center. What happens to your interest when the name is changed to Weight and Stress Control Center? The program is no longer about exerting physical energy; it is about getting body weight and stress under control. Now the "brand" is wellness rather than effort.

Another example is the leisure service agency that renamed an adult swim program for novices. The new title? Swimming for the Absolutely Terrified. The new choice was not only more descriptive but also more memorable. As a result, the program increased in popularity, and the agency has expanded the "absolutely terrified" naming theme to include programs on learning to ski, using computers and the Internet, and high school diploma exam preparation (McCarville, 2002).

From a communication perspective, naming a program focuses on developing "the hook"—something that gains attention. The most successful hooks focus on benefits (McCarville, 2002). The logic is simple: Programs that are named according to what the patrons want will attract more patron attention. Useful program names tell what the service will do and make it easy for patrons to visualize the benefits (Burton & Purvis, 1996).

Here is some specific advice on naming programs. Essentially, in order to be effective communication tools, names should pass four basic tests (Berry & Parasuraman, 1991). The first test is distinctiveness. The program name must clearly distinguish itself from other programs. The term *aerobics class*, for example, is descriptive but doesn't distinguish one fitness program from another. Instead, why not name this program Latin Explosion, Cardio Studio, or Fitness Jumpstart (Division of Recreational Sports, 2004)?

The second naming test is relevance. The program name needs to provide an image that is meaningful to the target constituency. The name must also be an honest representation of the program itself. For

---

What's in a Name?

Elderhostel is the world's largest education and travel organization for adults 55 and over. Since its founding in 1975, it has grown to offer more than 10,000 learning adventures each year in more than 100 countries. Here is a sampling of some of their programs. How distinctive, relevant, memorable, and flexible are these program names?

In the Footsteps of the Great Ice Age Floods: Northwest Landscapes
Color Country's National Parks: Bryce, Zion, Grand Canyon
Historic House Restoration for Dreamers and Doers
Al, Bing, and Frank
Toe Bone Connected to the Eyeball? Reflexology for Self-Care
Dancing for the Camera
Stories From the Midrash: Nourishing the Jewish Soul
From Lewis and Clark to Yellowstone Park
Song Catching: Ballads of the Appalachia
Introduction to Nature Art Quilts
Follow the Eagle's Spirit by Freighter and Ferry
Acting on Impulse: Theatre for Everyone
Thar She Blows: Whales and Shipwrecks

Elderhostel, 2003.

example, the titles Lifeguard Instructor Training and Water Safety Instructor Training provide a meaningful message about the differences in the two programs (Division of Recreational Sports, 2006). Memorability is the third test. Memorability refers to how easily the name is understood and remembered. This requires that the name be creatively interesting and to the point. Clutter and dullness are not memorable. For example, Owl Prowl, Classy Casting, and Rip Roaring Rapids are easy to remember because of the rhyming and alliteration (Bloomington Parks & Recreation, 2004).

For the fourth test, the name must be flexible enough to allow easy changes in program content or format over time. For instance, a program titled Yoga or Pilates Sampler enables programmers to alternate which fitness activity is offered from season to season without having to change the program's name (Division of Recreational Sports, 2006). For more information on this topic, see "Group Discussion Ideas," option 3, in chapter 10 of the CD-ROM.

Scheduling

Getting the word out about a program is also accomplished by how it is scheduled. Depending on the goals of the program, various scheduling schemes are available (e.g., annually, seasonally, weekly, and daily). Scheduling requires designating the length of the program as well as the day(s) of the week and time of day the program is offered. Appropriate scheduling is a strong determinant of a program's success in attracting participants.

Annual and Seasonal Schedules

Let's consider annual and seasonal scheduling first. Some programs are scheduled over the course of a year or multiple years. For example, a photography club at an older adults center might meet regularly for years. Its schedule is not affected by any geographical factors such as season, climate, and weather. This would probably also hold true for violin classes at the community center, water walking sessions at a YMCA, and poetry readings at the bookstore. The purposes of these programs are unrelated to the locale and season.

Other programs, on the other hand, are influenced by geographical and seasonal factors and are scheduled accordingly. For example, cross-country skiing clinics in North America are most likely scheduled in northern regions in the winter, and synchronized swimming competitions are most often held in the summer. Often, geographical considerations such as climate must be optimized in program scheduling, as demonstrated by the cruising schedule in table 10.1. Notice there are no cruises in the Caribbean during hurricane season!

There are other reasons to schedule programs seasonally. Children's programs typically mirror the local school district schedule, and, similarly, campus programs for college students reflect the semester calendar. For programs serving these clients, the three seasons most often used are fall, winter, and spring. In these seasons there is often a heavier emphasis on classes and clubs, with the summer season reserved for trips and day and resident camps.

Another factor that affects the seasonal scheduling of programs is tradition. This is particularly applicable to sports leagues

Programs such as indoor water walking can be scheduled without regard for locale and season.

TABLE 10.1

A Seasonal Schedule:
The Sailings of Three Cruise Ships of the Holland America Line

	MS Rotterdam	**MS Statendam**	**MS Prinsendam**
Spring	Transatlantic/European Capitals	Alaska	Mediterranean
Summer	Eastern Canada/New England	Alaska	Mediterranean
Fall	Caribbean/Panama Canal	Hawaii	Amazon River
Winter	Caribbean/Panama Canal	Hawaii	Grand World Voyage

Adapted from Holland America Line, Spring 2004, pp. 27-28.

and competitions. For example, there are traditional times of the year for basketball, soccer, and track and field. These traditional seasonal boundaries are fading somewhat, however. In basketball, the WNBA (Women's National Basketball Association) season is summer rather than winter, and many AAU (Amateur Athletic Union) leagues for children run basketball tournaments year-round.

Seasonal programming also includes scheduling special events around patriotic, religious, historical, or commercial commemorations, as well as to initiate or conclude regular-season programs. For example, a Martin Luther King, Jr. birthday celebration at the Boys and Girls Clubs in January could kick off a Black History Month program containing a whole series of special events for February. A camping and boating show at the state park could be scheduled for early March to officially start the camping and boating summer season, or a public exhibition of paintings could be scheduled in May around Mother's Day, culminating a mother–daughter water color class held all winter.

Monthly, Weekly, and Daily Schedules

Within an annual or seasonal schedule, program sessions or events that take place more than once must also be fitted into a monthly, weekly, or daily schedule. This usually depends on such factors as interest level, time requirements of the activity, and participant demographic characteristics. For example, adults-only lap swimming would be scheduled more frequently and for longer periods of time each day at a pool serving a retirement community and less frequently and for shorter periods of time each day at a pool located in a neighborhood with a high proportion of children. A high-impact, high-energy group workout at a fitness center might be more appropriately scheduled for 40 minutes daily, while a yoga class is best scheduled for 90 minutes twice a week.

Additionally, daily schedules with hour-by-hour activities must be developed for such programs as day and resident camps, all-day playground programs, after-school programs, tours, and weekend retreats. For this, great care must be taken to organize blocks of time—for rest, meals, activity, reflection, and housekeeping—that are balanced, flexible, and of the right length. For example, in a three-hour after-school program for children, an ideal schedule would begin with a snack and unstructured play time, followed by a highly organized physical activity, and end with a quiet homework assistance session.

A daily schedule is usually organized around distinct time periods. The morning session rarely begins before 9:00 a.m. and is typically used for physically active experiences. After the noon meal, the early afternoon session usually incorporates activity at a lower level or even rest and meditation. Next is the more productive time of projects in the late afternoon session. The early evening session follows dinner and is a popular time for social and interactive forms of recreation. Additionally, some constituent groups (such as athletic camps and health resorts) feature a prebreakfast "early bird" session of hiking, weightlifting, and so on. As well, socially oriented programs such as cruise ships normally offer a late evening session, which can extend even into the early morning hours.

Above all, the secret to successful program scheduling is that it complements the recreation needs and lifestyles of the clients. No amount of innovation will overcome an inappropriately scheduled program. This means that the preschool crafts program should not be scheduled in the evening, and the fitness program for employees of a company should not be scheduled midmorning. After all, the goal of scheduling is to bring the participant and the program together. For more information on this topic, see worksheet 10.2 in chapter 10 of the CD-ROM.

Promotion

Finally, communicating about a program typically requires promoting it. The purpose of **promotion** is to inform, persuade, remind, and educate people about the benefits of the program (Crompton & Lamb, 1986). Promoting a program may involve one or more of these efforts: advertising, publicity, and sales promotion.

"**Advertising** is communication that is paid for" (Russell, 1982, p. 249). For recreation programs, advertising is usually accomplished through such media as magazines, newspapers, radio, television, fliers, brochures, and billboards. It can also include such technologically based media as electronic kiosks, CDs and DVDs, the Internet, and even sky-writing. Advertising can be very effective in enabling your organization to rapidly reach large numbers of people.

Publicity, on the other hand, is news. If your programs create news, publicity is what communicates it to the potential participants. This promotion of an organization's successes is not usually paid for. In fact, the message in publicity is usually controlled by the medium itself. For example, a newspaper article on the upcoming art show in the park goes a long way in promoting the program. A public service announcement on the radio about the opening of the day-camp season will catch the attention of parents looking for possible day-care opportunities during school holidays. An appearance by one of your fitness leaders on a local television talk show will not only communicate how to keep fit but will also advertise the fitness program itself. As well, a glowing "letter to the editor" about a program is certainly helpful for getting the word out.

Indeed, nothing promotes a program better than favorable publicity. Unfavorable publicity can be just as effective, if not more so, but the response from potential patrons is not always positive. And don't forget, making the news does not mean staging the news. News is made by offering exciting and highly sought-after programs. You direct your efforts by keeping the media aware of them.

Finally, directly selling programs is an often-used promotion strategy. The point of a **sales promotion** is to stimulate program participation via direct and obvious communication. Coupons, giveaways, two-for-one deals, exhibits, demonstrations, speeches before groups and clubs, and T-shirts are often used to sell programs. Taster activities are another. Commercial health clubs provide a well-known example—many offer nonmembers a free day or week at the facility so they can "taste" the program service, with the hope that they will be satisfied with the experience and take out a membership.

Program Policies

For successful operation, recreation programs must have policies. **Policies** are detailed rules for the conduct of the program. They serve as a framework for maintaining staff efficiency and service quality (Kraus, 1997).

Program policies do not stand alone—they are a direct reflection of the values and ethical standards held by the program's sponsoring organization, which means they are often direct descendents of the mission and goals statements. In other programming situations, conversely, policies are unwritten, or implicit, values that have been developed over the years and that are an inherent part of the agency or the profession.

Generally, program policies are generic to all of an agency's program services and are assembled in leaders' manuals or operational handbooks used at staff orientation and in-service training sessions. A handbook for a summer day-camp program leader, for example, could cover policies for dealing with obscenities, wearing closed-toed shoes, throwing objects, keeping bathrooms clean, picking up trash, and being on time.

In many cases, program policies outline strict procedures in those areas that could result in lawsuits or other legal or social problems. For example, the materials for Girl Scout leaders include a policy on the place of religion in troop programs. For special events, agencies often maintain a separate set of policies covering everything from crowd control to parking to "rain dates." For travel programs, agencies develop policies governing such issues as the use of personal vehicles, route selection, and parent permission. For more information on this topic, see worksheet 10.3 in chapter 10 of the CD-ROM.

The point of establishing program policies is to control those aspects of the leisure experience that are controllable. To appreciate this it may be useful to consider the three types of program operation variables. First, there are **uncontrollable variables**, which include the weather, client attitudes and prejudices, and the actions of people outside the program and agency. Program policies may be developed to absolve the agency from responsibility for such uncontrollable variables. For instance, the Rivers Company cannot guarantee good weather for the white-water rafting trip on the New River in West Virginia and thus has a no-refund policy in case of rain.

Second, **influenceable variables** include staff motivation, number and types of participants in the program, access to the program site, and accidents. These factors can be influenced by the program's structure as well as its operational policies. For example, white-water rafting companies require participants to wear life jackets and helmets in order to decrease the likelihood of avoidable accidents.

Finally, there are **controllable variables** in a program's operation. Examples include staffing levels, thoroughness of staff training, equipment quality, registration system efficiency, and the tastiness of the food. Program policies seek to directly control such variables. White-water rafting programs usually enforce the policy that visual raft inspections are to be conducted by staff after each trip to be sure there are no holes or tears requiring repair. For more information on this topic, see "More Options for Individual Programming Practice," option 2, in chapter 10 of the CD-ROM.

Summary

This chapter discusses the operational decisions necessary to run a program. You should understand the following key points:

White-water rafting and kayaking programs have many policies that structure the experience for participants. These policies are directed at elements of the program the company can both control and not control.

* Programs must be budgeted.

* A program budget is an estimated plan for keeping expenses in line with income (i.e., balancing costs and revenues).

* When prices for participation are established, pricing strategies—such as penetration, neutral, and skim—differ in terms of how much of the cost of programs is assumed by participants.

* An important task in program implementation is assigning events and activities to specific facilities.

* Communication about programs requires creative attention to such details as naming, scheduling, and promotion.

* Useful program names tell what the service will do and make it easy for customers to visualize the benefits.

* Programs can be scheduled annually, seasonally, weekly, and daily. Scheduling also requires designating the length of programs and the day(s) of the week and time of day that programs are offered.

- Program promotions often include making arrangements for advertising, publicity, and direct selling.

- Policies, or rules for the conduct of the program, must also be established. Program policies serve as a framework for maintaining program staff efficiency and program service quality.

Glossary

line-item budget—A system that allocates specific amounts of money to each expenditure item.

zero-based budget—Each subunit of the organization is required to build its income and expenditures estimates beginning with zero amounts each year.

program budget—Money is allocated for expenditures according to major program areas.

budget—An estimated plan for keeping expenses in line with income.

cost allocation—Identifying and assigning costs to various resources needed to implement a program.

direct costs—Costs specifically assigned to a particular program.

indirect costs—Costs the organization incurs regardless of whether a specific program is offered.

cost tracking—Following the actual cost and use of a budget item over time.

pricing—Determining the amount of money to charge for the recreation program.

penetration pricing—Prices for programs are kept low in order to encourage wide participation.

neutral pricing—Prices for programs are a balance between high prices and low prices.

skim pricing—Prices for programs are intended to generate revenue.

pricing triangle—Using the criteria of agency priorities, the program requirements, and the marketplace to set program price.

taxes—Revenues provided by taxing citizens and tourists of a locale.

grants—Financial assistance from philanthropic organizations or government grant-in-aid programs.

contract programming—A legally sanctioned contract between a recreation agency and a commercial business firm for the delivery of recreation programs.

joint sponsorship—Cooperatively offering programs with other organizations.

special interest association—A private or commercial organization formed to support the expression of a particular leisure activity.

matrix—A chart with blank spaces representing days and times of day available for assigning programs to facilities.

promotion—Communication efforts directed at encouraging potential participants to become participants in a program.

advertising—Promotion that is paid for.

publicity—Promotion that is news based.

sales promotion—Stimulation of program participation via direct and obvious communication.

policies—Detailed rules for the conduct of the program.

uncontrollable variables—Elements of operating a program that cannot be controlled.

influenceable variables—Elements of operating a program that can be influenced by the program structure and operational policies.

controllable variables—Elements of operating a program that policies seek to directly control.

References

Berry, L., & Parasuraman, A. (1991). *Marketing services: Competing through quality.* New York: Free Press.

Bloomington Parks & Recreation. (2004, Fall/Winter). *The great outdoors* [Brochure]. Bloomington, IN: Author.

Brayley, R., & McLean, D. (1999). *Managing financial resources in sport and leisure service organizations.* Champaign, IL: Sagamore.

Burton, P.W., & Purvis, S.C. (1996). *Which ad pulled best?* Lincolnwood, IL: NTC Business Books.

Crompton, J., & Lamb, C. (1986). *Marketing government and social services.* New York: Wiley.

Division of Recreational Sports. (2004). *Membership application.* Bloomington, IN: Indiana University Publications.

Division of Recreational Sports. (2006). *Fall guide 2006, RSmag.* Bloomington, IN: Recreational Sports Marketing Department.

Elderhostel. (2003, Summer). *Elderhostel discover America. Summer outlooks, 6*(1).

GrandLuxe Rail Journeys. (2006). Home page. Retrieved August 25, 2006, from www.americanorientexpress.com/Index.html.

Holland America Line. (2004, Spring). *Mariner magazine,* 27-28.

Kraus, R. (1997). *Recreation programming: A benefits-driven approach.* Boston: Allyn & Bacon.

Los Angeles Philharmonic Association. (2006). LA Philharmonic. Retrieved May 22, 2006, from www.laphil.com/orchestra/laphilharmonic.cfm.

McCarville, R.E. (2002). *Improving leisure services through marketing action.* Champaign, IL: Sagamore.

Ries, A., & Trout, J. (1986). *Positioning: The battle for your mind.* New York: Warner.

Russell, R.V. (1982). *Planning programs in recreation.* St. Louis: Mosby.

Westerville Parks and Recreation Department. (July 26, 2004). *Personal interview notes.* Westerville, OH: City of Westerville.

Workamper.com. (1996-2006). Workamper news: The road to your dreams. Retrieved October 18, 2004, from www.workamper.com/workamperNews/WNIndex.cfm.

CHAPTER 11

Leading and Supervising Programs

- Determining staffing needs for program implementation
- Learning the expectations for program staff
- Receiving advice on recruiting, training, and supervising program staff

"**H**eritage is our legacy from the past, what we live with today, and what we pass on to future generations. Our cultural and natural heritage is an irreplaceable source of life and inspiration. Places as unique and diverse as the wilds of East Africa's Serengeti, the Pyramids of Egypt, the Great Barrier Reef in Australia and the Baroque cathedrals of Latin America make up our world's heritage" (UNESCO, 2006).

To honor and safeguard our heritage, the World Heritage program, sponsored by the United Nations Educational, Scientific and Cultural Organization (UNESCO), encourages the identification, protection, and preservation of cultural and natural sites around the world considered to be of outstanding value to humanity. These heritage places are considered to belong to all the peoples of the world, regardless of where they are located. Currently the World Heritage list includes 812 properties located in 137 countries. 628 of these sites are of cultural significance, 160 are of natural importance, and 24 are both.

Sites are selected by a group of volunteers who make up the World Heritage Committee. The committee consists of representatives from 21 countries, elected by the United Nations General Assembly for six-year terms. They meet once a year to carry out their responsibility for the implementation of the World Heritage Convention. Accordingly, they define the use of the World Heritage Fund and allocate financial assistance on request from World Heritage sites. The committee has the final say on whether a property is inscribed on the World Heritage list, and it examines reports on the state of conservation of these properties, asking countries to take action when sites are not being properly managed. The committee also decides on the inclusion (and deletion) of sites on the List of World Heritage in Danger. This international group of people—all volunteering their time and expertise—provide key leadership for the integrity of the World Heritage program.

In addition to its particularly beautiful scenery, Dinosaur Provincial Park—located in the heart of the badlands in the province of Alberta—contains some of the most important fossil discoveries ever made, in particular about 35 species of dinosaur, dating back some 75 million years. It is on the World Heritage list.

Making operational decisions for the implementation of recreation programs requires a determination of leadership needs. Will you need to hire additional lifeguards at the pool on the day of the aquatic sports festival? How much time is required of full-time staff members for the Friday lunches at the senior center? What will adding child-care programming at the beach resort mean for the number of part-time employees needed? Will the volunteers for the children's play program at the hospital be able to handle this new program? As the programmer for your organization, how much of your own time and energy will be required to manage other leadership staff for the planned program?

Staffing resources are needed at every step of the recreation program planning process. Specifically, directors, managers, supervisors, and leaders are needed for the following duties:

- *Planning the program.* Staff members are involved in assessing the needs and interests of clients and in developing recommendations for programs.
- *Implementing and monitoring the program.* Staff should assist in gathering program resources, promoting and publicizing programs, and making sure all needed supplies are available. Staff members are also typically needed to lead participants through program experiences.
- *Evaluating the program.* Once programs have been set in motion, staff members are responsible for carrying out systematic evaluations and preparing program reports.

In this chapter we focus on resources for staffing recreation program implementation. This includes determining the need for staff to carry out and monitor programs, designating optimal staff actions necessary for program success, and identifying how to acquire and keep program staff. For more information on this topic, see worksheet 11.1 in chapter 11 of the CD-ROM.

Determining Staffing Needs

Staffing needs for implementing and monitoring recreation programs include a wide array of well-prepared part-time and full-time employees and, frequently, talented volunteers. One of these staffing decisions is program and facility supervision.

Supervisors

Supervisors are assigned to manage the facilities where programs take place. They do not have direct activity leadership responsibilities; rather, they supervise tennis centers, golf courses, nature preserves, gymnasiums, community centers, art museums, climbing walls, and so on. They oversee the maintenance of these facilities, ensure the correct distribution of materials and equipment, check user permits, collect fees, see that agency policies are followed, and carry out other administrative tasks.

In addition to facility supervisors, program supervisors are often necessary for successful program implementation. These may include the aquatics supervisor for a city parks department, the special

group coordinator for a marine-themed park, or the wagon master for an RV caravan. Whereas facility supervisors are concerned about the use of a particular facility for programs, program supervisors see that the programs that take place at the facility are successful. Program supervisors typically focus on components of recreation programs, such as arts and crafts, sports, trips and tours, and aquatics, or on age-group categories such as youth and senior citizens. Either way, program supervisors are responsible for making sure program plans are carried out as prepared and that all leaders fulfill their responsibilities. For more information on this topic, see "More Options for Individual Programming Practice," option 1, in chapter 11 of the CD-ROM.

Program and facility supervisors may already be in place for the programs you plan; they are usually full-time permanent professional employees (e.g., the director of the cultural arts center, ice arena, or botanical gardens). On the other hand, some seasonal facilities, such as softball complexes and beach fronts, must hire seasonal employees. After that particular program season, staff may be reassigned to different facilities. For example, the supervisor of a nature center at a state park might be located at the center as the facility supervisor during the spring, summer, and autumn months; in the winter months he coordinates a traveling nature program that is held at area schools. For more information on this topic, see worksheet 11.3 in chapter 11 of the CD-ROM.

Activity Leaders

In addition to program and facility supervisors, **activity leaders** are often needed to implement recreation programs. Many leisure service organizations use part-time and volunteer employees to teach classes, lead events, and facilitate special interest groups. These staff may include playground leaders, camp counselors, lifeguards, interpretive naturalists, fitness specialists, outdoor adventure facilitators, dance instructors, craft instructors, golf starters, referees and coaches, and many others.

Activity leaders are carefully selected according to their backgrounds, skills, and credentials. As well, their recruitment, orientation, training, supervision, and evaluation are major functions in program implementation—including for volunteers and for seasonal and part-time employees. Activity leaders are usually managed by either program or facility supervisors.

The Programming Process: Determining Staff Resources

A couple of years ago, City of Westerville Parks and Recreation Department program supervisor Laura Horton was riding the crest of a major salsa dance phenomenon. Many adults wanted to learn how to do the latest Latin dances, and they also wanted social events so they could show off their dancing talents. As a result, Laura found herself scheduling more and more classes and dances. Music was purchased and special instructors were hired; but it seemed that no matter how many salsa events were planned, the department couldn't keep up with the interest.

After about a year, while studying the program enrollment data, Laura noticed an amazing thing: Participation in salsa dancing had leveled off and now seemed to be in a downward spiral. What should she do?

By studying what was currently popular in television programming, Laura jumped onto the next big phenomenon. Adults now want to know how to improve themselves, their homes, their children, and all aspects of their lives. So Laura now offers what she calls "life coaching" programs. For example, adult programs listed in the winter 2003-2004 catalog include Leading a Deliberate Life, Creating Your Path to a Perfect Life, Interior Design, and Organizing Matters. The catalog description of the Organizing Matters program follows:

Get started on the road to better organization. Professional organizer Mary Donovan will share proven strategies for managing time, clutter, and the never ending trail of paper. Participants will have the opportunity to share their own organizing challenges. (Westerville Parks and Recreation Department, 2003, p. 48)

Because of changes in program participant interests in Westerville, the supervisor had to let the salsa dancing instructors go and recruit life coaches instead.

Photo courtesy of Westerville Parks and Recreation Department, Westerville, Ohio.

According to Laura, "This program is such a hit due to the fact that everyone is in such a rush these days that they don't have time to get their act together. Just about every magazine you pick up has tips on how to get your life organized" (personal communication, July 10, 2004).

Of course, this new area of programming created a void in staffing. Laura had to let the salsa dancing instructors go and start recruiting life coaches. The mostly volunteer program staff now includes experts on interior design and life goals planning.

It is becoming more common for leisure service agencies to contract for program staff. For example, in Westerville, supervisors and activity leaders for the roller hockey program are provided by Skyhawks Sports, a commercial skating company. Contract program staff are not employees of the program sponsor; rather, they are given a flat rate or a percentage of the revenue generated from the program. This practice is controversial, of course. Although contracting for program staff reduces both direct costs

for the sponsoring organization and its exposure to the requirements of numerous employment laws (Moiseichik, Hunt, & Macchiarelli, 1992), it is more difficult to maintain control over the quality of the staff. Further, any problems in staff performance or in the provision of the program are contract violations rather than simply personnel problems.

When determining the need for program supervisors and activity leaders, decisions must be made regarding the number of staff needed and the special skills or credentials they should have (see the box on this page for sample qualifications). The **participant-to-staff ratio** for a program can be decided in several different ways. In many situations, personnel standards dictate the number of staff needed for specific programs. For example, the American Camp Association (ACA) has the following standards for accredited resident camps: one staff member for every 6 campers aged 6 to 8; one staff member for every 8 campers aged 9 to 14; and one staff member for every 10 campers aged 15 to 18. At day camps the ratios range from one staff member for every 8 campers aged 6 to 8; one staff member for every 10 campers aged 9 to 14; and one staff member for every 12 campers aged 15 to 18 (ACA, n.d.).

In comparison, Adventures Cross-Country (ARCC), a commercial company for adventure travel for teens, limits its group size to no more than 15 participants. "Our leaders cherish the time they have getting to know each student, which helps them tailor the adventure to meet your individual needs. ARCC adventures are not restricted by rigid schedules. Our group size allows us the flexibility to spend extra time cooling off in a trailside stream or celebrating at the top of a mountain" (ARCC, 2004b).

Without such agency-prepared and professional association standards to guide your decision about the number of leaders needed for a program, you'll have to rely on your own good judgment. Keep in mind that the ratio depends not only on the age of the participants but also on the nature of the recreation activity. For example, a program with activities requiring skill, such as rock rappelling, would probably require a small participant-to-staff ratio for both

Samples of Qualifications Listed in Job Descriptions

WILDERNESS LEADERS FOR ADVENTURES CROSS-COUNTRY

* Ability to carry a 55-pound (25 kilogram) backpack through rugged terrain for up to 12 hours per day
* Competence with backcountry map and compass techniques
* Familiarity with minimum impact camping techniques for backcountry travel
* Ability to plan the logistics (food, fuel, and so on) for 4- to 10-day backcountry trips for groups of 15 people
* Backcountry cooking skills
* Solid expedition behavior
* Ability to oversee (but not guide) outfitted activities such as rafting, rock climbing, sea kayaking, mountaineering, and so on (skill in these areas is helpful, but not required)

Adapted, by permission, from Adventures Cross-Country, 2004b, www.adventurescrosscountry.com/trip_lead.htm.

ARTS AND CRAFTS COUNSELORS FOR THE MONTECITO SEQUOIA SUMMER FAMILY RESORT

* Ability to handle a variety of activities such as face painting, tie-dying, creating beaded jew-elry, making ice candles, scrapbooking, copper enameling
* Ability to learn the popular crafts that are "in" this year
* Ability to work with all ages, including younger children and adults

Adapted, by permission, from Montecito Sequoia Summer Family Resort, 2006, www.resortjobs.com/do/details/238.

ASSISTANT AQUATICS COORDINATOR, UNIVERSITY OF CALIFORNIA AT BERKELEY

* Certifications in American Red Cross Water Safety Instructor, Lifeguard Training, and CPR for the Professional Rescuer
* Effective interpersonal and communication skills
* Ability to organize effectively, set priorities, take direction, and multitask in a fast-paced environment
* Experience supervising swim instructors, swimming lessons, and aquatics facilities

Adapted, by permission, from Cal Recreational Sports, n.d., http://calbears.berkeley.edu/insidepage.aspx?uid=33170984-95da-450f-8a3d-e9b23bb0b60e.

a group of 13-year-olds and a group of 55-year-olds. For more information on this topic, see "More Options for Individual Programming Practice," option 2, in chapter 11 of the CD-ROM.

Beyond determining the number of staff, programmers must also allow for the credentials needed by each program activity leader and supervisor. Will specific certifications be necessary, such as CPR (cardiopulmonary resuscitation) or Wilderness Rescue? Will computer skills or prior experience be important for the program's success? You likely will spell out such qualifications needed in a job description for the staff position. For example, in the box Samples of Qualifications Listed in Job Descriptions, staff requirement excerpts from three different job descriptions demonstrate great variety. In some programming situations, your organization may have already developed job descriptions for frequently offered programs. In other situations, you may need to develop new job descriptions, especially for new programs and special events. For more information on this topic, see "More Options for Individual Programming Practice," option 3, in chapter 11 of the CD-ROM.

Once you have determined the number and qualifications of the staff needed for a program, the next decisions require consideration of what staff will actually do—expectations for their duties—and how to recruit, train, and retain them. Let's consider program staff duties first.

Expectations for Program Staff

Recreation leaders and supervisors perform many tasks. They coordinate kite flying tournaments and summer musical performances in the park. They take penguins from the marine park to elementary school classrooms. They lead soccer programs for the children of military personnel stationed at an air base in Alaska. They direct outdoor trips for the student union at a university. They facilitate social programs for residential clients in a convalescent center. In fact, staff members who carry out leisure programs perform so many different tasks that listing them all is impossible.

More useful, then, is to consider the different functions of leaders according to categories. Hersey and Blanchard (1982) designate these categories as technical functions, human relations functions, and conceptual functions:

- *Technical functions.* The use of knowledge, methods, techniques, and equipment to accomplish specific tasks often requiring experience, education, or training. An example is the process of planning, carrying out, and evaluating leisure programs. Think of this book as providing the training necessary to perform a technical function—program planning.

- *Human relations functions.* Working with and for people in order to influence their behavior. For example, seeking and interpreting information about the clientele who use the programs and developing program goals to solve problems or meet needs require human relations skills.

- *Conceptual functions.* An understanding of the intricacies of the organization, how the organization relates to the world beyond it, and where your own role fits in. Delivering program services in the spirit of your agency's vision and mission, and according to a sound professional philosophy, are examples of functions requiring conceptual skills.

For more information on this topic, see "Can You Solve This Programming Issue?" and "More Options for Individual Programming Practice," option 4, in chapter 11 of the CD-ROM.

Within these categories of technical, human relations, and conceptual actions are many specific staff duties applicable to recreation programs. Program staff, for example, make decisions, solve problems, manage groups, communicate, lead change, innovate, inspire participant motivation, facilitate recreation behavior, resolve conflicts, ensure safety, teach, rally resources, use technology, and manage a workload—among other things. To offer a bit of elaboration on this, we feature the duties of facilitation, motivation, group dynamics, and behavior management.

Facilitation

Because recreation programs result in physical, social, emotional, and educational outcomes, supervisors and activity leaders have a responsibility to see that participants attain these benefits (Russell, 2005). This means program supervisors and leaders employ **facilitation techniques** to ensure that patrons have the best experience possible in the program. Facilitating involves calling patrons' attention to the nature of the experience and its meaning for them (Priest & Gass, 1997). Specifically, facilitation helps recreation program patrons do the following (Russell, 2005, p. 164):

- Evaluate the good and the bad about their experiences in the program
- Consider the impact of their actions and decisions during the program experience
- Anticipate consequences from the program experience
- Understand how they have learned or changed from the program experience
- Overcome barriers to participation in the program

Program staff can help participants achieve the benefits of a program in many ways. Some facilitation techniques are used before the program, some during, and some afterward. Here we discuss three facilitation techniques: discussion, frontloading, and feedback.

Most often used after the activity, **discussion** is an unstructured form of facilitation that encourages patrons to consider a leisure program experience and transfer what was learned to other aspects of their lives. In a discussion, the group verbalizes its reactions to an activity. The leader guides the con-

versation to make the content and format valuable to participants (Priest & Gass, 1997). Typically this is done according to ground rules that establish an atmosphere of trust, respect, equality, acceptance, and flexibility (Priest & Gass, 1997). Further, the discussion content should proceed from positive topics to negative ones, then return to a positive tone. This means that strengths, successes, and achievements, as well as mistakes or failures, are discussed.

In facilitating a leisure program through discussion, the leader usually poses open-ended questions. Plenty of time is allowed for participants to think and answer fully, all responses are acknowledged, and many are paraphrased to be sure everyone is understood. Sometimes such tools as the "talking stick" are passed around the group in order to invite quiet participants to enter the discussion without putting them on the spot and to stop participants who monopolize the discussion.

Using the **frontloading** facilitation technique means you hold the discussion before the recreation program. Frontloading involves punctuating the key learning points in advance of the recreation experience (Priest & Gass, 1997) rather than discussing the experience afterward. Sometimes this includes asking participants motivation questions that help them

Group discussion is an unstructured form of facilitation that encourages participants to consider a leisure program experience and transfer what was learned from it to other aspects of their lives.

think about what they want to experience during the program. Frontloading experiences can be thought of as programs themselves, where the goal is to prepare participants for the program in advance.

A final facilitation technique we'll consider is giving feedback. **Feedback** is verbal and nonverbal commenting on the behavior of others. Good feedback is descriptive rather than evaluative, and it is solicited rather than imposed. It is specific, well intended, and well timed (Russell, 2005). For example, "This activity seems to be challenging for everyone" allows recipients to use the information in a way that is most appropriate to them, and "I don't understand why you took off your life jacket" politely requests a positive change in behavior. For more information on this topic, see "Group Discussion Ideas," option 1, in chapter 11 of the CD-ROM.

In preparing to implement a recreation program, consider the role of facilitation techniques. If they would help ensure the safety and enjoyment of the experience, try to acquire staff with these abilities or this training.

Motivation

Another important function of staff is energizing participants, providing direction, and helping sustain recreational behavior (Russell, 2005). This is referred to as motivation. **Motivation** encompasses efforts to initiate, sustain, and stop behavior.

Because motivation is something within a person, we cannot describe the motivation of others directly. But research allows us to understand some principles of motivation. For example, positive reinforcement of a behavior increases the likelihood that the same behavior will be repeated, whereas negative reinforcement makes it more likely the same behavior will not be repeated.

There are two types of motivation: intrinsic and extrinsic. **Intrinsic motivation** means the behavior itself is positively reinforcing. Intrinsic motivation is doing something simply because it is interesting and personally meaningful. Ideally, all recreation participation is intrinsically motivated. Indeed, as Iso-Ahola (1982) explains, the participant initially chooses a recreation activity with the expectation that the activity will provide a feeling of freedom of choice and competence. On the other hand, **extrinsic motivation** comes from outside the behavior. The positive reinforcement is artificially established—a prize can be won, recognition can be awarded, weight can be

lost, others can be impressed. Recreation program staff are able to manage participant motivation through both intrinsic and extrinsic motivation.

Increasing intrinsic motivation revolves around strategies to increase participants' perceptions of success. Here are some suggestions (Weinberg & Gould, 1995; Bateman & Snell, 2002; Russell, 2005):

- Match skill levels of participants with the challenges required in the activity (e.g., use higher-classified white-water rivers for experienced boaters); see the box on page 163.

- Use verbal and nonverbal praise; this is especially important for participants who receive little recognition otherwise.

- Involve participants in decision making; people perceive they have greater competency when they make their own decisions, which in turn increases intrinsic motivation.

- Share the power with participants; confidence in one's worth is profoundly motivating.

- Be sure participants are ready to participate in the program (i.e., they have the knowledge and skills to enjoy a particular activity).

- Enhance the appropriateness of physical properties of the program setting (e.g., lower the lighting, turn up the music volume, and watch them dance!).

- Develop programs that include a planned progression. Some common examples are merit badges in scouting; A and B teams in sports; first, second, and third seats in an orchestra; and white, brown, and black belts in karate.

Using extrinsic motivation to guide recreation program interest and behavior is also common, especially when intrinsic motivation is not present. Here is a sampling of suggestions (Russell, 2005) for extrinsically motivating participation in recreation programs:

- Emphasize the status of the activity. Provide membership cards, mugs, uniforms, patches, T-shirts, well-maintained equipment, and other status symbols.

- Carefully employ well-planned and well-controlled competition. Although it runs the risk of going too far and becoming demotivating, competition can be used as an interest builder

How to Keep Competition's Motivational Potential

1. Determine individual participant stress thresholds in competitive activities.
2. Provide reinforcements for effort, sportsmanship, cooperation, most-improved player, and so on, in addition to winning.
3. Match ability levels.
4. Distribute the possibility of winning by establishing more classes separating ability or age.
5. Avoid programming only for the skilled.
6. Handicap those who have achieved mastery.
7. Increase the number of winners.

For more information on this topic, see "Group Discussion Ideas," option 2, in chapter 11 of the CD-ROM.

(see "How to Keep Competition's Motivational Potential" on this page).

- Capitalize on people's desire to be part of a group. Peer pressure is a motivator in much the same way as announcing, "Only a few tickets left."
- Offer prizes and rewards directly associated with the activity; blue ribbons, door prizes, gold stars, free gifts, coupons, and certificates are the most common.

In preparing to implement a recreation program, consider the role of intrinsic and extrinsic motivation techniques. If they would help ensure the safety and enjoyment of the experience, try to acquire staff with these abilities or this training.

Group Dynamics

Recreation programs are usually implemented for people in groups. According to Niepoth (1983), such participant groups exist because of a common interest in a recreation expression. This means that recreation groups are likely to be higher in cohesiveness, morale, and productivity. Recreation groups also tend to have clearer norms for appropriate behavior and an explicit group structure. In other words, recreation groups often work better than other types of groups, such as those formed for accomplishing jobs.

But, suppose you are leading a small group of young adults on a tour of western national parks in Canada. Because some of the group's members have brought along more spending money than others, a splinter group forms. Those travelers with more spending money have begun to break off from the rest of the group for extra shopping and different restaurant choices. Some have even discussed leaving the tour for a three-day helicopter side trip (Russell, 2005).

Is this group effective in making it possible for the tour participants to enjoy the trip? Is there anything the trip leaders should do to improve the group? **Group dynamics** is the study and practice of improving group effectiveness. A successful tour group, chess club, scout troop, audience, and soccer team must have a quality of interaction among its members that enhances the recreational value of the experience. It is the responsibility of program staff to manage for the group's success.

There are several rules for leading successful groups that program staff can follow. These include the following (Russell, 2005):

- Group goals must be clearly understood, be relevant to the needs and interests of group members, and be highly committed to by every group member.
- Group members must be able to effectively communicate their ideas and feelings.
- Power and influence based on ability and expertise needs to be equitable throughout the group.
- Group members need to like each other, and every group member should want to continue as part of the group.
- Group problems must be resolved early and with minimal energy.
- There must be high interpersonal cohesion among group members.
- Controversy and conflict need to be interpreted by group members as a positive indication of the group's effort.

For more information on this topic, see "Group Discussion Ideas," option 3, in chapter 11 of the CD-ROM.

A successful tour group must have a quality of interaction among its members that enhances the recreational value of the experience. It is the responsibility of program staff to manage for this.

more fun when no one is fighting. Young adults enjoy a wilderness adventure program more when everyone feels confident in themselves and each other. Team members in lacrosse enjoy a higher-quality experience when winning and losing are put in proper perspective. The efforts of program staff to encourage all these behaviors are referred to as behavior management. **Behavior management** uses both preventive methods and discipline to guide recreation program participants' actions.

The idea of preventive behavior management is to minimize or prevent behavior difficulties before they occur. This basically means the leader monitors and responds to participants' emotions in a timely way—such as giving encouragement for feelings of self-doubt. In fact, one of the most important skills for the program leader in managing participants' behavior is appropriately responding to the actions and words that carry their emotions. If the leader gives understanding responses, a participant will be encouraged to go on with the activity. If the leader gives judgmental responses, a participant might resort to quitting the activity or throwing a temper tantrum. Table 11.1 highlights some types of responses of program leaders, according to Vinton and Farley (1979).

Beyond responding appropriately to participants, what are some specific preventive behavior management techniques? There are many, and which one you use depends on the situation. Here are some techniques used in many recreation program settings (Russell, 2005):

In preparing to implement a recreation program, consider the role of group dynamics techniques. If they would help ensure the safety and enjoyment of the experience, try to acquire staff with these abilities or this training.

Behavior Management

Participants behave in a wide variety of ways in recreation programs. Program staff work with children who fight and children who are afraid to fight, people who seek the spotlight and those who are shy, people who possess an exaggerated sense of confidence and those with no self-confidence at all, and people who lose their heads when they lose a game and others to whom defeat is of relative unimportance (Russell, 2005). Some program participants are afraid, angry, depressed, sad, anxious, doubtful, and frustrated, while other program participants feel awe, delight, pleasure, excitement, enthusiasm, tenderness, and happiness. Behavior in the recreation program is influenced by all these feelings.

Program staff are interested not so much in controlling others' behaviors (although sometimes this may be needed) but in guiding people's actions in order to maximize the recreational experiences of the program. Children in an after-school program have

- *Structure the physical environment.* Arranging the program space appropriately (chairs in a circle, proper lighting, adequate room size) can increase the likelihood of desired behaviors.

- *Clearly state privileges.* If participants understand the acceptable behavior limits in the program, they won't be tempted to test them;

TABLE 11.1

Types of Responses and Program Participant Reactions

Response type	Defined	Participant's reaction
Judging	Placing a negative evaluation on the participant	Feels put down
Topping	A form of one-upmanship	Feels deflated and unimportant
Giving advice	Suggesting what possible action can be taken to solve a problem	Usually ignores the advice if she doesn't first feel accepted and understood
Interpreting	Giving facts and opinions intended to give insights to the situation	May better understand that his behavior is not typical for the situation
Understanding	Active listening	Opens the door to further communication

Adapted from D.A. Vinton & E.M. Farley, 1979.

yet too many rules will encourage rebellious behavior.

- *Clarify benefits of desirable behavior.* Point out the positive consequences of good behavior.

- *Clarify consequences of undesirable behavior.* The enforcement of consequences should be immediate, nonpunitive, and consistent.

- *Model the behavior.* Continually display the behaviors expected of others.

- *Create contracts.* Establish a written or verbal agreement with each participant, stating the expected behavior and the resulting benefit.

- *Use regulated permission.* Provide socially acceptable outlets for undesirable behavior, such as encouraging a child to punch a boxing bag instead of another child.

- *Tolerate some undesirable behavior.* Too much attention paid to undesirable behavior may only encourage more undesirable behavior.

- *Use nonverbal cues.* Before responding verbally, use eye contact, a frown, or your body position to discourage undesirable behavior.

- *Change the activity.* Change to another activity or modify the current activity in order to either increase or reduce the challenge.

- *Use time-out procedures.* Place the person exhibiting the undesirable behavior in a temporary and separate location from the rest of the program participants.

Although well-planned and well-led recreation programs that match the needs and interests of participants go a very long way toward minimizing the probability of behavioral problems, behavior requiring discipline can occur. If disruptive behavior is not adequately dealt with, it can ultimately diminish the value of the experience for all participants.

"**Discipline** is a set of assertive methods used in behavior management to maintain orderly behaviors" (Russell, 2005, p. 186). Discipline can include direct instruction to enforce compliance as well as the use of punishment. When punishment is necessary, such as in situations involving safety, it should be used with caution—and only as a last resort. Many leisure service organizations provide specific guidelines that outline procedures the program staff should follow in cases requiring punishment. For more information on this topic, see worksheet 11.2 in chapter 11 of the CD-ROM.

In preparing to implement a recreation program, consider the role of behavior management techniques. If they would help ensure the safety and enjoyment of the experience, try to acquire staff with these abilities or this training.

Recruiting, Training, and Retaining Staff

Because staff persons ultimately determine program success or failure, programmers are frequently involved in staffing responsibilities. You will often need to select people to fill jobs, train and orient new staff, and evaluate employee performance. This is called **staffing** (Russell, 2005), and your primary goal is to obtain a "good fit" between the person and the job. Your responsibilities for staffing will vary from organization to organization and likely from program to program. Regardless, typical tasks include recruitment, selection, training, supervision, and performance reviews.

The first step is to prepare and approve job descriptions in order to attract a pool of qualified applicants. After the application materials are received, interviews, reference checks, and sometimes testing may be undertaken (e.g., for lifeguards). These recruitment efforts ultimately lead to the hiring decision. After the selections are complete, new staff persons are oriented to the job, coworkers, and the organization. Often, they must also be trained in leading the program activities. Training of staff may occur away from the job, using such resources as conferences and workshops. Or training may take place on the job, either before the program begins or while it is under way. Program staff must also be supervised while performing their duties. Staff supervision means guiding people to perform well—communicating with them and handling problems. Finally, the staffing process culminates in conducting performance reviews. This involves conferring with your staff on areas of satisfactory performance and areas that need improvement.

A special resource for staffing recreation programs is volunteers. **Volunteers** are individuals who perform services without financial reward. When volunteers provide programming services such as coaching a masters swim team, driving backpackers to the trail head, teaching about the Internet at the senior center, and helping hospital patients write letters, they extend an organization's programming services tremendously. For example, with volunteer assistance it may be possible for you to initiate a teen theater workshop program, sponsor a bicycle race, provide vegetable-growing classes at the town garden plots, raise funds for an arts day camp, or

Successful management of volunteers must include formal and informal recognition.

mail out brochures promoting the new spa services at the health club.

The staffing process of recruitment, selection, training, supervision, and reviewing is exactly the same for program volunteers as for paid staff. However, there is one special consideration for managing volunteers that is perhaps unique. Successful management of volunteers must include formal and informal recognition. To reward and retain positive volunteer contributions, systems for their recognition must be developed (Russell, 2005). Some commonly applied strategies are identifying volunteers with badges or uniforms, holding award meetings, featuring volunteers in organization newsletters, awarding certificates, sending letters of appreciation, and sponsoring volunteer parties or picnics.

Summary

This chapter focuses on staff resources for recreation programs. You should understand the following key points:

- Staffing resources are needed at every recreation program planning step, including preparation, implementation, and evaluation.

- At the program implementation step, both supervisors and activity leaders are needed to deliver the program events and services to participants.

- Determining the need for program staff includes decisions about both the number of staff and the credentials desired.

- Program staff duties can be categorized into technical, human relations, and conceptual functions.

- Specific program staff duties within these categories include participant facilitation, participant motivation, group dynamics, and behavior management.

- The staffing process for both paid and volunteer program staff entails recruitment, selection, training, supervision, and performance reviews.

- Systems of recognition are also important when staffing with volunteers.

For more information on this topic, see "Group Discussion Ideas," option 4, in chapter 11 of the CD-ROM. •

Glossary

supervisors—Trained staff who oversee facilities or the efforts of activity leaders.

activity leaders—Trained staff who work directly with patrons in facilitating the leisure program experience.

participant-to-staff ratio—The number of participants in a program with respect to the number of staff for the program; usually expressed as so many participants per staff member (e.g., 20:1).

facilitation techniques—Methods to ensure that participants have the best experience possible in the program.

discussion—The program group verbalizes its reactions to an activity.

frontloading—Briefing about the key points in advance of the recreation program.

feedback—Verbal and nonverbal commenting on the behavior of others.

motivation—Those factors that initiate, sustain, and stop behavior.

intrinsic motivation—The behavior itself is positively reinforcing.

extrinsic motivation—Something outside the behavior is positively reinforcing.

group dynamics—The study and practice of improving group effectiveness.

behavior management—Using both preventive methods and discipline to guide recreation program participants' actions.

discipline—A set of assertive methods used to maintain orderly behaviors.

staffing—Selecting people to fill jobs, placing people in jobs and orienting them, training new staff, and evaluating their performance.

volunteers—Individuals who perform services without financial reward.

References

Adventures Cross-Country. (2004a). ARCC trip leader positions. Retrieved May 27, 2006, from www.adventurescrosscountry.com/trip_lead.htm.

Adventures Cross-Country. (2004b). What is ARCC? Retrieved May 27, 2006, from www.adventurescrosscountry.com/about.htm.

American Camp Association. (n.d.). Standards at a glance. Retrieved May 27, 2006, from www.acacamps.org/parents/accreditation/stdsglance.htm.

Bateman, T.S., & Snell, S.A. (2002). *Management: Competing in the new era*. New York: McGraw-Hill.

Cal Recreational Sports. (n.d.). Retrieved May 27, 2006, from University of California at Berkeley Web site: http://calbears.berkeley.edu/insidepage.aspx?uid=33170984-95da-450f-8a3d-e9b23bb0b60e.

Hersey, P., & Blanchard, K.H. (1982). *Management of organizational behavior: Utilizing human resources* (4th ed.). Englewood Cliffs, NJ: Prentice Hall.

Iso-Ahola, S.E. (1982). Intrinsic motivation: An overlooked basis for evaluation. *Parks and Recreation, 17*(2), 32-33.

Moiseichik, M., Hunt, S., & Macchiarelli, D. (1992). Recreation sports officials: Contractors or employees? *Journal of Park and Recreation Administration, 10*(1), 62-70.

Montecito Sequoia Summer Family Resort. (2006). Job descriptions. Retrieved May 27, 2006, from www.resortjobs.com/do/details/238.

Niepoth, E.W. (1983). *Leisure leadership: Working with people in recreation and park settings.* Englewood Cliffs, NJ: Prentice Hall.

Priest, S., & Gass, M.A. (1997). *Effective leadership in adventure programming.* Champaign, IL: Human Kinetics.

Russell, R.V. (2005). *Leadership in recreation* (3rd ed.). New York: McGraw-Hill.

UNESCO. (2006). World heritage. Retrieved May 27, 2006, from http://whc.unesco.org/en/about.

Vinton, D.A., & Farley, E.M. (1979). *Camp training series, module 5: Dealing with camper behavior.* Lexington: University of Kentucky; available from American Camp Association, Martinsville, IN.

Weinberg, R.S., & Gould, D. (1995). *Foundations of sport and exercise psychology.* Champaign, IL: Human Kinetics.

Westerville Parks and Recreation Department. (2003). *Winter 2003-2004* [Catalog]. Westerville, OH: City of Westerville.

CHAPTER 12

Program Monitoring

In this chapter, you can look forward to the following:

- Discovering the importance of program monitoring
- Learning how to manage registration and reservation information
- Learning the advantages of participant program orientation
- Discovering how to assess the effectiveness of a program promotional campaign
- Understanding the value of databases in marketing to user groups
- Becoming familiar with the common methods and tools for keeping program records
- Appreciating the value of keeping accurate and thorough program records

al Recreational Sports, which represents the recreational sports opportunities at the University of California at Berkeley, features a wide array of programming services, including aquatics, fitness, group exercise, intramural sports, sport clubs, open recreation, outdoor, martial arts, mind and body, massage, and youth programs. Its urban location allows for a relationship with the nearby community, providing opportunities not only for Cal Berkeley students but also for the city of Berkeley and surrounding areas. Such an approach necessitates systems to monitor programs. For example, monitoring programs for safety and security includes requiring proof of membership (all users carry identification cards) and providing supervision for all activities (Cal Recreational Sports, n.d.).

Monitoring a group exercise class for safety and security might include requiring proof of identity.

Program monitoring involves a system of checks and balances that allows for the smooth operation of programs. Any monitoring system developed for a program needs to be efficient and effective in a way that does not interrupt a program unless absolutely necessary. All programs should be monitored, and the system for such monitoring should be incorporated into the training of all staff. For more information on this topic, see "Group Discussion Ideas," option 3, in chapter 12 of the CD-ROM.

The monitoring systems you develop are intended to prevent issues that arise from becoming eligible for crisis management. This chapter shows how programs are monitored and describes several advanced technology packages tailored to leisure service delivery that can make program monitoring easy. For more information on this topic, see worksheet 12.3 in chapter 12 of the CD-ROM.

The Importance of Program Monitoring

Program monitoring allows programmers to regularly check progress and proper implementation of services. Once a program monitoring system is in place, program success is reviewed regularly. As with summative and formative evaluation (discussed in chapter 14), information noted in reports and program files allows for changes in both current and future programs. For example, it may be noted that there were too many participants in a fitness program, and the new program could adjust the total number of individuals allowed to register for the next class.

Evidence from program monitoring reports may also provide information about safety or a problem associated with a program. The greater the documentation, the greater the chance of solving such problems when they arise. It is also much easier to hold parties accountable for what occurred in a program if there is sufficient documentation.

Through program monitoring, staff receive a cross-sectional view of program success, typically in terms of goals achievement, budget, performance, efficiency, effectiveness, and stewardship. We'll review each of these elements in turn.

Goals Achievement

Program monitoring allows for the review of goals and objectives attainment. Once goals are set and measurable objectives determined, they may be checked to determine if they are being met. The box on this page shows a sample of some initiatives for monitoring taken in the facilities division of the Westerville Parks and Recreation Department. These and other mechanisms allow program staff to continually review their goals and track progress in their programs on a regular basis.

Budget

A system of monitoring also enables cost analysis and tracking. In this way, programmers may track the budget and make adjustments as necessary to expand or reduce services according to budgetary feasibility. As demonstrated in table 12.1, budget tracking allows a supervisor to see the financial status of each program monthly, quarterly, biannually, or annually. By

---

City of Westerville Parks and Recreation Department: Major Initiatives for 2004 for the Facilities Division

- Develop benchmark reports on pass retention rates, online registration versus walk-in, peak community center usage times.
- Develop matrix schedule for all recreation facility inspection requirements.
- Develop and document preventive maintenance schedule.
- Implement bulk purchasing procedures.
- Implement the RecTrac facility scheduling module.
- Update all operations manuals including EAP, aquatics, money handling, opening, closing, maintenance procedures.
- Track cost the benefit of the follow-up promotional incentive for past Community Center pass holders.
- Implement budgeting tracking system in conjunction with the AS400.
- Complete quarterly walk through audit checks at each recreation facility.

City of Westerville, March 2000.

TABLE 12.1

Budget Tracking for Programs for Fiscal Year FY2004

Account number	Account description	FY2004 original budget ($)	FY2004 adjusted budget ($)	2004 YTD actual ($)	% of budget actual	2003 YTD current encumbrances ($)	Unencumbered/ Unexpended balance ($)
		FUND 128 P&R INCOME TAX DEPT 51 PARKS & RECREATION DIV 60 RECREATION ADMINISTRATION					
138–5460–334.60–00	Arts programs	58,500	58,500	30,305	51.80	0	28,195
138–5460–334.60–02	Arts events sponsorship	5,500	5,500	5,350	97.27	0	150
138–5460–334.61–00	Children's support programs	24,200	24,200	14,576	60.23	0	9,624

(CONTINUED)

TABLE 12.1 *(CONTINUED)*

Account number	Account description	FY2004 original budget ($)	FY2004 adjusted budget ($)	2004 YTD actual ($)	% of budget actual	2003 YTD current encumbrances ($)	Unencumbered/ Unexpended balance ($)
138-5460-334.62-00	Children's programs	42,000	42,000	19,490	46.40	0	22,510
138-5460-334.63-00	Preschool programs	55,000	55,000	29,494	53.63	0	25,506
138-5460-334.64-00	Youth programs	153,500	153,500	148,376	96.66	0	5,124
138-5460-334.65-00	Teen programs	6,000	6,000	5,426	90.43	0	574
138-5460-334.66-00	Adult programs	15,000	15,000	6,520	43.47	0	8,480
138-5460-334.67-00	Special interest programs	7,500	7,500	4,977	66.36	0	2,523
138-5460-334.68-00	Sports programs	188,500	188,500	111,557	59.18	0	76,943
138-5460-334.69-00	Fitness & wellness programs	0	0	0	0.00	0	0
138-5460-334.70-00	Miscellaneous revenues	13,000	13,000	7,049	54.22	0	5,951
138-5460-452.51-10	S & W regular FT	315,666	315,666	131,002	41.50	0	184,664
138-5460-452.51-11	PT wages	232,575	232,575	61,860	26.60	0	170,715
138-5460-452.51-12	Overtime	3,000	3,000	432	14.40	0	2,568
138-5460-452.51-13	Other pay	4,300	4,300	972	22.60	0	3,328
138-5460-452.51-14	Longevity pay	3,275	3,275	0	0.00	0	3,275
138-5460-452.51-15	Pay in lieu of vacation	1,250	1,250	0	0.00	0	1,250
138-5460-452.51-25	Personal services	75,890	75,890	26,323	34.69	0	49,567
138-5460-452.51-26	PERS city liab. RC Sec 145	0	0	4,187	0.00	0	−4,187
138-5460-452.51-30	Police pension	0	0	0	0.00	0	0

DETAIL BUDGET SUMMARY FOR FISCAL YEAR FY2004							
Account number	Account description	FY2004 original budget ($)	FY2004 adjusted budget ($)	2004 YTD actual ($)	% of budget actual	2003 YTD current encumbrances ($)	Unencumbered/ Unexpended balance ($)
138-5460-452.51-40	Unemployment compensation	0	0	0	0.00	0	0
138-5460-452.51-45	Workers' compensation	10,634	10,634	2,810	26.42	3,434	4,390
138-5460-452.51-60	Hospitalization	63,709	63,709	22,916	35.97	0	40,793
138-5460-452.51-65	Life insurance	1,281	1,281	450	35.13	0	831

Account number	Account description	FY2004 original budget ($)	FY2004 adjusted budget ($)	2004 YTD actual ($)	% of budget actual	2003 YTD current encumbrances ($)	Unencumbered/ Unexpended balance ($)
138-5460-452.51-70	Dental insurance	5,401	5,401	2,085	38.60	0	3,316
138-5460-452.51-80	Vision insurance	1,657	1,657	637	38.44	0	1,020
138-5460-452.51-90	Medicare	8,121	8,121	2,795	34.42	0	5,326
* Personal services		726,759	726,759	256,469	35.29	3,434	466,856
138-5460-452.60-01	Budget contingency acct.	0	0	0	0.00	0	0
138-5460-452.60-05	Office supplies	1,300	1,547	451	29.15	49	1,047
138-5460-452.60-10	Cleaning supplies	100	100	0	0.00	0	100
138-5460-452.60-30	Fuel, oil, & lubricants	800	800	245	30.63	0	555
138-5460-452.60-35	Clothing & uniforms	2,500	3,592	1,092	30.40	1,586	914
138-5460-452.60-40	Printing & reproduction supp.	2,900	2,900	467	16.10	851	1,582
138-5460-452.60-45	Concession supplies/food	12,000	12,513	4,724	37.75	2,554	5,235
138-5460-452.60-60	Paint & painting supplies	100	100	0	0.00	0	100
138-5460-452.60-65	Building materials & supplies	1,000	1,012	12	1.19	0	1,000
138-5460-452.60-80	Small tools & minor equipment	2,000	2,156	1,383	64.15	0	773
138-5460-452.69-80	Other operating supplies	4,000	4,808	1,299	27.02	314	3,195
138-5460-452.69-88	Participants' T-shirts	14,000	15,270	9,043	59.22	1,910	4,317
138-5460-452.69-89	Program expenses & trips	65,000	66,974	14,288	21.33	12,902	39,784
* Supplies & materials		105,700	111,772	33,004	29.53	20,166	58,602
138-5460-452.70-01	Budget contingency acct.	0	0	0	0.00	0	0
138-5460-452.70-09	P&R contract. entertainment	13,000	13,000	2,169	16.68	5,470	5,361
138-5460-452.70-20	Other prof. & consult. services	5,000	5,000	0	0.00	0	5,000

Reprinted, by permission, from Westerville Parks and Recreation Department, 2004a.

tracking budget totals and the percentage of budget available, it is possible to determine how well the budget target is being met.

Performance

How well individuals perform a particular task, attainment of scores, and other measures may also be compared from program to program or year to year. For example, how many participants passed swimming lessons this year as compared to last year?

Such participant performance standards are created in the first program planning step when objectives are stated. As well, performance standards for staff are usually established at the time of hiring and in regular reviews. The following areas are most suitable for developing guidelines for tracking performance:

- Participation increases
- Facility and area maintenance time decreases
- Participation return rate increases
- Accident rate decreases
- Employee retention increases
- Employee sick days decreases
- Improvement of efficiency of program delivery
- Expansion and effectiveness of marketing program

These examples allow for the development of tracking mechanisms that allow programmers to show progress or determine weaknesses and needs for improvement.

Efficiency

Are resources being used efficiently? A program monitoring system allows for certain measures of efficiency to be tracked and compared. Goals may then be revised to allow for changes and adjustments. For example, time taken to enter program registrations may be monitored; efficient handling of questions for online enrollment may reduce participant inquiries for assistance; time taken to register and travel, along with other considerations, may be monitored and then reduced by switching to a new agency; and facility usage may be monitored to determine the most efficient hours of operation.

Data from an annual art fair event such as this can be compared from year to year.

The Programming Process: Helping the Internet Help Program Participants

As you can easily judge from the many examples in this chapter, the Westerville Parks and Recreation Department's use of the Internet for monitoring programs is extensive. Here are more examples of how this award-winning department's Web site improves the efficiency of online program enrollments. These examples also demonstrate the FAQ strategy (frequently asked questions) of improving potential program participant understanding in using the Internet service:

- **I do not have a computer at home or do not have access to the Internet. May I still register online?** Yes. You may register online by utilizing the computers at the Westerville Public Library (126 South State Street), but you still must submit an online registration form at the Westerville Community Center first. The library has 23 computers in the Adult Tech Center, 7 computers in the youth area, and several catalog computers online that are available to the public at no charge on a first-come, first-serve basis. Printing cost is 10 cents per page. Library hours are Mondays through Thursdays, 9:00 a.m. to 9:00 p.m.; Fridays and Saturdays, 9:00 a.m. to 6:00 p.m.; and Sundays, 1:00 to 5:00 p.m.

- **When I click on the "$" note button to find out the cost of a class, why does it say "applicable discounts not applied"?** This statement is part of the online registration software package that is used by other city agencies who apply discounts for varied reasons. This statement alerts users that the discount is not applied here, but is applied later in the registration process. Westerville Parks and Recreation does not offer discounts; therefore, this statement does not apply.

- **I registered for a class online and now I want to change classes or cancel the class and get a refund. May I do that online?** No. You can only register for classes online. If you need to change classes or cancel a class, please come in person to the registration desk at the Community Center (350 N. Cleveland Avenue). You may change your registration online prior to proceeding to "Checkout."

- **One family member who will be taking a class has special needs. How do I notify staff so needed special accommodations can be made?** After putting the class you want in your shopping cart, click on "Shopping Cart." The classes you register for will be listed with a note under each that reads, "Update Note/Info for Staff." Click on this note under the class where you require special assistance, and type in a note for staff describing the assistance required before you proceed to checkout.

Westerville Parks and Recreation, 2004b.

Effectiveness

If something is efficient, is it effective? For example, opening the pool to a maximum number of swimmers may be an efficient way to run a pool in terms of gaining the maximum amount of funds; however, crowds may prevent the pool from running effectively because mishaps may occur within crowded conditions. When considering changes to make a program more effective, you must take into account how the changes will affect client satisfaction, staff ease in programming, safety, skill attainments and other variables. Therefore, an increase in the number in an aquatics class that results in compromising safety results in failure to meet program effectiveness criteria.

Stewardship

Stewardship implies that programmers will protect human and natural resources, spend funds wisely, and provide for the overall health of a community. The degree to which fiscal and environmental resources are being used may be monitored through environmental impact statements or fiscal reporting mechanisms. These and other monitoring measures may determine the degree to which the funds entrusted to programmers are used. It is the overall responsibility of leisure service organizations to safeguard the land or fiscal resources entrusted to their care through taxes, community funds, memberships, or consumer spending.

Stewarding the environment is not just "a walk in the park!"

© Will & Deni McIntyre/CORBIS.

Specific Program Monitoring Systems

This section identifies monitoring systems used by many leisure service organizations. Monitoring systems often serve a primary purpose, but some also create a **database**, or an organized body of information, that may be used for ongoing monitoring and evaluation.

Registration and Reservations

A typical leisure service delivery system, whether it is a public agency emphasizing parks or a commercial enterprise emphasizing membership-based programs, may operate most effectively with an efficient system for reservations and registration.

A **registration system** provides a way to sign participants up for programs in advance. It can be done via manual or computerized systems. A **reservation system** refers to declaring priority for the use of recreation space, such as picnic shelters and meeting rooms. Table 12.2 identifies the variables that may be tracked through the information provided through a registration system.

Many combinations of detail can be studied with a database that contains this information. In considering these data, what are the forms of monitoring that may take place? Here are just a few ways a programmer may monitor a program using a registration database:

- *Distance from program.* How far did each person travel to participate in a program? This information gives the program personnel an idea about where to distribute future programs.

- *Demographic details.* What is the nature of the people who participate in each program? Are there any gaps in programming for specific age groups? What are the market targets being reached, and what are their characteristics?

- *Roster information.* How many people have been enrolling, and is there a waiting list that provides an indicator of demand for services? These figures are valuable when planning for unmet market need.

- *Fluctuations in participation.* Are there changes in the amount of participation or the type of participant? If so, do these changes

TABLE 12.2

Example of a Program Registration Form

Name of registrant:		Name of child or other family member registering:	
Today's date:		Age:	
Home address:		Grade:	
City:		Phone:	
State:		E-mail:	
Zip:		Web address:	
Program code:		Payment method:	
Program title:		Amount:	
Program date:		Affiliation:	
Program time:		Other:	

indicate trends that should be tracked? A programmer may find this information useful for future marketing and for planning changes in program offerings. Moving a program from one center to another may be useful; changing the type of program to meet higher demand for services is another issue.

Several credible recreation management software companies offer efficient and highly detailed registration and reservation systems, and you may benefit from using a canned program. Others develop their own computer capability and add to it as needed. In addition, a corporate or government program may need to use what is available in that jurisdiction because programs may need connectivity to other organizational functions outside of a department or division.

Examples of computerized registration and reservation systems include the following:

- *RecWare*. This system handles registration, reservations, maintenance planning, scheduling, timetables, and budgets and has a number of other capabilities. The program may be custom designed to meet agency needs, and it may be adjusted to suit expansion of programs and services.
- *RecTrac*. Similar to RecWare, this program is used by Westerville to monitor recreation.

This system is used by private and commercial clients as well. For more information, see the box on page 178.

- *Class*. This registration and permitting system is available for use in the public, private, non-profit, and commercial sectors.
- *Custom Built System*. Benefits of this form of database is that an agency can customize the software to accommodate its unique needs.

The box on page 178 shows one way a system has been implemented in leisure programs. In the box, the city of Decatur, Georgia, announces the implementation of RecTrac. This program integrates all operations into one seamless process that creates an enormous database for the system. More details about the RecTrac and RecWare systems can be found later in this chapter under Program Contracts in the section on computer-based records.

Participant Program Orientation

Another mechanism for monitoring programs is to provide participants and related groups, such as coaches and parents, with an orientation before and during participation. This is a form of **program control**, whereby checks and balances are installed to ensure accuracy, safety, and fiscal responsibility. For example, parental pressure and disrespectful behavior have been noted as problematic aspects of youth sports programs, two of perhaps many factors that contribute to sport mishaps. Training and development for volunteer coaches as well as orientation meetings for parents and other adults help set codes of conduct to avoid conflicts that defeat the recreational purpose of the program. Sport programmers benefit from sharing requirements for proper conduct of coaches, team members, individual members, parents, and other adults. An orientation meeting provides rules and regulations within the sport itself, behavior codes, expectations for volunteers, support mechanisms provided by the sponsor, rosters, practice schedules, and other important information items.

An orientation program prepares people for participation, analyzes their expectations, and ensures safety in the implementation of the program. For example, many outdoor recreation programs require preparation in the form of proper clothing, equipment, and food. Participants ordinarily do not come to a program with all the knowledge they need about preparing for such programs. An orientation program will alleviate many of these issues and help prepare staff for ways to work with problem clients.

A typical orientation schedule for a soccer program may include general information, introduction of key members, contact data, and other important information. Then specific sport information, schedules, rules and conduct information, equipment needed, and coordinating information may be shared.

Marketing Program Delivery

Another way to establish a monitoring process is through ongoing assessment of the marketing plan. How effective is the **promotional campaign** message delivered on the Web site or through print and broadcast media? The number of visitors to a Web site and analysis of where these individuals come from and what they sign up for are an effective means of monitoring how the message is received.

In addition, feedback may automatically be built into the promotional message, such as a code for a discount, a survey about where the client heard about the program, the submittal of coupons, or early-bird sign-ups known only by those who were sent the message.

It is important to gauge the response to the promotional message that is sent. How effective are mailed brochures, online registration, program-specific fliers, and other mechanisms to advertise a program or an array of services? Identifying the most efficient and effective message is an important feature of a marketing plan. The plan identifies the goals, and monitoring may gauge to what extent the goals are being met.

Such **database marketing** is also an effective way to analyze the nature of the users through information collected in the normal process of interacting with participants. As noted earlier in the chapter, specific information gained through registration generates a profile of the typical participant and allows for adjustments to be made.

Mining the program database achieves answers to many questions, a few of which are noted here:

* What are the characteristics of the average participant in the program?
* What groups are not being served in the program?
* Are there any characteristics of the users that need further attention when developing programs?

What prompts people to select a particular program or destination?

- Where do most participants come from for the program?
- Are there any participation patterns that require adjustment?
- Are there any common complaints that need to be taken care of?
- Are there any potentially dangerous situations that need to be addressed?
- Is supervision adequate for each program?
- Are there any lifestyle features that affect program planning?
- Have there been significant declines in programs when changes have been made?
- Is there anything to suggest that a program may have reached the decline phase of the program life cycle?

The database is rich with detail regarding the characteristics of the participant, the nature of the program, the nature of scheduling the program, the instructor or leader needed, and many other factors. Using existing data is of essential value in program planning.

The database can reveal where gaps exist and identify possible nonparticipant groups. Of course, nonparticipants are harder to reach, but a database search will reveal who they may be, and then singular strategies may be employed to reach them.

Other Program Monitoring Systems

The successful programmer of organized leisure experiences must accomplish some desk work—it simply cannot be avoided. The most typical reason for hanging out at your office desk is record keeping. To do it well, thorough and up-to-date program records must continually be kept. To enjoy doing it, a systematic approach with helpful tools is needed.

Keeping program records may not directly benefit the recreation program you're working on at that moment or even the one set to start next week. Think of record keeping in general as helping the overall success of your organization and your future programs. For this, you must keep a whole series of accurate records.

Some records relate to personnel: job descriptions, resumes, copies of certifications, letters of recommendation, job performance reviews, hourly time cards, and disciplinary action records for your program staff and leaders. You must also retain insurance records, facility maintenance records, equipment inventories, facility rental receipts, and telephone and fax records.

Keep parent permission forms for minors, parent sign-in and sign-out sheets, the agency's risk management plan, and documentation of program marketing and promotional efforts. Maintain and file the program plan itself (see chapter 9), as well as the program evaluation reports that you'll learn about in part IV of the book. For more information on this topic, see "More Options for Individual Programming Practice," option 1, in chapter 12 of the CD-ROM.

Preregistration records help assure that participants are matched with appropriate program levels, such as swim levels.

For this chapter, however, we focus on the most commonly required records during program implementation: registration, accident and incident, expenditures, attendance, and program contracts. We conclude the discussion with ways to use computers to make these records easier to prepare and more accurate and reliable.

Registration Records

You will often want participants to register in advance for programs. Many reasons exist for this program implementation decision, including the need to make sure there are not too many participants in a class, which creates a safety hazard, or too few participants in a class, resulting in a waste of instructor time and expense. For example, because the swim instruction program at Westerville carries a participation fee ($35 for residents), preregistration is also an effective way of collecting the money. As well, the registration process helps programmers assign clients to the appropriate swim level. The "tiny tot swim lessons" help 6- to 18-month-olds (along with a parent) become comfortable in the water, while "whale and shark swim lessons" are for older children who are learning more advanced skills, such as the butterfly stroke.

In other words, the ultimate point of program registration is to develop a list of persons qualified to be in the program. Also, if such a list does not enhance the program's ability to meet participant needs, then registration should not be undertaken. Not all programs benefit from participation registration.

Staff with the specific expertise and credentials (such as swim instructors) don't have to be contracted until the class fills.

Registration may be handled in several different ways, usually according to how an agency or business is equipped to carry out the process. Often, this is determined through a study of efficient and effective ways to handle those who register.

Central Location Registration

In-person program registration at a central location has historically been the most typical method used by recreation organizations. This central location is often the agency office or headquarters, but it can also be a recreation center, school building, or other facility. Designated staff and all registration materials are provided at this one location. In some cases an actual event is made of the process, with specific dates and times extended for conducting the registration.

The central location in-person method requires that plans be made and implemented for adequate parking, organized lineups, collecting and handling money, and perhaps even extra restrooms and accessibility solutions. Staff members who are working the centralized registration also need to be well informed about all the programs and able to find answers to questions they cannot answer themselves.

Program Location Registration

A variation of in-person registration at a central location is in-person registration at the program location. Participants enroll at the program site (e.g., the swimming pool, tennis court, or camp). This is perhaps a preferred method when it is important for potential participants to see the program site before signing up or when the event takes place for a limited time, such as one day. For example, it may be comforting if young children see the playground and all its exciting equipment and toys as part of registering for a summer day-camp program, or all the "loved ones" can be most efficiently registered for the "pet appreciation fair" at the park before the program begins. But because of its decentralized approach, this registration method usually means more work for staff and concern for such issues as how money is managed.

Mail-In Registration

In the mail-in method of program registration, participants complete a registration form and mail it, along with any payment required, to the agency. This method provides a centralized system that is equally accessible to everyone throughout the service area. It does not require transportation and is therefore convenient for clients. It is also more convenient for programmers because it allows for more staff flexibility in handling the registration forms and fees. However, registration by mail requires establishing policies about refunds if programs become filled, and confirmation of enrollment is either not possible or requires extra staff effort.

Telephone and Fax Registration

With the telephone method of registering for recreation programs, participants simply make a call, usually to the agency's main office. This improves on the mail-in method because staff members have an opportunity to interact with participants, answering their questions and passing on important information about program details. If a fee for the program is involved, however, collecting it over the telephone is difficult unless the agency accepts credit card payments. Similarly, the fax method of registration requires fee payment via credit card; but a staff member does not have to attend to the telephone, instead taking the faxes off the machine when convenient. On the other hand, interaction with program staff is not an option with this method.

The method of program registration used should be appropriate to the program itself. For example, registration for a fishing tournament would likely require a mail-in approach.

Computer-Based Registration

Finally, many organized leisure sponsors are now employing computer-based registration methods. A major convenience for people with Internet access, this method enables participants to register whenever they desire—usually 24 hours a day, seven days a week. Registrants also receive an automatic confirmation. A disadvantage of this method is that poorly designed Web sites can be frustrating to users and result in poor public relations for the agency. Further, this method typically requires the purchase of special computer software, a financial capability many agencies may not have.

To register for programs online, Westerville participants must initially complete an information card and submit it in person at the community center. For one year thereafter, they will be able to register for future programs by going to www.westerville.org and clicking on eServices, then Parks Online Registration. We discuss specific computer-assisted registration utilities at the end of this chapter.

Many leisure service organizations use multiple methods for program registration. Yet offering several options requires a well organized and thoroughly planned system, particularly through the ongoing reporting mechanisms that are available. For more information on this topic, see "Can You Solve This Programming Issue?" in chapter 12 of the CD-ROM.

Accident and Incident Reports

Recreation programs involve risks to health and safety. Even the most comprehensive, professionally prepared program can result in an **accident** or unanticipated **incident**. It is imperative to have a risk management plan in place that works toward a high level of safety and accident prevention. (We discuss such a plan in chapter 13.)

Most organizations rely on a variety of forms to manage program risks. Typically, assumption of risk forms, as well as limited liability waivers and medical releases, are used to help manage accidents and incidents that occur during programs.

These "in advance" forms can be helpful in communicating safety concerns to participants and as a result may reduce the frequency and severity of accidents, but they do not prevent accidents from occurring. They do not absolve you or your organization of negligence either. Only sound and safe program operations, thorough facility maintenance, and well-trained and responsible program leaders can protect against treating participants negligently.

Nonetheless, accidents will happen. Responding to them requires another category of reports and forms. You must keep accurate records of accidents that occur as well as records of noninjury forms of incidents, such as participant fights, racial or ethnic slurs, lost participants, disciplined participants, theft, and policy violations. Most leisure service organizations have prescribed accident and incident forms for you to use. See page 184 for a sample accident report form.

The computer-based registration process can store data effectively and efficiently for monitoring uses.

Accident and incident reports must be filled out as soon and as thoroughly as possible. All known details should be recorded. Further, on a regular basis (such as after each programming season), program supervisors should review all reports to identify patterns that could guide a program operation change or correction. For more information on this topic, see "Group Discussion Ideas," option 2, in chapter 12 of the CD-ROM.

Expenditures Records

Records that monitor expenses are also commonly kept in recreation programs. Regardless of the program budgeting approach used by your organization (see chapter 10), an accounting of money spent for supplies can be useful during implementation of the program to ensure that expenditures meet the budget. This can be as simple as a running list of the date, program supply purchased, and cost.

Attendance Records

Information should also be kept on how well your recreation programs are attended. Russell (1982, p. 277) stresses the importance of keeping attendance records:

> Elaborate attendance or activity participation records are also a popular documentation required in programming. In fact, programmers have a tendency to rely heavily on attendance records to define everything from the program's popularity to its ultimate value.

Attendance information also plays a useful role in program evaluation and therefore should be as efficiently kept as possible; but as you'll learn in the last section of the book, it is not the only source of determining program worth.

In some cases it can be difficult to keep precise participation statistics because of the size of the event or the program format. When program preregistration is required, it is easy to keep complete and accurate records of attendance, but when the format is open facility, such as on a playground, attendance can be much more difficult to determine. See page 185 for an attendance report form used for Westerville's Kids Fun Club summer program. In addition to keeping track of the number of children participating, the form also logs volunteer involvement. Program leaders complete this form on a weekly basis.

Program Contracts

Contract programming entails a legally sanctioned **contract** between a recreation agency and a commercial business firm. The commercial firm has a program service it specializes in performing, and the recreation organization contracts to purchase it. The most prevalent examples are the contracts signed for concession services such as park restaurants, boat docks, marinas, park bus lines, golf, and ice skating. Advantages to contract programming have also been found for preschool day care, skiing instruction, marathon road races, and outdoor adventure programming. According to Russell (1982), contracting for program services has gained popularity recently. It applies more to a deficit in facility or leadership resources than to a lack in fiscal resources because contract programming often carries a price tag.

Contract programming can operate the other way as well. Recreation agencies can provide the complete planning, organization, and implementation of recreation programs to other entities. For example, company picnics can be offered by a leisure services organization that, for an agreed-upon price, provide for all the details. Westerville residents can rent "picnic packs" containing a variety of sporting equipment suitable for picnics and family outings.

Further, recreation agencies can enter into contractual agreements with other organizations to jointly sponsor programs. For example, Ja-Mar North Travel Park in Florida contracts with local travel agents to jointly sponsor tours for guests.

For every type of contractual agreement, it is important that the details be precisely spelled out. The major details in most contracts include the length of the arrangement, with exact dates for specific actions; the responsibility for inspecting and maintaining program equipment and facilities; standards of performance; the charges arising from vandalism and accidents; the nature of the program advertising and promotion; and the nature of the cost of services based on a flat fee, a percentage of sales, or net profit (Kraus & Curtis, 2000).

Heydt (1986) outlines some important principles for program contracts:

- *Read and understand the contract.* Be sure you are clear on all its terms and conditions. A contract is an active document to be used, not left in the desk drawer. "Active" means a continual referral to points listed in the agreement

Sample Accident Report Form

Today's date _____   Time of accident _____

Name of injured _____   Parent/Guardian if minor_____

Address _____   Telephone number _____

Description of accident (How did it happen? What was the participant doing? What equipment was involved?)

Nature of injury (check all that apply)

___ scrape / abrasion   ___ puncture   ___ burn   ___ sprain

___ possible fracture   ___ cut / laceration   ___ bump / bruise

___ other _____

Location of injury (place an X on the body)

Staff member(s) first on scene _____

Immediate action taken _____

First aid provided _____

Subsequent action taken ___ home   ___ doctor   ___ hospital   ___ emergency squad

Were parents or guardians notified?   ___ yes ___ no

Name of person making report _____

Supervisor signature _____   *Date* _____

Sample Attendance Report Form, Westerville

Kids Fun Club Attendance Report

Kids Fun Club _____

Week of _____

	Monday		Tuesday		Wednesday		Thursday		Friday	
	a.m.	p.m.	a.m.	p.m.	a.m.	p.m.	a.m.	p.m.	a.m.	p.m.
Daily attendance										
Volunteers										

Total attendance this week:

Total attendance to date:

Total overall attendance:

Registrations this week:

Registrations to date:

Total registrations:

Volunteer's name   # of hours per week

_____   _____

_____   _____

_____   _____

_____   _____

_____   _____

_____   _____

_____   _____

From R. Russell and L. Jamieson, 2008, *Leisure Program Planning and Delivery* (Champaign, IL: Human Kinetics). Reprinted, by permission, from Westerville Parks and Recreation Department, 2004c.

Contracting an instructor for a water aerobics class can be a good source of revenue cost tracking.

so that details are provided in the planning and implementation of the program.

- *Document meetings and conversations.* Record details about the history of the contracting process, including all meetings, conversations, and modifications.

- *Keep a record of performance.* A detailed log of the contractor's performance should also be kept so that a proper case for breach of contract may be made if necessary. Track the contracted tasks to determine if they are being performed correctly and on schedule.

- *Head off performance failures early.* At the first signs of lack of performance, take positive steps to either solve the problem or terminate the contract.

For more information on this topic, see "More Options for Individual Programming Practice," option 3, in chapter 12 of the CD-ROM.

Computer-Based Records

Most recreation programmers use technology to help with all their record keeping. Leading the way is the computer, which can provide registration, attendance, accident and incident, expenditure, and contractual records assistance. Computers can make these records easier to prepare and more accurate to rely on. For more information on this topic, see worksheet 12.2 in chapter 12 of the CD-ROM.

For example, RecTrac is a **software** package that provides a full-service database system for leisure service organizations. Established by Vermont Systems, it consists of "fully integrated software that increases your efficiency and productivity, while providing management with extensive reporting and statistical data" (Vermont Systems, 2006b). RecTrac offers computer software that assists with program registration, facility reservation, photo ID and pass management, point-of-sale inventory and tickets, league scheduling, equipment and site scheduling, court reservations, locker rentals, and trip reservations (see figure 12.1 for a sample screen from the program).

Vermont Systems also offers WebTrac, an Internet-based tool applied to activity registration, tee-time reservations, facility reservations, pass registration and renewal, court reservations, trip reservations, locker rental and renewal, equipment and site rental, personal trainer reservations, and league schedules and standings (Vermont Systems, 2006c). The advantage of this software is it allows your clients 24/7 access to your services.

GISTrac is another source of computer-based assistance. Also available through Vermont Systems, GISTrac is an integrated mapping software that can help you analyze park usage and population characteristics, find suitable land for new parks, locate users according to specific characteristics, and create mailing labels for nonpark users (Vermont Systems,

2006a). Vermont Systems also offers GolfTrac (golf course management) and FinTrac (financial management) software.

A similar computer-based record-keeping tool is RecWare. Specific packages include RecWare Safari, RecWare Pro, and RecWare Online. For example, RecWare Safari is software that provides assistance with program enrollment, facility reservation, point of sale, membership sales, and financial reporting. At this writing, even more technology resource capabilities are expected as RecWare merges with Class Software Solutions.

Another tool is WebRegistration by AEK. The AEK WebRegistration system allows patrons to log on via the Internet to register for activities and classes (see figure 12.2), reserve facilities, and review their past registration activity. Programming staff can use the system to monitor registration activities as well as handle walk-in, mail-in, and phone-in registrations.

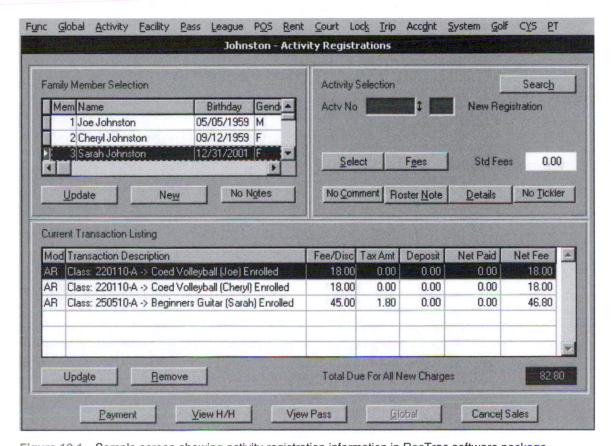

Figure 12.1 Sample screen showing activity registration information in RecTrac software package.

From Vermont Systems RecTrac Application.

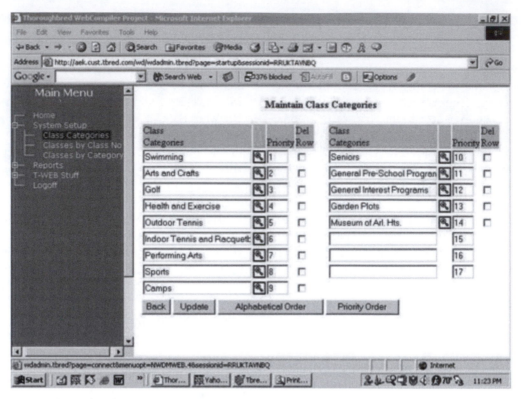

Figure 12.2 Sample registration screen from AEK's WebRegistration system.

Reprinted, by permission, from AEK Computers.

The advantage of this system is that the application is maintained at a central data center in New Jersey, thus your organization does not need to maintain the hardware, software, and security issues. For more information on this topic, see "More Options for Individual Programming Practice," option 2, and "Group Discussion Ideas," options 1 and 4, in chapter 12 of the CD-ROM. ◉

- Program monitoring infuses the system with information that drives necessary changes.

- Thorough and up-to-date program records must be kept at all times.

- The most commonly required program records are registration, accident and incident, expenditures, attendance, and program contracts.

Summary

This chapter focuses on the records programmers typically produce and manage. Most recreation programmers use technology, especially the computer, to help with their record keeping. You should understand the following key points:

- Creation of a consistent set of records allows for comparison from program to program or year to year.

- Reviewing program and operational success on a regular basis can be achieved through many means.

Glossary

program monitoring— Seeing that the program is accomplishing what is intended and customers are satisfied.

database—An organized body of related information.

registration system—A process of signing up individuals for programs, ranging from manual to computerized systems.

reservation system—A process of reserving space for events, programs, outdoor picnics, and other forms of recreation.

program control—The method by which checks and balances are installed to ensure accuracy, safety, and fiscal responsibility.

promotional campaign—A marketing plan that uses print and broadcast media to target markets and the general public.

database marketing—The use of existing programmatic information to create an understanding of the types of clients who use recreation programs and services.

accident—A mishap causing injury or death.

incident—A public disturbance.

contract—A legally binding agreement.

software—Computer-based procedures performing a database task.

References

AEK Computers. (2006). Hosted WebRegistration. Retrieved July 1, 2005, from www.aek-recreation-fund-accounting-software.com/datasheets/aekwebregistration_hosted.html.

Cal Recreational Sports. (n.d.). Students. Athletes. For life. Retrieved June 26, 2006, from University of California at Berkeley Web site: http://calbears.berkeley.edu.

City of Decatur. (2005). RecTrac registration system. Retrieved January 13, 2005, from www.decatur-ga.com/cgs_citysvcs_rec_rectrak.aspx.

City of Westerville. (2000). *Parks Recreation Open Space (PROS) 2000.* Columbus, OH: Edsell.

City of Westerville. (n.d.). Online registration FAQs. Retrieved February 16, 2007, from www.ci.westerville.oh.us/Default.aspx?tabid=116.

Heydt, M. (1986). Ten principles for contract administration. *Parks and Recreation, 21*(2), 48, 51.

Kraus, R.G., & Curtis, J.E. (2000). *Creative management in recreation, parks, and leisure services* (6th ed.). Boston: McGraw-Hill.

Russell, R.V. (1982). *Planning programs in recreation.* St. Louis: Mosby.

Vermont Systems. (2006a). GISTrac. Retrieved October 26, 2004, from www.vermontsystems.com/scripts/vsiweb.wsc/gistrac.htm?xxpref=gi.

Vermont Systems. (2006b). RecTrac. Retrieved October 26, 2004, from www.vermontsystems.com/scripts/vsiweb.wsc/rectrac.htm?xxpref=rt.

Vermont Systems. (2006c). WebTrac. Retrieved October 26, 2004, from www.vermontsystems.com/scripts/vsiweb.wsc/webtrac.htm?xxpref=wt.

Vermont Systems. (n.d.). Johnston: Activity registrations. Retrieved October 17, 2006, from www.vermontsystems.com/webtest/images/screens/rtactivityReg.jpg.

Westerville Parks and Recreation Department. (2004a). *Detail budget summary for fiscal year FY2004.* Westerville, OH: City of Westerville.

Westerville Parks and Recreation. (2004b). *The FAQs of On-line Registration: Frequently Asked Questions.* Westerville, OH: City of Westerville.

Westerville Parks and Recreation. (2004c). *Sample Attendance Report Form, Westerville.* Westerville, OH: City of Westerville.

CHAPTER 13

Managing Risk in Leisure Programs

In this chapter, you can look forward to the following:

- Learning how to ensure the reasonable safety of program participants
- Applying risk management practices for program conduct and supervision
- Developing a risk management manual for program operations
- Understanding the three key components of risk management in programming: the plan, conduct, and supervision

In 1937, through an act of Congress, the National Gallery of Art was formed "for the people of the United States of America" (National Gallery of Art, 2006). Since then, the gallery has been a centerpiece of the cultural experiences available to visitors to the nation's capital and to those who reside in the Washington, D.C., residential area. The vast collection, which features paintings, sculptures, works on paper, photographs, and decorative arts and architecture from American European and Northern European artists, is open 363 days a year at no charge to visitors. This art collection, considered one of the finest in the world, features more than 110,000 objects and images. Handling millions of people per year as well as protecting the collections requires a great deal of planning, particularly to deal with risk factors associated with crowds, persons with disabilities, theft and vandalism, varying visitor languages, groups of children, and other issues. In addition, plans for the safety and security of all federal buildings have been modified radically since 9/11 to complement national security issues.

People enjoy the many works of art at the National Gallery of Art in Washington.

Another important consideration in program implementation, then, is safety. Is the environment of the program activity safe? That is, is it free of unreasonable risk and foreseeable harm? Although the risk of injury or death is highest in such outdoor recreation activities as skydiving, mountain climbing, scuba diving, and hang gliding, or in team sports such as ice hockey, soccer, football, or basketball, the reality is that any recreational pursuit can become a safety hazard. Arts and crafts often use chemicals, power tools, and implements for cutting; travel can result in transportation accidents; and social and performance dance may produce all manner of body injuries. For more information on this topic, see "Group Discussion Ideas," option 1, in chapter 13 of the CD-ROM.

A programmer has not only a professional and moral duty to manage risk but also a legal obligation. Lawsuits have become a way of life in North America, and recreation programs have often been targeted. The courts have awarded sizable monetary compensation for such accidents as a sport camp trampoline accident resulting in paralysis from the chest down, the death of a boy hit in the head with a golf club swung by another class participant, a toy rocket launcher taking out a child's eye in an after-school program, and a head injury suffered by a college student during a beer company–sponsored spring break beach volleyball tournament (Russell, 1982). For more information on this topic, see worksheet 13.1 in chapter 13 of the CD-ROM.

Minimizing the threat of such accidents, and therefore the threat of lawsuits, is a part of the

Risky programming situations may result in lawsuits.

everyday life of programmers in leisure services. Yet it need not be overwhelmingly difficult. The secret is the management of risk. Risk managers generally define **risk** as the possibility of receiving harm from a hazard. Essentially there are two types of risk: (1) financial loss to the organization or agency and (2) injury to participants, users, visitors, volunteers, and employees (Kaiser & Robinson, 1999). Although programmers are certainly concerned about the fiscal risks of their program services (see chapter 10), our focus here is on risks associated with possible injury to program patrons. Your task as a programmer is to reduce the frequency and severity of injuries and to take care of known hazards and situations that may potentially lead to harm. Managing risk does not mean seeking to eliminate all risk; instead, it involves providing a balance and understanding the risks inherent within the program services you offer.

How do you accomplish this? Recreation program planners minimize the threat of accidents in these basic ways: by initiating and maintaining an up-to-date and systematic risk management plan, by ensuring that all programs are conducted with care and consistency, and by following established procedures governing the behavior of participants and their supervision by leaders.

Developing a Risk Management Plan

The process of managing risk is called **risk management**. Risk management means anticipating what might go wrong, planning ways to avoid something going wrong, and developing ways to respond appropriately when something does go wrong (Riddick & Russell, 1999). Having a risk management plan means you and your organization are taking a **proactive**, or forward thinking, approach to safety—it is a planned system for protecting against undue risk to patrons.

Reducing the incidence of accidents and the severity of injuries from these accidents is a shared responsibility between the park and recreation agency and the program participants. In situations where legal action is taken against you and your organization, a thorough and followed risk management plan is evidence of intent to act professionally, and this intent is usually all that is needed to avoid lawsuits awarded against you. Negligence law requires agencies to act with only reasonable care and prudence to prevent unreasonable harm to patrons, and correspondingly, the law stipulates that patrons must assume their own responsibility for making good behavior choices in recreation programs.

The risk management plan has three phases: anticipating, planning, and responding. These three phases are depicted in figure 13.1; let's consider each.

Anticipating

The first phase, anticipating, involves risk identification and assessment. Here the various types of hazards associated with recreation programs and services are identified and categorized. A **hazard** is an activity, event, or condition that poses a possibility of harm to participants. For example, failing to use spotters in a trampoline program may result in a hazard to a participant. Placing participants too closely together as they practice golf swings also produces a hazard, as does the presence of a lot of alcohol in a beach volleyball tournament.

Establishing a systematic procedure to ensure a total analysis of risk for program services is important. One aid in attaining such completeness is a hazards typology. Typically, five types of hazards are common

to leisure services: environmental, infrastructure, programmatic, emergency care, and transportation (see table 13.1).

- Environmental hazards are associated with natural conditions. You must assess the degree of danger they pose to participants as well as the characteristics of participants that contribute to their risk (Kaiser & Robinson, 1999). For example, the location for the children's day-camp program should be assessed for the presence of poison ivy, holes and protrusions, steep slopes, and dangerous water conditions. For more information on this topic, see "Can You Solve This Programming Issue?" in chapter 13 of the CD-ROM.

- Infrastructure hazards involve all facilities, buildings, fields, roads, and trails constructed and used for programs. Overall, most lawsuits have involved man-made or substantially altered activity sites, such as swimming pools with diving boards, prepared athletic fields, and groomed ski areas. In most of these cases, the facility had a dangerous obstruction or defective equipment or was in poor condition in general. Although the potential for hazards is greatest when recreation facilities are improperly designed and constructed, the main source of infrastructure hazard to patrons is the lack of regular and thorough inspection and maintenance.

- Programmatic hazards occur when activities are not organized and conducted properly. Activities should be well planned and led by an adequate number of well-trained leaders. Programmed activities must also match participants' skill and experi-

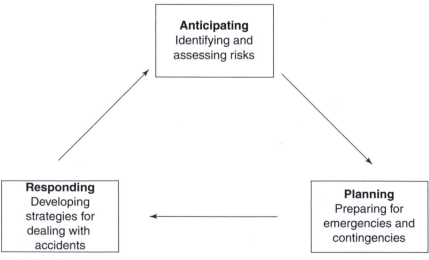

Figure 13.1 Phases of the risk management plan.

TABLE 13.1

Examples of Types of Hazards

Hazard type	Examples
Environmental	• Slippery surfaces • Weather • Steep slopes • Dangerous animals • Poisonous plants • Shallow and deep water • Currents
Infrastructure	• Stairs • Moving parts • Overhead objects • Sharp edges and protrusions • Design defects • Fences
Programmatic	• Improper supervision • Unenforced safety rules • Lack of safety devices • Failure to warn participants of dangers • Inappropriate activity selection for age, ability, experience of participants
Emergency care	• First aid not administered • Untrained personnel • Inappropriate treatment applied
Transportation	• Vehicle not maintained • Driver with inappropriate or no license

ence levels. Reasonable attention must be paid to the adequacy of activity instruction, including offering lead-up skill practice if needed. Promotions and advertising should offer an accurate and truthful representation of the program and include warnings of any potential dangers inherent in participating. If appropriate, protective devices (such as helmets, goggles, and life jackets) should be provided for participants.

• Emergency care hazards and information can and do change frequently. Talk with your recreation department supervisor about your department's current emergency care hazards.

• Transportation hazards are associated with moving program participants around. Liability can be avoided in this category only by not providing transportation. When transportation services are necessary, great care must be taken to obey all traffic rules and to properly and regularly maintain vehicles. Drivers should be trained and supervised. Usually participants should not serve as drivers. For more information on this topic, see "More Options for Individual Programming Practice," option 3, in chapter 13 of the CD-ROM.

According to this hazard typology, what do programmers specifically need to do in the first phase of risk management? Identifying the presence of hazards in program situations is, of course, the most important thing, but in addition you should assess their probability and severity. The probability of a hazard is how frequently it occurs. Some agencies rate hazards as high (accidents are expected), medium (accidents occasionally happen), or low (accidents are unexpected but not impossible). To determine how severe the consequences might be, consider the extent of the injury for the participant. Severity of potential hazards can also be rated on a scale—fatal (deaths likely), severe (extensive hospitalization or permanent disability), major (temporary disability yet not life threatening), and minor (requiring first aid).

Planning

The second phase of risk management is planning. The planning phase involves preparing for contingencies and emergencies; establishing rules and regulations; adopting routine and systematic methods for safety inspections; determining practices for releases, waivers, and agreements to participate in programs; and developing a comprehensive program of in-service risk management training for staff members.

The content of your risk management plan is typically a function of the nature of your organization and its program services, but there are a few details you should always consider:

• *Adopt a philosophical statement.* Your organization's beliefs about loss prevention and safety control are important for a workable risk management plan. This might include your organization's policies on sexual harassment; rights to participate; discrimination in employment and facility use; and punishment for the physical or sexual abuse of children, persons with disabilities, the elderly, or any other participant. Have your governing authority formally adopt these philosophical statements.

- *Pay attention to requirements.* All relevant ordinances, charters, master plans, professional standards and regulations, and health and safety laws must be directly reflected in a risk management plan. This also includes the specifications of leasing and rental agreements, contracts, and insurance riders. In the United States, for example, almost half the states have a ski responsibility law that defines the operators' duties and the skiers' responsibilities (Kaiser & Robinson, 1999).

- *Put it in writing.* Risk management plans are usually organized and presented to staff in the form of a risk management manual. It is one thing to adopt policies and procedures for reducing the potential harm of hazards and yet another to make sure they are carried out. This is helped by developing a carefully referenced and well-written handbook for employees and volunteers. Many professional and agency accrediting organizations, such as the American Camp Association for camps, the National Recreation and Park Association for city and county departments, and the Association for Experiential Education for adventure programs, provide specific recommendations regarding how to conduct their programs. A generic outline for a risk management manual is found in "Typical Contents of a Risk Management Manual" on this page.

- *Conduct regular reviews.* Once the plan is adopted and put into practice, do not consider the assignment completed. To be effective, risk management is an ongoing process—the plan must be systematically evaluated and adjustments made accordingly. Establish periodic review procedures for checking your plan's ability to meet the risk management needs of your programs. Revise any aspects of the plan that are not working well.

Beyond the very important function of protecting participants from unreasonable hazards, planning for risk management also provides a practical and philosophical base for building a solid public relations strategy (Riddick & Russell, 1999). Although there is no substitute for showing genuine concern for an injured person after an accident, a good risk management plan can help reduce unhappy feelings that may later lead to a lawsuit. As well, a risk management plan provides stewardship of the organization's financial, physical, and personnel assets by reducing the frequency and severity of potential hazards (Kaiser &

Typical Contents of a Risk Management Manual

1. Philosophical statement (priority risks, role of employees)

2. Policies related to contracts (licenses, leases, permits, rentals, insurance)

3. Conduct of programs and services (professional standards, ADA, warnings, medical and health exams, joint sponsorships, use of waivers, participant forms)

4. Human resources policies (occupational safety standards, sexual harassment, workplace violence)

5. Supervisory functions (discipline, crowd control, sport violence, rules enforcement)

6. Emergency or contingency response protocol (participant injury, rendering first aid, accident reports, large-scale disasters such as earthquakes and tornadoes, evacuation procedures, civil disturbances such as bomb threats, runaway children, fires and power failures, releasing minors to proper adults, and wandering elderly)

7. Protection against criminal acts (terrorism, guns and knives, law enforcement, illegal drug and alcohol use)

8. Transportation (vehicle maintenance, traffic laws, driver's licenses)

9. Developed areas and facilities (lighting, signage, sanitation, smoke alarms, maintenance, inspection)

Many of these topics are covered in more detail later in this chapter.

Reprinted, by permission, from R. Kaiser and K. Robinson, 1999, Risk Management. In *Management of Park and Recreation Agencies* (Ashburn, VA: National Recreation and Park Association), 732-733.

For more information on this topic, see worksheet 13.2 in chapter 13 of the CD-ROM.

Robinson, 1999). It contributes to the effective and efficient operation of the agency. Bluntly put, a risk management plan is good professional practice.

Responding

Finally, the risk management process includes a responding phase. Sometimes, even with an excellent risk management plan, accidents happen. Accidents are inherent in leisure experiences. Indeed, patrons in certain leisure pursuits are motivated by their potential for risk. Wisely managing this risk requires its anticipation, planned avoidance, and reduction as well as strategies for responding to emergencies. Frequent training and review in first aid and rescue techniques, properly equipped first aid kits, and well-maintained rescue equipment are all vital for efficient emergency response.

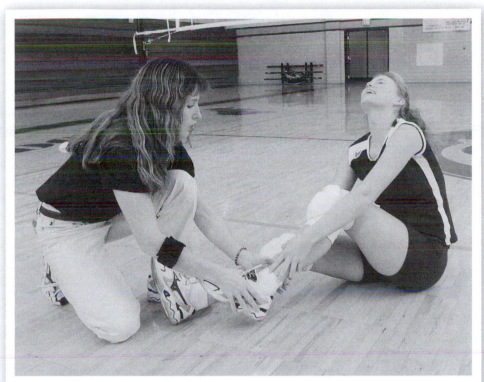

The ability to respond to accidents quickly and while under pressure is important in an emergency response situation.

© Human Kinetics.

If the risk management plan is thoroughly prepared, the responding phase usually means simply following through on the emergency and contingency plans. This requires that policies and procedures for responding, as well as proper arrangements, be well established before an accident or other emergency. Such responses as first aid, calling 911, contacting families, and area evacuation are all included in the plan. Staff and patrons must know what to do and who should do it. Who will render first aid? Who will continue on-site care until emergency medical technicians (EMTs) arrive? Who will accompany the ambulance? Who will remain behind at the program site to care for the noninjured participants? For more information on this topic, see worksheet 13.3 in chapter 13 of the CD-ROM.

All this information is usually found in the risk management plan as the emergency or contingency response **protocol** (see "Typical Contents of a Risk Management Manual" on page 196). For some programs, such as backpacking, rock climbing, and white-water kayaking, procedures for search and rescue should also be included. Regardless, a response protocol documents the approach taken by program staff in case of an accident or other emergency. It should include the following:

- Priority of response actions (what to do first, second, and so on)
- First aid and EMT provisions
- Evacuation options
- Police and fire department phone numbers
- Local hospital or doctors' phone numbers
- Other relevant contact numbers (e.g., park ranger)
- The program supervisor's mobile phone number

The responding phase also involves reporting. This requires documenting the dates and content of regular safety checks of facilities and equipment, as well as recording accidents or other emergency incidents. Accident reporting forms are integral to any risk management plan. There are typically four types of forms—accident, treatment, statistical, and

Information Needed on an Accident Report Form

- Identification information (identifying information about the injured, name of the person in charge, date and time of accident, witnesses and their addresses)
- Location of accident (a specific diagram of where the injured, leaders, other participants, and witnesses were)
- Action of injured (what the injured person was doing when the accident occurred)
- Program context (previous activity instruction, experience level of the injured person, warnings issued by leader, preventive measures taken by the injured person)
- Procedures followed in rendering aid (first aid, emergency care, physician diagnosis, follow-up contacts)

Adapted from van der Smissen & Gregg, 1999, p. 294.

insurance (van der Smissen & Gregg, 1999). The form of most interest in risk management is the accident form (see also chapter 12), which provides information about the circumstances of the injury. Some organizations require that "near misses" be recorded as well so that corrections can be made to programs or additional training be required of staff. The box on this page lists the information needed on an accident form. Accident reports should be kept for the number of years specified by your governing or legal authority statute. When a child is involved, forms should typically be kept for at least two years after the child reaches the age of majority, or the age he or she is considered to be an adult.

Sometimes accident and treatment reports are combined on the same form. Essentially, how the accident happened, the physical or emotional injury resulting from the accident, and how the injury was treated are documented. Depending on the nature of the program, treatment reporting may be more or less extensive. For example, the treatment form for a resident camp with a health center or for a sport program with an athletic trainer will be much more extensive than that of a weekly crafts program with a first aid kit.

Conducting Programs With Care

The second basic way recreation program planners minimize the threat of accidents is by ensuring that all programs are conducted with care and consistency. Properly conducting programs is one of the most important aspects of a risk management plan. How should a playground program be conducted to make it as safe as possible for the children? What special precautions should be taken at the camp waterfront program to reduce the risk of drowning? Does the management of special events require special precautions?

Playground safety is the chief concern of public recreation and park programmers. To meet this, in the United States the National Playground Safety Institute and the U.S. Consumer Product Safety Commission have published extensive guidelines and standards about playground inspection, staff training, and recommended procedures for preventing injuries (Kraus, 1997). In conducting playground programs, the development and enforcement of safety rules are particularly important. No bicycling, skateboarding, or in-line skating, for example, except in specified areas, is universally appropriate. As well, requiring appropriate safety equipment, such as batting helmets, and having strict rules for the use of dangerous materials in arts and crafts are important for playground safety. Separating activity areas, such as baseball from free play, is also a useful and important safety measure. For more information on this topic, see "Group Discussion Ideas," option 2, in chapter 13 of the CD-ROM.

Dr. Betty van der Smissen, the foremost authority on accident liability in leisure services, maintains that no matter the type of agency, it is the legal responsibility of programmers to know and understand the participants and to conduct recreation activities in accordance (van der Smissen & Gregg, 1999). Some essential aspects include the maturity and condition of participants (i.e., their age, developmental stage, and size). The physical, mental, emotional, and social capabilities of participants, as well as their experience and skill in the activity itself, are also important to consider when conducting recreation programs. Is the program format (e.g., competition) appropriate? Program objectives should reflect the most up-to-date and best professional practices so as not to set the participant up for the likelihood of injury.

Safety gear is an important feature of conducting programs with care.

© Human Kinetics.

Dr. van der Smissen also emphasizes that you consider the adequacy of activity instruction and the learning process, including skill and judgment progression, instruction for safety, rules for participant conduct in the activity, protective equipment, and rules of the activity itself (van der Smissen & Gregg, 1999). Are participants properly informed about the nature of the activity and its inherent risks? Are they warned about what injury might occur if they do not follow instructions? Program patrons who do not understand the nature of the activity do not comprehend the risks. Some organizations have an "Agreement to Participate" form to ensure that patrons assume their own responsibility in recreation programs.

Program instruction is an important aspect of risk management. Programs that involve complicated activities or that rely heavily on equipment should be conducted specifically to maximize proper preinstruction and skill progression. For example, before programming a week-long backpacking trip in the Canadian Rockies, organize several overnight and weekend trial runs for the group, and provide orientation to such factors as weather changes at high altitudes.

Supervising Participant Behavior

Closely aligned with how programs are conducted is the establishment of procedures governing supervision and participant behavior (also see chapter 11). Supervising participants as they engage in recreation activities is an important element in risk management. Plainly, when a recreation, park, sport, or tourism organization sponsors and conducts recreation programs, supervision is required (Russell, 2005).

Various elements of a recreation program determine the nature of the supervision (Jordan, 2001). For example, suppose you take the children, aged 7 through 11, who are participating in a day-camp program on a trip to a nearby state park. At the park you visit two areas: the swimming beach on the lake and the historical interpretation village where craftspeople demonstrate pioneer customs. Will there be a difference in the degree of your supervision of the children at the lake and at the village? Most likely, yes. Why? Because the environments and the activities performed at each are different. The beach poses more inherent risk than the village setting, and swimming is more difficult than walking around and watching craftspeople spin yarn and make apple butter. Thus the supervision at the beach will be more specific, and the supervision at the village will be more general.

Let's consider more carefully both types of supervision: general and specific. **General supervision** involves overseeing a broad area of activity. The leader of the day-camp trip to the state park might stand in the center of the interpretive pioneer village and watch the children as they enter and leave each of the craft cabins on their own. You might provide general supervision of the gym while adult-league volleyball is under way and general supervision of youth campers setting up their tents at a campout. With general supervision, you would notice if someone is playing too aggressively or if a thunderstorm is approaching quickly, plus you would be visibly available for participant questions and problems. Under general supervision, visual and voice contact is easily maintained with patrons (Russell, 2005). For more information on this topic, see "More Options for Individual Programming Practice," option 1, in chapter 13 of the CD-ROM.

A common general supervision issue is crowd control. Although there is no one way to manage a crowd

of people, factors that affect crowd behavior can be managed (Edginton & O'Neill, 1999). Programmers of special events in particular need to prepare to handle crowds effectively. The time of day, the size and age of the crowd, the physical layout of the facility, and the type of activity or entertainment all affect crowd behavior. People can become confused, frustrated, or frightened in crowds. Reducing such anxieties is accomplished by using clear signage, lighting dark areas, providing information over a public address system, maintaining wide aisles of seats, having multiple exits, providing ushers who give directions, and using uniformed security personnel (Edginton & O'Neill, 1999). The point is, plans and procedures must be developed and implemented in order to reassure program clients and therefore lessen the potential for problems.

Recreation leaders engage in **specific supervision** when there is skill instruction involved, when participants are young or have little skill, and when the activity has inherent risk (Jordan, 2001). Specific supervision involves direct and close visual and voice contact with participants. Examples include spotting in gymnastics, coaching a sports team in skill development, or giving instructions to novice rock climbers. Table 13.2 indicates the level of required

TABLE 13.2

Degree of Supervision

Factors	Specific supervision	General supervision
PARTICIPANTS		
Age	Very young	Adult
Skill level	Low	Advanced
Previous experience	None	Plenty
ACTIVITY		
Complexity	High	Low
Difficulty	High	Low
Inherent risk	High	Low
ENVIRONMENT		
Condition	Poor	Excellent
Participant familiarity with space	None	High

Adapted from D.J. Jordan, 2001.

Terrorism Preparedness Tips

- Listen to the radio or television for current information and instructions.
- Be alert to suspicious activity, and immediately report anything suspicious to the proper authorities.
- Close the program if recommended by appropriate authorities.
- Ask for an identification check (e.g., driver's license) of anyone who enters the program as a nonparticipant and is unknown to staff.
- Be prepared to handle inquiries from anxious participants, parents of participants, staff, and the media.
- Include emergency response procedures in your organization's risk management manual.

For more information on this topic, see "More Options for Individual Programming Practice," option 2, and "Group Discussion Ideas," option 3, in chapter 13 of the CD-ROM.

supervision according to participant, activity, and environmental factors.

Also, more recent events have prompted general and specific supervision with regard to terrorism threats and issues. The first box on this page lists numerous methods that can be employed to protect against security threats.

Your organization's policy for general versus specific supervision of program participants, as well as procedures for managing crowds, demonstrations, traffic, and other public safety matters, is outlined in a **supervisory plan**—a written statement of supervision goals. For example, an end-of-season sports banquet can require supervision of people who attend in addition to players. Which areas and activities will be under general supervision and which under specific supervision? The number of staff necessary and their competence and suitability are also designated in the supervisory plan. Then, for each program season or new program offering, specific staff members are assigned to cover specific areas or activities. See "Risk Management Checklist for a Special Event" for an example of a supervisory plan.

Risk Management Checklist for a Special Event

When programming large-scale programs attracting hundreds or even thousands of participants, the following guidelines are useful in managing supervision.

- __ Plans are prescreened by both the program supervisor and the agency director.
- __ Plans are also reviewed by local law enforcement and community officials.
- __ If necessary, permits are acquired for use of the facility or area for the event.
- __ A map of the location of specific activities, traffic flow, parking, ticket sales, event entrances and exits, and so on is included in the plan.
- __ Activities are checked for appropriateness for age, gender, experience, and probable number of participants.

- __ Event leadership ratio (employee and volunteer) is adequate in number and is specifically trained for the event.
- __ In case of adverse weather, alternatives are developed and communicated.
- __ A crowd control plan including use of fences, ropes, and other control barriers is devised.
- __ Police coverage for traffic entrance and exit is arranged.
- __ Sufficient portable toilets are rented if needed.
- __ EMT or first aid personnel are arranged to be onsite.
- __ All incident and accident forms are completed at the event's conclusion.

Adapted from Kraus, 1997, p. 227.

Photo courtesy of Westerville Parks and Recreation Department, Westerville, Ohio.

The Programming Process: Keeping It Safe

Lyn Kiger, a program supervisor for the Westerville Parks and Recreation Department, tells an interesting story. It has become a tradition for Westerville teens to celebrate the end of the school year with a shaving cream fight around the town streets. To help manage this risky behavior, the department's aquatics staff planned and implemented a "school's out celebration" at the city pool, including the "world's largest shaving cream fight." Their goal was not to squelch the teens' fun but to manage it so that behaviors could be more safely controlled and the risk of damage to community property contained. The program became very successful—in fact, too successful as more and more middle school kids showed up to sling shaving cream at each other in the pool. After several years, the programmers decided they could no longer adequately implement this program.

In considering the safety implications of the shaving cream fights according to the department's risk management plan, the staff decided to stop sponsoring the "school's out" program at the pool. It was their judgment that it would be impossible to continue the pool-based party without the shaving cream fight, and they considered their liability risk for that activity too high. Now, Westerville teens hold their end-of-school celebration back on the town streets.

Ultimately, the shaving cream fight at the pool's "school's out" celebration forced the program to be canceled because it overstepped the protocol of the department's risk management plan.

Summary

This chapter advocates the practice of risk management in program implementation. You should understand the following key points:

- Recreation programs need to be free of unreasonable risk and foreseeable harm.
- Programmers minimize the threat of accidents by developing an up-to-date and systematic risk management plan, conducting programs with care and consistency, and effectively supervising participant behavior.
- A risk management plan has three phases: anticipating, planning, and responding.
- Appropriately conducting programs involves consideration for participant skills and experiences as well as for adequate activity instruction.
- A supervisory plan should specify circumstances for general and specific overseeing of participants.

Glossary

risk—Possibility of harm from a hazard.

risk management—Systematic planning that anticipates, avoids, and responds to the potential of harm to program participants.

proactive—Acting in anticipation of future problems, needs, or changes.

hazard—An activity, event, or condition that poses a risk to participants.

protocol—Procedure or set of rules that guides safety and effectiveness of programs.

general supervision—Overseeing a broad area of activity.

specific supervision—Direct and close visual and voice contact with participants.

supervisory plan—Written statement of participant supervision goals.

References

Edginton, C.R., & O'Neill, J.P. (1999). Program, services, and event management. In B. van der Smissen, M. Moiseichik, V.J. Hartenburg, & L.F. Twardzik (Eds.), *Management of park and recreation agencies* (pp. 175-240). Ashburn, VA: National Recreation and Park Association.

Jordan, D.J. (2001). *Leadership in leisure services: Making a difference.* State College, PA: Venture.

Kaiser, R., & Robinson, K. (1999). Risk management. In B. van der Smissen, M. Moiseichik, V.J. Hartenburg, & L.F. Twardzik (Eds.), *Management of park and recreation agencies* (pp. 713-742). Ashburn, VA: National Recreation and Park Association.

Kraus, R. (1997). *Recreation programming: A benefits-driven approach.* Boston: Allyn & Bacon.

National Gallery of Art. (2006). About the National Gallery of Art: A brief history. Retrieved June 26, 2006, from www.nga.gov/ginfo/aboutnga.shtm.

Riddick, C.C., & Russell, R.V. (1999). *Evaluative research in recreation, park and sport settings: Searching for useful information.* Champaign, IL: Sagamore.

Russell, R.V. (1982). *Planning programs in recreation.* St. Louis: Mosby.

Russell, R.V. (2005). *Leadership in recreation* (3rd ed.). Boston: McGraw-Hill.

van der Smissen, B., & Gregg, C.R. (1999). Legal liability and risk management. In J.C. Miles & S. Priest (Eds.), *Adventure programming* (pp. 287-301). State College, PA: Venture.

Program Evaluation

Known as program evaluation, the third step in the program planning process is crucial for programming success. Attendance in the adult fitness program is soaring, and no one has come to complain to you about anything. The program must be a huge success, right? Well, maybe. How can you really tell you are providing the quality program services you think you are? These last chapters feature a systematic process for judging the quality of programs. Our intent here is to delve into the logic, as well as the procedures, for evaluating recreation programs.

- Chapter 14 introduces this final planning step by overviewing its rationale, approaches, obstacles, and types. Why should we evaluate, and what are our options for approaching the process?

- Chapter 15 outlines the specific steps of evaluation. What are the research rules that must be followed?

Evaluation Approaches

In this chapter, you can look forward to the following:

- Learning the value of systematic inquiry about program success
- Becoming familiar with the various evaluation approaches
- Understanding the preliminary preparations needed for evaluation projects

The Lodge and Conference Center at Geneva State Park, located on Lake Erie near Cleveland, Ohio, offers a three-star experience at an affordable price. The lakeside destination is striking, and the award-winning lodge makes a breathtaking impression with its sculpted stone exterior and cathedral-like lobby and a dramatic fireplace spanning four stories. Suggesting a new direction for state-operated recreation services, this state park lodge features finely appointed guest rooms and suites, an upscale restaurant with a spectacular lake view, a lounge, a wine-tasting room, a gift shop, a conference and banquet center, a game room, a glass-enclosed spacious indoor pool and hot tub, and a fitness center. Other recreational program services include massage, golf, bike rentals, boating, fishing, and more (Lodge and Conference Center at Geneva State Park, 2006).

Another difference is that the operation of this state park lodge is managed by a commercial hospitality corporation. Delaware North Companies and its more than 30,000 employees manage travel destinations in Europe, Canada, Australia, and New Zealand as well as more than 40 destinations in the United States. The corporation also makes arrangements for sports stadiums and arenas, national park inns, theme parks, airport hospitality, and even the guest experience for NASA at the Kennedy Space Center.

How do both the state of Ohio and Delaware North Companies know that such a partnership is worth it? They evaluate.

We have come to that step in the program planning process where program services are evaluated. **Program evaluation** is a judgment about the worth and value of your programming efforts. The results determine how to improve the quality of program services as well as whether to continue or terminate them. Because evaluation ultimately measures the extent to which program goals have been achieved, the results of evaluation are crucial.

Yet, even though evaluation is one of the most important tasks in leisure programming, it is also one of the least understood (Russell, 1982). Perhaps this occurs because we expect so much from it. For example, you may think of evaluation as a "professional judgment on the merits of a program" (Bannon, 1976, p. 267) and at the same time consider it a matter of mathematical measurement. Also, evaluation is expected to determine the worth of a program in order to improve it or to cancel it—both desirable and undesirable consequences. Finally, evaluation is the complex merging of the final step in the program planning process with the first step, as evaluation findings cycle back to inform program preparations.

At one time leisure programmers evaluated their programs simply by counting the attendance, but the current mandate for accountability and professionalism means you must develop and use both qualitative and quantitative evaluation measurement approaches to assess how efficiently programs were carried out and what happened to the participants as a result of experiencing the program (Russell, 1982). For more information on this topic, see "More Options for Individual Programing Practice," option 1, in chapter 14 of the CD-ROM.

Therefore, we propose the following definition of evaluation in recreation programming:

> [Evaluation is] a continuing, ongoing function whereby pertinent information is gathered in order to assess the efficiency of program conduct and the effect of the program on the participant; this information is then used to determine the adequacy of the program in reaching its stated goals so that future program decisions may be wisely made. (Russell, 1982, p. 284)

This means evaluation is a continual process, determining both program efficiency and effectiveness. Its purpose is to compare program results against goals and objectives in order to make decisions about the future.

Timetables for Evaluation

To demonstrate the ongoing nature of program evaluation, we can distinguish two different timetables. These we refer to as formative and summative evaluation.

Formative Evaluation

Formative evaluation means that information about the program's usefulness is collected as the program is implemented. Measurement of an ongoing activity or event is valuable for modifying the program while it is still under way. When the summer day-camp staff meet at the end of each day to make recommendations for changes in the next day's program plan, they are conducting formative evaluation—daily or weekly fine-tuning to improve the program while it is in progress (Stumbo & Peterson, 2004). Or, in the case of a special event, formative evaluation can take place immediately. For example, if 4 participants come to an event designed for 50, program changes are made right away. This does not mean that programmers career out of control, changing program content or format on a whim, but it does imply that skilled professionals are able to adapt to a changing situation. For more information on this topic, see "Group Discussion Ideas," option 1, in chapter 14 of the CD-ROM.

The box on this page provides an example of a short questionnaire distributed each July to regular pool-pass holders of the Westerville Parks and Recreation Department. It illustrates a formative evaluation because its purpose is to determine changes necessary while the summer aquatics season is still in session. Last year, as a result of pool-user responses, staff ordered more food for the concessions on weekends, initiated an hourly bathroom inspection and cleaning schedule, and held a midseason staff

---

Midseason Pool Satisfaction Survey for Westerville: A Formative Evaluation

Overall, how would you rate the Highlands Pool facility?

___ Poor
___ Needs improvement
___ Average
___ Good
___ Excellent

Please explain:

How would you rate the service you receive by the pool staff (e.g., lifeguards, front desk, concessions)?

___ Poor
___ Needs improvement
___ Average
___ Good
___ Excellent

Please explain:

Could you suggest any improvements that can be made at the pool this season?

A formative evaluation questionnaire conducted midsummer helps Highlands Swimming Pool staff realign programs and services right away so that participant satisfaction is improved.

Reprinted from Westerville Parks and Recreation Department, 2004.

"refresher" course focused on customer relations and service.

Summative Evaluation

Summative evaluation, on the other hand, is conducted at the conclusion of a program and provides useful information for the next time the program is offered. The results instruct the next "season" of programming—they enable organizations to compare programs and determine those that are most worthwhile to offer again. For example, the responses given on an end-of-semester course evaluation questionnaire typically benefit students who will take the course next year. Interviews with former clients in a recreation therapy program can be very helpful in preparing for the next group of clients in the program. If clients who have completed the program indicate they did not learn how to use assertiveness skills in social situations, let's suppose, changes can be made to the program content or format to try to achieve this goal the next time around.

Compared with formative evaluation, summative evaluation is usually considered more formal and systematic, but there are no rules requiring this distinction. In fact, the same evaluation steps explained in chapter 15 apply equally to both. The only real distinction is how much time it takes. Formative evaluation is usually done much more quickly than summative evaluation.

Rationale for Evaluation

The importance of evaluating recreation programs cannot be overemphasized. Because effective evaluation provides the means to learn from experience—both successes and failures—it is a critical component of providing leisure services.

There are many reasons to evaluate a recreation program, including the sincere and logical as well as the cosmetic and appealing. Evaluation results can be used to simply justify a program's costs or to satisfy a supervisor's request for proof of the worth of your efforts. On the other hand, evaluation results can also address the complex task of demonstrating what happens to participants as a result of participating in the program. Ideally, the rationale for program evaluation is providing a systematic appraisal of the program in order to determine whether it is doing what it is intended to do. Thus, the ultimate reason for evaluation is to help the programmer become more proficient and more effective in meeting participants' and society's needs.

What specific lessons from evaluation accomplish this? We consider four primary ones. First, valuable understanding can be gained about *what happens to people* as a result of recreation programs. This requires determining the experiences of individuals in the program as well as the whole program experience. Accordingly, program evaluation should employ both quantitative measures—ones that measure specific effects of the program on participants—and qualitative measures that seek out the holistic impact of the program experience overall. For example, in an outdoor adventure program, using a questionnaire to determine changes in participants' self-esteem does not provide a complete picture. Adding insights gained through face-to-face interviews with participants rounds out the programmer's understanding of the quality of the overall experience.

It follows, then, that the second reason to evaluate recreation programs is *program improvement*. From the evaluation, you can develop strategies to solve programming problems and make informed decisions about program expansion, alteration, or cancellation. These decisions improve not only the programs offered but also the agency itself. Thus, evaluation becomes part of a systematic decision-making process. It stimulates the quality of all the services the agency provides. How is this accomplished? When used wisely, evaluation can promote staff growth and training, determine the flexibility of policies and internal systems, appraise personnel quality, develop a firmer foundation for the agency's philosophy, appraise the adequacy of existing physical properties, and avoid unnecessary or wasteful financial expenditures. For more information on this topic, see "Can You Solve This Programming Issue?" in chapter 14 of the CD-ROM.

These two lessons—understanding what happens to participants and making decisions about improvement—boil down to assessing the *achievement of program goals and objectives*. This is the third reason for evaluation. Is the program achieving its intention? Indeed, the ultimate goal of evaluation is to provide evidence of the program's ability to achieve what it promised. This links evaluation back to the first step of the program planning process. The program goals and objectives are now called forth for assessment against the program's results. The goal and objective statements written earlier in program preparation now provide a yardstick for measuring program success. Indeed, according to Theobald (1979), determining whether program objectives are met offers the programmer another chance to study the objectives themselves. Therefore, the evaluation step can occasionally result in a redefinition of objectives.

Finally, a fourth reason that supports the importance of program evaluation is the contribution made to the professional leisure services *body of knowledge*. Outmoded concepts, invalid ideas, and inadequate understanding are replaced through evaluation. This makes professional practice knowledge based—current practice is tested so that the profession becomes broader and stronger.

Obstacles to Evaluation

It all seems so obvious, doesn't it? What could be more logical than to emphasize quality, take responsibility for improvement, and use knowledge wisely? It turns out, however, that evaluation is easier to advocate than to accomplish. Indeed, assessments of the leisure services fields consistently indicate that a low percentage of organizations engage in ongoing and systematic program evaluation. Recent surveys suggest that more than 80 percent of wilderness programs for university students, more than 80 percent of adventure programs for substance abusers, and more than 50 percent of wilderness therapy programs are not conducting systematic evaluations (Warner, 1999). There are two primary reasons for this—psychological obstacles and structural obstacles. Psychological obstacles are perhaps the most powerful. Let's explore these first.

Psychological Obstacles

Professional recreation programmers—like all human beings—must believe in what they are doing. In fact, believing that a program is important is much more important for predicting its success than any other factor. There is, of course, a flip side to this. Believing strongly in the worth of something can also interfere with objectivity. This is a **psychological obstacle** to program evaluation (Warner, 1999).

Tallies of the leisure services fields, including high-risk outdoor adventure programs, consistently indicate that a low percentage of organizations engage in ongoing and systematic evaluation.

© PhotoDisc.

Most programmers are eager to make program adjustments when they happen to notice difficulties, but are they willing to move beyond their own biases to seek out trouble spots? The role of evaluation in providing a new perspective is often proclaimed, but when push comes to shove, because of insecurity in knowing, evaluation just isn't carried out.

A second psychological obstacle often blocking programmers from making more commitment to evaluation is fear of the jargon and technical procedures often used in evaluative research (Warner, 1999). Some programmers are convinced they do not have the expertise to conduct evaluations correctly. But identifying the key issues, acquiring information about these issues, and figuring out what the information says about the issues are really not very difficult. You do not need to conduct a major research project to produce meaningful evaluation conclusions.

Structural Obstacles

Structural obstacles also restrict evaluation efforts (Warner, 1999). For example, a very legitimate complaint among programmers is that there is simply not enough time for thorough and systematic evaluation given other responsibilities. Some leisure services programs are run on a shoestring budget, and some programmers juggle hundreds of different programs at a time. Thus, evaluation can be easily sacrificed to other priorities and programming efforts. For program evaluation to have a rightful place in the organization's operation, there must be incentives and payoffs for programmers. For example, salary increases could be awarded to programmers who consistently carry out evaluation studies (but the rewards are not attached to the results of the evaluation). Or release time from usual duties could be granted to programmers in order to have larger blocks of time to design and write about the results of program evaluation studies.

Developing a meaningful and constructive program evaluation system requires overcoming these psychological and structural obstacles. One key way of reducing psychological threats is to integrate research and evaluation into the professional training process. This is why you (typically) are required to complete course work in research methods and statistics. If you are given a firm grounding in the needed research tools, your confidence in your ability to conduct program evaluation will soar.

The structural obstacles can be confronted by setting aside time and resources for evaluation work. Professionals can do this by requiring that evaluation plans be included in new program proposals and by building the cost of evaluation into program budgets. Programmers may also pool resources, cooperate with universities, and work with outside consultants to increase priority on program evaluation. For more information on this topic, see "Group Discussion Ideas," option 3, in chapter 14 of the CD-ROM.

Types of Evaluation

Basically, there are two types of evaluation needed in recreation and park programs. First, evaluation must ask about the outcome, or benefit, of services. Second, evaluation must provide information about the process, or effort, of implementing these services.

Benefits Evaluation

Benefits evaluation, also known as outcomes analysis, impact evaluation, or effectiveness evaluation, documents the effect of a service on the individual client. You might also say that benefits evaluation measures the "outputs" (Russell, 2005). What happened to the participants as a result of being in the program? Did they learn anything, develop a skill, or become healthier? This type of evaluation is directly linked to the goals and objectives set forth in the planning of a program.

Park, recreation, tourism, sport, and related services benefit both individuals and collections of individuals—neighborhoods, communities, and other organizations. For example, an employee sports league may lower absenteeism for a corporation. Or a conservation program may result in cleaner roadsides, which lead to more town pride felt by citizens. Each particular program results in a range of short-term and long-term benefits, and these must all be assessed through the evaluation process. This can be as simple as counting the "billions served" at McDonald's or as complex as a full cost–benefit analysis. Either way, such measurements attempt to assess program patrons. For more information on this topic, see worksheet 14.3 in chapter 14 of the CD-ROM.

Implementation Evaluation

On the other hand, **implementation evaluation** focuses on how programs are conducted within an organization. It may also be labeled efficiency analysis, effort evaluation, or process evaluation. This approach determines whether the resources used to create the services have been applied in an efficient, legal, and ethical manner. Implementation evaluation judges the worth of a program's operation; it measures the "inputs" (Russell, 2005). For example, an implementation evaluation might focus on whether staffing policies were followed. Were there enough lifeguards at the waterfront this summer? Were the lifeguards adequately recruited and trained? Was the compensation adequate for reducing midsummer staff turnover, without exceeding the budget and without reducing the satisfaction of pool users?

Strategies for Benefits and Implementation Evaluation

Under the umbrella of the benefits and implementation evaluation types, specific strategies are available.

Following is an abridged list of the various options for focusing evaluation. Some are useful for benefits evaluation, while others serve the purpose of implementation evaluation. Various approaches are often used together within the same evaluation study or in sequence over a period of time. Indeed, an ideal evaluation includes approaches that address both implementation and benefits outcomes. Table 14.1 outlines each approach.

- *Accreditation and certification.* Does the program meet minimum standards for agency or personnel accreditation or licensing? Those working in leisure services fields obey a variety of professional standards, operational principles, codes of ethics, and credentialing rules. For example, the American Therapeutic Recreation Association (ATRA) and the National Therapeutic Recreation Society (NTRS) develop and publish the minimal programming actions expected of agencies across the United States. Every therapeutic recreation specialist is required to conduct services accordingly. As well, the Association for Experiential Education has established an accreditation method for outdoor

TABLE 14.1

Summary of Evaluation Approaches

Approach	Description	Purpose
Accreditation and certification	Measures program success against professional standards	Implementation evaluation
Balanced scorecard	Management process for balancing performance and vision	Implementation evaluation
Benchmarking	Compares programs across different agencies	Implementation evaluation
Effort evaluation	Measures the effort made by an agency in sponsoring a program	Implementation evaluation
Cost–benefit analysis	Monetarily measures the relationship between service costs and benefits to participants	Implementation and benefits evaluation
Trend analysis	Compares program elements across time	Implementation and benefits evaluation
Goals achievement	Determines if the program met its stated intention	Implementation and benefits evaluation
Participant satisfaction	Measures participant opinions through questionnaires	Benefits evaluation

adventure programs. This includes standards for providing program participants with a high level of quality assurance as well as sound environmental practices for the natural resources used. Evaluation provides a tool for determining how well these best-practice standards are met.

- *Balanced scorecard.* Does the program meet the organization's vision and strategic goals? The balanced scorecard approach to evaluation is actually more of a management process. The task is to balance performance with vision. Derived from total quality management (TQM), this process directly measures achievement of a program's strategic goals. Performance metrics are organized on the scorecard according to such categories as finances, customer satisfaction, internal planning processes, and learning and growth. Tracked continually over time, the comparison of objectives against performance enables programmers to look for trends, best and worst practices, and areas of improvement.

- *Benchmarking.* Does the program compare favorably with the best of its kind in another organization or service sector? Adams (2002) distinguishes between benchmarking and benchmarks. Benchmarks are the statistical figures for comparing programs, while benchmarking is determining best practices for programs. There are basically three steps in benchmarking. First, decide what to compare. Such factors as budgets, number and qualification of personnel, salaries, fees charged, number or square footage of facilities, and number of patrons served are often benchmarked. The second step is determining which and how many other agencies to include in the comparison. Should only those operating in your area or region that are of similar size and that are recognized for high-quality operations be included in the comparison? The third step is to design a questionnaire to send to the chosen agencies according to the points of comparison. Once it is determined which agencies are achieving at the highest levels, their methods, policies, and processes can be mimicked.

- *Effort evaluation.* This approach to evaluation focuses on the effort made by an organization in sponsoring a program. This frequently refers to the percentage of staff members who are involved in planning and directing the program. One way of measuring staff effort is through **full-time equivalents (FTE)**. FTE is the sum of part-time and full-time workers. For instance, an evaluation reports that it takes 6 FTE to operate a youth soccer program on a weekly basis. In this example, and in FTE nomenclature, this translates to 240 hours per week—6 people multiplied by a 40-hour work-week, or 12 persons multiplied by a 20-hour work-week, or any applicable combination.

- *Cost–benefit analysis.* How do program costs compare with their benefits? Concern for program efficiency has led to the use of cost–benefit ratios. To calculate, program costs in dollars (including for staff, facilities, and supplies) are first determined. Then the dollar value of the program's benefits is determined, and a resulting ratio is established between the two. If the cost–benefit ratio is too high, the programmer works to reduce it—ideally without disturbing program quality. For more information on this topic, see "More Options for Individual Programming Practice," option 2, in chapter 14 of the CD-ROM.

- *Trend analysis.* This form of comparison helps programmers determine what the future might hold according to changes recorded from the past. It is applicable to any information that can be measured over time, such as spending, revenues, number of people served, and number of accidents. For example, a resort swimming pool recorded over the years the number of gallons of water used each season. After the information was corrected for the number of days open each year, it became clear that more water was being used in later years. It was concluded that this increased water usage indicated leaks in the pipes and systems, which became part of the justification for a new pool.

- *Goals achievement.* Did the program achieve the goals and objectives set forth during the initial planning step? Perhaps the most important, this approach to evaluation determines if the program met its stated intention. Answering this question requires accurate and clear preparation of goals and objectives at the outset. This means it must be possible to measure such outcomes as participant skill mastery, social behavior change, personal values or self-concepts, and other desired program benefits.

- *Participant satisfaction.* Did the participants like (appreciate, enjoy, have fun in) the program? Typically using questionnaires or rating scales, program patrons express their opinions about the program. Was the program affordable? Was it offered at convenient hours and locations? Did it meet expectations?

The Programming Process: Evaluation Approaches

How successful is Westerville's arts programming? There seem to be many offerings for preschool-aged participants, including Carebear Creations and Piano Playtime. And drama, ballet, tap, and clay classes are provided for youth. For participants between 6 and 10 years of age, there's even a celli class, which teaches the Irish dance form made famous by Riverdance. Dance for teen and adult participants seems plentiful, too, with classes in ballroom, swing, polka, belly dancing, rumba, waltz, and salsa. Adults can also choose classes such as Drawing for Personal Expression, Painting Landscapes and Seascapes, and Introduction to Watercolor.

Indeed, there seems to be a variety of arts classes available, but what about the other programming formats? For example, should there be more special events than the Big Band Bash and the Sounds of Summer concert series offered in summer? "Our program philosophy in the arts is to offer tastes of things," says Laura Horton, program manager for adult programs. "This is because we are in a very arts-focused community. There are lots of dance studios and art galleries" (personal communication, June 2002).

To evaluate whether the department's arts program offerings were successful, a benchmarking study was conducted. Staff sent a brief questionnaire asking about numbers, depth, staffing, locations, and formats of arts programming to other cities of similar size and socioeconomic makeup. Results not only provided a comparison of how well Westerville's arts programming was doing according to its "sister" recreation and park departments but also generated ideas for expanding and changing the arts programming for participants of all ages. For example, Westerville now offers more performance and exhibit forms of arts programming.

Is Westerville's provision of arts programming enough? Program offerings are primarily beginner-level instructional. For a city of if its size and type, should more in-depth arts programs be provided?

Developing an Evaluation System

In an ideal world, recreation programs would be continually and thoroughly evaluated. Yet, without a systematic plan for evaluation, you and your organization will be left with only the best of intentions.

Many details must be considered when developing such a plan. Foremost are the elements of staffing, funding, and timing, as well as considerations for integrity and ethics. Overall, these are managed through a set of guidelines for establishing an evaluation system (see the form on page 216).

Checklist for Developing a Systematic Evaluation Plan

[ ]   Link evaluation projects.

[ ]   Gain administrative support.

[ ]   Designate staff.

[ ]   Involve program participants.

[ ]   Define roles and clarify authority structures.

[ ]   Provide adequate funding.

[ ]   Ensure adequate time.

[ ]   Provide useful feedback.

[ ]   Prepare an evaluation project proposal.

[ ]   Keep evaluation projects going.

[ ]   Conduct evaluations ethically and with integrity.

From R. Russell and L. Jamieson, 2008, *Leisure Program Planning and Delivery* (Champaign, IL: Human Kinetics). Adapted from Riddick & Russell, 1999.

• *Link evaluation projects.* Specific efforts to evaluate specific programs should be connected in an interwoven system that focuses on a joint and coordinated effort. This requires open communication among programmers and a transparent vision for organization-wide evaluation. For example, information collected in a summative evaluation for one program might be helpful when planning an evaluation project for another program. Or questionnaires prepared for one program's evaluation might also be used to evaluate another program. Individual program evaluations should answer questions about program service success for the entire organization. Overall, are you achieving your mission?

• *Gain administrative support.* Your supervisors should be involved in planning specific evaluation projects as well as the entire evaluation system. Also, an advisory committee may be useful in helping with individual evaluation projects and overseeing the overall evaluation system for the organization. Communication with administrators or an advisory group can help you develop insights and gain commitment to the study. For example, organization directors may be crucial for getting the cooperation of other program staff for an evaluation effort. Involving them will also mean a greater likelihood that the results from the evaluation will be used to improve programs and upgrade program policies.

• *Designate staff.* Your organization should designate a person who is ultimately responsible for program evaluation. This is essential for any coordinated and systematic evaluation effort. Sometimes the programmers themselves may fill this role, or when more sensitivity is needed, outside consultants or research specialists may be called in. As well, sometimes a staff member is appointed to oversee the organization's entire evaluation system, or an individual is designated for a specific program evaluation project.

Ideally, persons responsible for evaluation should be well versed in both qualitative and quantitative inquiry methods, should be able to analyze and interpret data, and should have excellent written and verbal communication skills (Russell, 2005). They should also be able to work objectively, not trying to prove a particular finding or distort or promote a specific conclusion. As well, they should be thorough, meticulous, and able to design and carry out evaluation studies using precise methods in order for the results to have any real value to the organization.

• *Involve program participants.* There are many reasons for involving program participants in evaluation. Involving them early and often can help them gain understanding of what the evaluation is all about, ultimately increasing their support for the study and the program. Program participants can learn why the evaluation is being conducted and how it will proceed. This may help them feel less threatened. It will also help them understand what the program is trying to accomplish. Best of all, including participants in program evaluation can vastly improve the evaluator's understanding of the worth of the program.

• *Define roles and clarify authority structures.* At the outset, those involved in an evaluation project—administrators, staff, and participants—should be very clear with each other about what is expected from them. The scope and limits of their roles need to be declared, ideally in written form. This not only helps ensure completeness—the elimination of gaps in the evaluation study—but also helps solve disagreements if they arise.

• *Provide adequate funding.* Costs of evaluation should be included in organizational operations budgets. Depending on their scope and method, evaluations can potentially be expensive. Personnel costs, in particular, must be considered in an evaluation budget because they are often the major expense category. Also, some supplies can be purchased inexpensively or are free, but others will require specifically earmarked funds. For example, some equipment, such as computers, may already be available, but specialized software, such as statistical and graphing programs, may need to be purchased. To augment organization-provided general operations budgets, grants can be a source of evaluation funding. In fact, most grants that fund programs require an evaluation component in the grant proposal. Regional foundations and state, provincial, and federal government agencies will sometimes fund entire evaluation studies. Evaluation expenses that should be included in an organization's budget or grant proposal include the following:

Specific staff members should be designated to assume program evaluation responsibilities in their job description.

- Sample selection costs
- Travel expenses for interviewer(s)
- Materials costs for pretesting the evaluation procedures
- Supervisory costs for hiring an outside consultant and overseeing his or her work
- Staff training costs
- Labor and material costs for data entry
- Analyst costs for preparing tabulations and special data analyses
- Labor and materials costs for report preparation
- Telephone charges, postage, reproduction, and printing costs

• *Ensure adequate time.* Evaluation takes time. Some projects require several months to complete at a certain time of year, while others may take only a day and can be done during any season. For example, if you are interested in assessing downhill skiers' satisfaction with instructional programs at the ski resort, then administering a questionnaire to participants may take only a couple of days, but it will need to be done during the winter.

As well, since evaluators and decision makers have different time schedule demands, you should estab-lish an agreed-upon time frame for the completion of an evaluation project (Riddick & Russell, 1999). Estimate how much time is needed for recruitment of study participants, data collection, data analysis, preparation of the final report, and so on. Planning for evaluation therefore requires development of a timetable, or **time budget** (Riddick & Russell, 1999). Both calendar and clock time need to be budgeted. A mistake many evaluators make is underestimating the time needed, resulting in late delivery of the report or missing the deadline altogether. We recommend that the time budget include a 20 percent "extra time" factor to compensate for this.

• *Provide useful feedback.* Programmers are most appreciated by supervisors, advisory and policy groups, participants, and other program staff when the information gathered in the evaluation is perceived to be valuable. For example, suppose you wish to determine guest satisfaction with state park cabins. Measuring overall satisfaction is important, but even more useful information is possible by measuring specific satisfaction with such details as cabin design, cleanliness, linen service, the registration system, and proximity to park activities. These more targeted results increase the evaluation's value to a wider array of staff.

Some seasonal programs require special attention to timing an evaluation study.

• *Prepare an evaluation project proposal.* An evaluation plan benefits from documented decisions about the purpose of a project and how it will be carried out. A formal proposal—a written description of the intentions of the evaluation—is useful for communicating your plans to others in the organization.

In addition, the process of writing a proposal helps you think through the research steps you'll follow, helping you be more efficient in carrying out the study. It is much easier to find flaws in the evaluation project and correct them before beginning to collect information than it is to discover and correct problems after you have started.

• *Keep evaluation projects going.* Successful evaluation projects start out well organized and stay on track through the finish. Usually the person who develops the project proposal is the one who has the responsibility of seeing it through to completion. This might mean taking care of such logistics as recruiting respondents to questionnaires, printing and distributing questionnaires, monitoring the evaluation budget, and seeing that the final report is timely.

• *Conduct evaluations ethically and with integrity.* Integrity and ethics are essential for conducting a valid evaluation. **Integrity** refers to the validity of the information that is collected to determine the value of a program. **Ethics** is concerned with the treatment of the participants in the evaluation process.

First, how can you maintain evaluation integrity? Those who use the evaluation results want the information to be accurate; they apply what Weiss and Bucuvalas (1980) call truth tests in deciding how seriously to pay attention to an evaluation outcome—or its validity. Typically, a program evaluation is **valid** if it is "true, credible, and right" (House, 1980, p. 250). This means the nature of the evaluation process, the study design, the data gathering, and the way results are reported are honest. Both the evaluation (action) and the evaluator (person) must be perceived as trustworthy for the evaluation to have high validity (Russell, 2005). Only an honestly conducted evaluation can provide useful information and help an organization achieve its goals. The box on this page provides two illustrations of the negative effect an evaluation that lacks integrity can have. For more information on this topic, see worksheet 14.1 in chapter 14 of the CD-ROM.

Second, what are sound ethical practices in evaluation? Conducting ethical evaluations requires doing everything possible to treat the people, programs, and organizations studied graciously and honorably, including providing an environment that is safe and free of discrimination. One way to accomplish this is through **informed consent**—communication that ensures a potential evaluation respondent has sufficient information to decide whether to participate in the study. Typically, the respondent reads and signs a statement agreeing to participate in the study. The statement should describe the essential details of the study, including an explanation of the procedures, the potential benefits and risks of participation, the participant's rights to confidentiality, and the choice to participate. When children are involved in an evaluation, parents or guardians should sign an informed consent. Government-sponsored evaluations, as well as most professional associations, require informed consent. For more information on this topic, see worksheet 14.2 in chapter 14 of the CD-ROM.

Another factor that helps ensure an ethical evaluation is an approving authority. An **approving authority**, such as a special committee within or outside the organization, can review evaluation project proposals for fair treatment of the people and programs studied as well as for honorably collected information. For example, universities all have institutional review committees that must give approval for studies that use human subjects. Elementary and secondary school systems have committees to review studies that outside groups, such as park and recreation agencies, want to conduct within the schools. Similarly, hospitals have review committees that must give approval for studies done with patients. For more information on this topic, see "Group Discussion Ideas," option 2, in chapter 14 of the CD-ROM.

Summary

This chapter introduces the evaluation step in recreation program planning. You should understand the following key points:

- Evaluation is the third step in the cyclical program planning process.
- Evaluation is systematic, assessing both program efficiency (implementation) and effectiveness (benefits).
- The two timetables for evaluation are formative and summative.
- There are many reasons to evaluate a recreation program, including the sincere and logical as well as the cosmetic and appeasing.

- In spite of its importance, evaluation is not yet a vital professional skill in leisure services because of both psychological and structural obstacles.

- Approaches to evaluation include accreditation and certification, balanced scorecard, benchmarking, effort evaluation, cost–benefit analysis, trend analysis, goals achievement, and participant satisfaction.

- Successful evaluation ensures coordination, personnel, funding, timing, use, integrity, and ethics.

Glossary

program evaluation—A systematic process for judging the achievement of program goals.

formative evaluation— Ongoing assessment of the program's success while the program is in progress so that changes or corrections can be made during program implementation.

summative evaluation— Conducted at the end of the program to provide useful information for determining the program's success.

psychological obstacles—Programmers' own beliefs in the worth of their efforts obstruct the systematic evaluation of programs.

structural obstacles—Organizational barriers to systematic evaluation of programs.

benefits evaluation—Documenting the effect of a program on the individual client.

implementation evaluation—Documenting the conduct of the program.

full-time equivalents (FTE)—The sum of part-time and full-time employees.

time budget—A projected timetable for carrying out the evaluation steps.

integrity—The validity of the information collected.

ethics—Treating evaluation participants well.

valid—True, credible, and right.

informed consent—Communication that ensures a potential respondent has sufficient information about the study.

approving authority—A special committee that reviews evaluation project proposals for fair treatment of the people and programs studied.

References

Adams, J. (2002, Winter). Benchmarking for best practices. *California Parks and Recreation, 59*(1), 28.

Bannon, J.J. (1976). *Leisure resources: Its comprehensive planning.* Englewood Cliffs, NJ: Prentice Hall.

House, E.R. (1980). *Evaluating with validity.* Beverly Hills: Sage.

Lodge and Conference Center at Geneva State Park. (2006). Lodge overview. Retrieved July 5, 2006, from www.thelodgeatgeneva.com/lodge_overview.asp.

Riddick, C.C., & Russell, R.V. (1999). *Evaluative research in recreation, park, and sport settings: Searching for useful information.* Champaign, IL: Sagamore.

Russell, R.V. (1982). *Planning programs in recreation.* St. Louis: Mosby.

Russell, R.V. (2005). Evaluation. In B. van der Smissen, M. Moiseichik, & V.J. Hartenburg (Eds.), *Management of park and recreation agencies* (2nd ed., pp. 655-677). Ashburn, VA: National Recreation and Park Association.

Stumbo, N.J., & Peterson, C.A. (2004). *Therapeutic recreation program design: Principles and procedures.* San Francisco: Pearson/Cummings.

Theobald, W.F. (1979). *Evaluation of recreation and park programs.* New York: Wiley.

Warner, A. (1999). Improving program quality through evaluation. In J.C. Miles & S. Priest (Eds.), *Adventure programming* (pp. 299-308). State College, PA: Venture.

Weiss, C.H., & Bucuvalas, M. (1980). Truth tests and utility tests: Decision makers' frame of reference for social science research. *American Sociological Review, 45*(2), 302-313.

Westerville Parks and Recreation Department. (2004). *Midseason Pool Satisfaction Survey for Westerville: A Formative Evaluation.* Westerville, OH: City of Westerville.

CHAPTER 15

Evaluation Steps

In this chapter, you can look forward to learning about the following:

- Preparing an evaluation proposal
- Designing the study
- Selecting a sample
- Collecting information
- Interpreting the information gathered
- Preparing the final report
- Putting the findings into action

Therapeutic recreation programmers Linda Buettner and Suzanne Fitzsimmons conducted an evaluation of a bicycle program in Fort Myers, Florida. They carried out a controlled clinical investigation of the effectiveness of wheelchair bicycles in treating depression in long-term-care residents with dementia. The wheelchair bicycle program included both a small-group activity and one-to-one bike rides with a staff member. The evaluation revealed that depression levels were significantly reduced in the patients, even after only 2 weeks of the program, and were maintained for 10 weeks after the program ended (Buettner & Fitzsimmons, 2002).

The recreation programming process ends with an evaluation of the program, such as for this therapeutic recreation program.

Now we are ready to overview the steps for systematically evaluating programs. Remember, programming is both a science and an art. This chapter focuses on the "science" of the evaluation phase: the recurring process of collecting new information that ultimately results in changes to program plans. The list of steps can differ from evaluator to evaluator, but we've included those that are minimally necessary. While you read the chapter, however, keep in mind the "art" of evaluation as well. That is, good evaluation also requires creativity and responsiveness. You must remain open to the need for adjusting each step according to the unique situation of the evaluation study (Riddick & Russell, 1999).

Step 1: Preparing an Evaluation Proposal

The first step in conducting a program evaluation is to prepare a **proposal**—a written description of how you intend to carry out the evaluation study (Riddick & Russell, 1999). A proposal not only keeps your organization's director and other staff informed, but also the process of writing a proposal helps you think through the research design and the most appropriate methods to use. Once the evaluation study is under way, the proposal can also serve as a guide to keep you on track and provide a head start to writing the final report (Gall & Gall, 1996). This all means that ultimately the evaluation proposal becomes part of a "contract" between you and your organization. It ensures accountability for the expenditure of time, staff resources, and funds.

An evaluation proposal usually contains the following sections: introduction, literature review, study design and methods, time line, personnel, budget, and dissemination plan. Some of these sections are identical to those you will use in the final evaluation report, while a few are specific to the proposing of an evaluation.

Let's overview each of these proposal sections separately. First, the introduction states the purpose, significance, and objectives of the evaluation study. Your goal is to lead the proposal reader unfailingly to the same decision you made: A study must be done now and with these aims. Sometimes the study's aim is written in the form of research questions. For example, the box on page 223 illustrates some of the

© Jacques Pavlovsky/Sygma/CORBIS.

Examples of Evaluation Questions

- Did the volunteers for the senior center learn emergency care procedures from the in-service training?

- Are the methods being used to teach swimming at the pool in conformance with American or Canadian Red Cross standards?

- Did the fitness class participants reach the goal of 1 percent loss in body fat over the three months of the program?

- Are the assisted living residents more likely to attend programs if refreshments are served?

- Does participation in the leisure education program decrease the probability of subsequent drug abuse by the outpatient psychiatric patients?

- Which type of training is most effective in increasing knowledge about young adult development for program staff?

- Did increasing the number of trash containers along the park trails reduce littering behavior of hikers?

- Would tour participants recommend the Mackinaw Island tour to their friends?

- Do the weekend adventure outings help first-year students adjust to college life?

---

typical research questions posed in program evaluations by leisure services organizations.

The second section is a review of related literature. Its purpose is to show you have taken into account previous research on the topic of your evaluation study. The **literature review** also provides a context for how your study will fill the gaps in what is understood from previous research (Riddick & Russell, 1999). Your evaluation study should build on the work of others—the findings from your program's evaluation add to what we know. For example, from the findings presented in this chapter's opening case, we know that bicycle riding is effective as an intervention against depression resulting from dementia.

Writing a literature review requires that you first cull through publications, such as professional journals, academic books, and organization files, to find information related to your evaluation topic. In the proposal, the literature review is relatively brief—just long enough to provide an understanding of the existing knowledge base for your research questions. Later, in the final report, your literature

Your plans for carrying out the evaluation, including how you will analyze the information you collect, must be established in the proposal.

© PhotoDisc.

review will likely be expanded. For more information on this topic, see worksheet 15.1 in chapter 15 of the CD-ROM.

The next section presents the study design and methods. Here you go into some detail about the procedures you propose to use. What are your intentions for the research design, the sample, instrumentation, and data analysis? Even though the analysis of collected data seems a long way off, it is important to develop a data analysis strategy before starting the study because sample size, data collection methods, and other decisions hinge on it. Later steps explain all this more fully.

As advocated in the previous chapter, to maximize your organization's resources, the study time line, personnel needs, and cost must also be determined ahead of time and explained in the evaluation proposal. In a time budget, estimates are given for the project deadlines and the duration of each research step in the entire project. A personnel budget estimates the kinds of people and the skills needed to complete the evaluation project. And, of course, a monetary budget for accomplishing an evaluation study is typically presented in the proposal. The budget should include not only the direct costs of carrying out the study, such as questionnaire printing, postage stamps, and a video recorder, but also such indirect costs as office space and use of computers. Table 15.1 illustrates some of this in a handy matrix form.

Finally, the proposal should include a plan for dissemination. **Dissemination of study findings** entails how the results and recommendations are to be communicated and implemented. How will what was learned from the evaluation be applied to improve programs and their delivery? What program policies and practices should be changed as a result of the study's recommendations? When will these changes be made, and by whom? Without dissemination your evaluation efforts will remain "entombed in a very formal, and often seldom-read, document" (Moore, 1987, p. 76). Obviously, dissemination should begin within your organization. The results should also be passed along more broadly, perhaps, such as submitted to professional journals and magazines or delivered at professional conferences and seminars.

Although writing an evaluation proposal is valuable in helping you develop and clarify how the study will be conducted, it is frequently also used for communicating with other people both internal and external to your organization. The proposal often becomes a sales tool, used to convince the people who have approval authority or financial backing that the study is worth doing. Expect that your proposals will be keenly judged, particularly when applying for government grants.

Step 2: Designing the Study

Similar to barbecue, where there is more than one good recipe, there is also more than one way to design a program evaluation study. In fact, many more designs are available to the evaluator than we have room to overview here. We'll discuss several evaluative research designs in a moment, but first here are the factors to consider when adopting a particular design (Weiss, 1972, p. 4):

TABLE 15.1

Matrix of Responsibility for Evaluating the Mackinaw Island Tour

Person in charge	Writing proposal	Design and sampling	Data collection tools	Data analysis	Writing final report	Application of results
Agency director						X
Tour planner	X	X			X	X
Tour leaders		X	X			X
Business manager	X			X		
Marketing director			X			X

- *What are the information needs of the programmers and agency?* More information requires more complex designs.
- *What are the evaluation project constraints—time, personnel, money?* Limited resources require quickly conducted designs.
- *How can you best protect study participants?* Some designs are more intrusive on program patrons than others.
- *How rigorous must future program decisions be?* The more rigorous the design, the more accurate the resulting program solutions.

From the long list of all possible study designs, we overview these six: control group pretest–posttest, one-group pretest–posttest, survey, ethnographic study, case study, and content analysis.

Control Group Pretest–Posttest Design

For the **control group pretest–posttest** design there are two samples, one we call experimental and the other we call control. Both samples are measured before the program and after the program, but only the experimental sample participates in the recreation program. Then, a comparison is made between the pretest and posttest data; if the difference is larger for the experimental group, it is concluded that the program was effective. For example, two groups of college students are given a questionnaire that measures adjustment to college, first in late August just after arriving on campus and again in early December as the first semester comes to a close. One group (the experimental group) participates in an outdoor adventure club program sponsored by the student union, and the other group (the control) does not. If the group that participated in the program shows higher scores for adjustment to college between the beginning of the semester and the end of the semester, while the control group does not, then it is concluded that the outdoor adventure club accomplished its goal.

Many different research designs are available to programmers for evaluating the effectiveness of programs.

One-Group Pretest–Posttest Design

In a **one-group pretest–posttest** design, only one sample receives a pretest before experiencing the program and a posttest after concluding the program. There is no control group. For example, suppose in a fitness program the aim is to lose 1 percent body fat in three months. Using this design, the participants' body fat is recorded on the first and last days of the fitness program and then compared. Any changes are assumed to be the result of the program, which can be problematic if participants lose body fat for reasons other than the program, such as from dieting.

Survey Design

The survey design is one of the most common approaches in the evaluation of recreation programs (Riddick, DeSchriver, & Weissinger, 1991). In a **survey**, respondents are interviewed or questioned in order to determine their attitudes, preferences, and self-reported behaviors. This means that surveys are not a direct measure of knowledge gained, skills developed, or other outcomes of the program. Surveys require the programmer to estimate this from the participants' perspectives. For example, assisted living residents could be asked if they are more likely to participate in recreation programs if refreshments are served. Or participants in an in-service training session on emergency care procedures could be asked how confident they feel in administering first aid. In these situations, you do not have a direct measure of what motivates resident participation in the program or what the in-service training participants learned about emergency care; rather, you need to infer such information from their responses.

Surveys can be conducted via mailed or e-mailed questionnaires, face-to-face interviews, or telephone interviews. Critically important to the integrity of all these methods is response rate. **Response rate** is one way to determine the representativeness of a sample of respondents. A high response rate is achieved when almost everyone who was asked to answer the questions does so. If a high response rate is obtained for a survey, there is less chance that the sample is biased. What is a high response rate? The experts do not agree on this; but one rule of thumb is that 50 percent is considered adequate, 60 percent is good, and 70 percent is very good (Babbie, 1998).

Ethnographic Study Design

In an **ethnographic study**, the programmer attempts to obtain as complete an understanding as possible of program services. The emphasis is on learning the regular, everyday experiences of program participants by intensely observing or interviewing over a sustained period of time (Miles & Huberman, 1994). To illustrate, suppose an evaluator of an outpatient psychiatric leisure education program wants to know about the experience of being in the program. To accomplish this, the evaluator could regularly attend the programs, observing and interviewing participants as well as staff over a long period of time. Ethnographic study is essentially a discovery and descriptive process (Miles & Huberman, 1994). The idea is to uncover what is typical about the program setting or situation studied—not to explain or justify it.

A special kind of ethnographic study is the evaluation of a single program participant. This is called a **case study**. Suppose there is one patient in the psychiatric outpatient leisure education program who seems to be responding particularly well. To explore this further, the evaluator could conduct a case study on just this one individual to discover how and why the program is working so well for her. She could be observed and interviewed on a regular basis. Also, the woman's friends, family members, and the program staff might be interviewed regarding their observations about her. Through this method of studying a unique individual, the programmer gains insights that may suggest ways to help other patients make the most of the program (Riddick & Russell, 1999).

Finally, **content analysis** is a special kind of case study. Instead of studying a single individual, the evaluator examines a document. Content, or document, analysis is the study of the contents of a written, visual, or recorded document. Meeting minutes, long-range plans, newspapers, speeches, advertisements, promotional videos, children's drawings, indeed any written or visual communication can be studied. For example, to determine if the methods used to teach swimming at the pool are in conformance with American or Canadian Red Cross standards, the lesson plans of instructors could be analyzed. This may involve tallying the number of times the lesson plan content refers to a specific standard. For more information on this topic, see "More Options for Individual Programming Practice," option 2, in chapter 15 of the CD-ROM.

Step 3: Selecting a Sample

A deceivingly important step in evaluation is the selection of respondents. Respondents can be individual people, classes, teams, communities, organizations, or other groups. An evaluation answers the question of how well the program is working. This means that selecting a sample of study participants first requires answering the following question: From whom do you want to know how well the program is working? A **sample** is a subset of everyone of interest to you. A sample could be a subset of all programming staff working in the after-school program, a subset of participants in the annual Renaissance Faire, a subset of the members of the senior citizen club, or even a subset of all "letters to the editor" about your organization.

The most important consideration in selecting a sample is **representativeness**. The sample of respondents must be a good "likeness" of the total group from which it was selected in order for the evaluation to be accurate. There are many ways to accomplish this—all with both advantages and disadvantages. Some sampling methods are based on pure chance, so everyone in the total group has an equal likelihood of being chosen for the sample. But these methods can be time consuming and expensive to accomplish. Other methods provide the advantages of ease and low cost, but they are not as likely to produce representative samples. To illustrate, let's consider simple random sampling, stratified random sampling, systematic random sampling, purposive sampling, and snowball sampling.

Simple Random Sampling

Simple random sampling produces a subset of respondents for an evaluation study by pure chance. With this method, all members of the study population have an equal opportunity to be chosen. There are several ways to accomplish this, but the simplest is to put the names of all potential respondents in a hat and draw out the names one by one until the desired sample size is reached. Also, a table of random numbers or a computer-based selection program can help.

Stratified Random Sampling

However, it is not always possible to select a sample of respondents with complete randomness. In this situation the stratified random sampling method can be used. In **stratified random sampling**, the overall population of respondents is divided into several different subgroups according to common characteristics such as gender, age, ethnic identity, or socioeconomic status. Random samples are then taken from each subgroup in proportion to the subgroup's total size.

Another type of stratification involves sampling over time or by services offered. For example, sampling on site at a fitness club may require stratification by activity. This type of sampling often needs to be varied by season, time of week, and time of day. The fitness club may offer indoor swimming that is used

by 10 percent of club members, with 65 percent of that usage occurring after 5:00 p.m. So, 10 percent of a sample of club members should be sampled at the swimming pool, and 65 percent of that 10 percent should be sampled after 5:00 p.m. (Riddick & Russell, 1999). This method makes it possible for a cross section of respondents to be selected according to their representativeness from the overall group.

Systematic Random Sampling

Another sampling method, called **systematic random sampling**, is mostly used when the total program group is very large. The basic idea is that every nth person is selected. This nth could be set at every 2nd person, every 10th person, every 25th person, or whatever. Once the number (nth) has been determined, a list of the total group membership is used to designate those names at the chosen nth position. Customarily, the list of names is first arranged alphabetically.

The three sampling methods outlined so far can be labeled probability samples because every member of the total population, or program group, has the same chance of being chosen for the sample. Probability samples are more likely to be representative.

Purposive Sampling

There are also sampling methods not based on probability. In **purposive sampling**, evaluators purposively seek out respondents they believe, based on judgment or intuition, will best answer the evaluation questions. This may be especially important when little is understood about the program or service being evaluated (Russell, 2005). For example, you interview users of the swimming pool's diving well because you want to evaluate how well this part of the facility serves these patrons. In this case, it would not make sense to draw a random sample of all swimming pool users because, for this evaluation project, you are interested only in those who regularly use the diving area.

Snowball Sampling

Finally, another nonprobability sampling method is **snowball sampling**. This technique involves identifying the next respondent in the evaluation based on the recommendation of the previous respondent. Like a chain reaction, you first identify one or two people to interview. In addition to asking these persons questions pertinent to the evaluation, you also request the names of other people to include in the study. This second wave of interviewees also has a dual involvement—to contribute their information to the study and to inform the evaluator about additional people to interview. The procedure continues ("snowballs") until you stop learning new information.

Step 4: Collecting Information

There is a variety of ways to collect information to answer evaluation questions; some methods will result in quantitative data, and others will produce qualitative data. This section of the chapter focuses on questionnaires and structured interviews, unstructured interviews and focus groups, observations, document studies, and nonreactive measures.

First, **questionnaires** and **structured interviews** are probably the most common ways of gathering information in a recreation program evaluation project. These data collection tools allow evaluators to quickly determine wide-ranging aspects of a program's success. Questionnaires and structured interviews can measure facts, knowledge, behaviors, attitudes, beliefs, and practices (Russell & Bixler, 1999).

Customarily, questionnaires are distributed to individuals by way of mail or within a preformed group; when conducted face to face or over the telephone, they become structured interviews. Although questionnaires vary greatly in length and complexity, there are several important rules to follow:

- Begin with short, easy, and familiar questions that are nonthreatening.

- Give complete directions on how questions are to be answered.

- Make the questionnaire as brief, simple, and attractive as possible.

- Group questions into subparts according to similarities in content and in question format.

- Avoid vague terms. For example, in asking how often a particular service is used, how often is "often"?

- Avoid questions that show bias, such as "How good do you think this program really was?"

- Avoid questions that could have multiple responses. For example, each choice in the following question should be asked about sepa-

The Benefits of Pilot Testing

An evaluator sat down individually with 15 adolescents and went through a questionnaire with them. As they answered each question, the evaluator asked the respondents to state in their own words why they answered the way they did. One set of questions asked for participation rates in various outdoor activities. Most of the pilot test group reported having participated in tent camping but explained that their tent camping experience consisted of staying in a tent during a slumber party in the backyard of a friend's home. Since the evaluator wanted to know about the usage of parks, the question was modified to "Have you ever been tent camping in parks or forests?"

rately: "Do you prefer the program to be held on weekends, weekdays, or nights?"

Getting accurate and useful answers requires thoroughly planning the questionnaire. You might want to work with another staff member experienced in questionnaire design or with a research specialist in your organization. As the box on this page illustrates, pilot testing the questionnaire can help correct any problems with clarity, language, or time. For more information on this topic, see worksheet 15.2 in chapter 15 of the CD-ROM.

Unstructured interviews, unlike structured interviews, ask more flexible and open-ended questions. This is actually a conversation that proceeds more spontaneously. Although the interviewer typically uses an outline of possible questions, the respondents answer the questions in their own words, with the interviewer asking follow-up questions that may not be in the original outline.

One form of unstructured interview is the **focus group** (also presented in chapter 7). Focus groups generally involve 7 to 12 people who discuss a particular topic under the direction of a facilitator, who promotes interaction and ensures that the discussion remains on topic. A typical focus group session lasts from one and a half to two hours. Moderating a focus group can look deceptively simple, yet it requires a wide range of interview skills and knowledge of group dynamics. For more information on this topic, see "Group Discussion Ideas," option 3, in chapter 15 of the CD-ROM.

Because people's actions are a central aspect of virtually any evaluation, another technique for collecting information is watching what people do. One of the more common types is **participant observation**. This form of watching is done from the vantage point of the program participants, using different levels of involvement. At the highest level, complete participant observation, the observer acts as naturally as possible, seeking to become a full member of the program group. The marginal participant, on the other hand, is in an observation situation where there is a lower degree of participation. This can be done by adopting the role of a peripheral, although completely accepted, participant (e.g., a spectator at a sports event). An alternative to the complete and marginal participant roles is that of the passive participant. Here the observer is present at the scene of the action but does not participate or interact with the program participants (e.g., the observer sits on a bench at the edge of a children's playground). For more information on this topic, see "More Options for Individual Programming Practice," option 3, in chapter 15 of the CD-ROM.

On the other hand, a great deal can be evaluated without ever observing people or asking them questions. Archival sources, such as documents and records, can be studied. The two forms of archival sources are continuous documents and episodic records. **Continuous documents**, which tend to be public, include actuarial records (marriage), political and judicial records (votes), other government records (city budgets), crime records, and mass media archives (newspapers). **Episodic records** are more discontinuous and private; they include letters, memos, drawings, speeches, and personnel disciplinary action files.

Finally, there is another way to gather information in an evaluation without having contact with people. This requires the use of unobtrusive **nonreactive measures**—so labeled because they do not alter the natural actions of people. When you ask people questions, you make them aware they are being studied, and sometimes this sets into motion new attitudes or atypical responses. This can compromise the validity of the evaluation results. Customarily, nonreactive measures are used in tandem with other data-collection strategies.

One of the more common nonreactive measures is collecting physical traces. Physical tracing is the visible evidence of behavior. These are pieces of information not specifically produced for the evaluation but nonetheless available to be studied. The debris from a party provides a trace about what happened; graffiti on the recreation center restroom walls offer a clue as to the concerns of youth; food waste in the summer camp dining hall adds to your knowledge of menu popularity; wear on floor tiles in front of selected museum exhibits serves as an index to popularity. Physical traces are inconspicuous and anonymous; those who left them usually have no knowledge of their potential for evaluation.

Although they are easy to gather, there are limitations to the usefulness of nonreactive measures. First, extensive time is required to collect some traces (such as the abrasion of the metal on a weightlifting machine). As well, there is often a lack of understanding about the intentions of the people who left the traces. Why did the weightlifting participants choose

From studying the "physical trace" on this weightlifting machine at the fitness center, you can determine the most popular amount of weight used by participants.

such a low amount of weight to lift? Does this suggest the program attracts only beginners? It is impossible to tell from these measures. For more information on this topic, see "Group Discussion Ideas," option 1, in chapter 15 of the CD-ROM. 💿

Step 5: Interpreting the Information Gathered

Evaluation information is essentially numbers or words—the number of participants in an after-school program, the percentage of health club members who prefer longer operating hours, the adjectives written down by district supervisors on playground leaders' performance forms, the ideas for new programs contained on slips of paper in the suggestion box at the resort. When you gather information from questionnaires, focus groups, participant observations, nonreactive measures, and so on, it is disarrayed. Ordering and then analyzing such information is necessary because data in their "raw" form do not tell you very much.

A vast extended family of analysis tools exists, so don't expect mastery of this evaluation step right away. Like so many other elements of evaluation, data analysis takes training and experience. Seek the help of a colleague or consultant who has this experience if you need to. Meanwhile, to give you an idea of what analysis entails, we'll overview some of the basics.

First, when data are in the form of numbers, you apply **quantitative data analysis**. Essentially, there are two ways to analyze quantitative data: describing and inferring.

When you want to numerically describe the main features of the program, you calculate **descriptive statistics**. For example, in a sample of children in an after-school program, you might be interested in describing their average age, the most typical number of hours per day they spend in the program, percentages of boys and girls, the frequency of their participation in physically active sports, and so on. You have available four tools for describing the children.

1. *Frequency distributions.* These are simply lists of the information categories and the number of responses that correspond to the categories. Figure 15.1 provides an example.

Frequency distribution in table form:

Disability type	Frequency
Motor	8
Hearing	4
Visual	3
Multiple	2

Same distribution in graphic form:

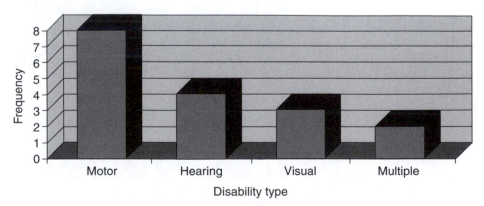

Figure 15.1 Frequency distribution example—disability types for program participants.

2. *Measures of central tendency.* A frequency distribution's center, or middle, is a measure of its central tendency. A single number is used to indicate the distribution's center, usually via a mean, median, or mode. The mean is computed by adding all the scores in the distribution and dividing by the number of scores. The median is the middle value in the distribution when the values are placed in numerical order. That is, the median is that score that divides a distribution exactly in half. The mode is the most common response in the distribution—the most popular category or most frequently occurring score. See figure 15.2 for examples of the mean, median, and mode measures of central tendency.

3. *Measures of variability.* A summary of the spread of individual scores is a measure of their variability. For example, the range of the ages in figure 15.2 is 6 (oldest age [11] minus youngest age [5]). Another measure of variability is the standard deviation, which indicates the spread of the scores by accounting for the distance between each score and the mean. It is the average distance of scores from the mean. The closer individual ages are to the mean, the less the variation and thus the lower the standard deviation. For example, consider two resident camp sessions; if the standard deviation for "miles campers traveled to attend camp" for the first session is 22.5 miles (36 kilometers), and the standard deviation for "miles campers traveled to attend camp" for the second session is 42 miles (67.5 kilometers), you know that the second camp session attracted more campers from farther distances. The standard deviation is the most common and preferred measure of variability (Russell, 2005).

4. *Measures of relationship.* Measures of relationship determine how closely associated two or more variables are to each other. For example, a programmer may wish to know the relationship between operating hours at the indoor climbing wall and revenue generated. To answer the question "Are longer operating hours worthwhile for generating user-fee receipts?" numerous quantitative tools are available. The two most common are the chi-square test (which determines the relationship between two variables that are named, such as gender and neighborhood of residence) and Pearson correlation (which determines the relationship between two variables that are numerical, such as length of operating hours and revenue in dollars).

A second way to analyze quantitative information is by inferring. Known as **inferential statistics**, these tools measure differences between variables.

Figure 15.2 Central tendency example—children's ages in an after-school program.

Reprinted, by permission, from R.V. Russell and R. Bixler, 2005, Evaluation. In *Management of park and recreation agencies,* edited by B. van der Smissen et al. (Ashburn, VA: The National Recreation and Park Association), 675.

For example, a program evaluator may need to know if the daily exercise program at the convalescent center made a difference in patient health. That is, do the patients who participate in the program have lower blood pressure than the residents who do not participate? To answer the question, the evaluator collects blood pressure information on two samples of patients—those who regularly participate in exercise and those who do not. These are compared with their blood pressure readings from before the program started. An inferential statistical procedure is used to test for the difference. If the value obtained is statistically significant, the evaluator can infer that the exercise program contributes to the difference in patients' blood pressure. There are many inferential statistical tools. Perhaps the most commonly used in program evaluation are the t-test and analysis of variance (or F test). For more information on this topic, see worksheet 15.3 in chapter 15 of the CD-ROM.

Statistics are useful for answering many evaluation questions, but not all information collected in an evaluation study is in numerical form. Data are often qualitative—that is, they are in text, photographic, or video form (Russell, 2005). This calls for **qualitative data analysis**. Suppose you have interviewed parents of the children who participate in the traveling soccer program. The information gathered is in the form of words written down in interview notes. How do you make sense of these words?

With qualitative information, the analysis begins as soon as the first bits of data are gathered. It continues in a parallel way throughout the collection of the rest of the data. Although there is room for creativity in qualitative data analysis, a systematic approach is needed. Here is one approach:

1. *Prepare notes.* Notes made during observations or interviews are in condensed form. Afterward you need to expand the notes into a full account by filling in details and recalling things not yet written down. As the number of expanded accounts begins to grow, you will also need to make decisions about note management. This involves developing a system for keeping notes tidy (such as placing them into files), a way to cross-reference information between the files, and a mechanism for labeling the files (Russell & Bixler, 1999).

2. *Focus the data.* Early in the data collection, researchers should pause to consider the main themes learned. This involves focusing the data in your notes by preparing a summary, coding, and memoing. Writing a series of preliminary summaries on a card or piece of paper creates a focused summary. It serves as a guide for planning the next observation or interview. Codes are tags or labels for assigning meaning to the information compiled in the expanded account notes. Usually written in the margin of the notes, codes help keep track of the meanings of the information in the notes at a quick glance. Memoing is another strategy for focusing the data. Memos are personal notes—little descriptions of how, at this point in the study, you would tie together different pieces of information in the notes into some kind of general understanding.

3. *Display the data.* Display the data in a visual chart that systematically presents the information from interviews and observations. The purpose of data displays is to develop and verify descriptive conclusions. Although there are various types of display formats, the matrix is one of the more popular options. A matrix display is essentially a way of pulling together two lists. List number one contains the categories possible for information, and list number two identifies the attributes useful in describing the information. You'll find an example of a matrix display in figure 15.3.

Suppose the categories determined to be useful in describing the types of parents whose children participate in the traveling soccer program are:

- The "coaches" (those parents who actively involved themselves in the soccer program)
- The "spectators" (those parents who were not actively involved)

These two categories become list number one. The parents' attributes list, list number two, could include such elements as age range of the parents, occupational type, and gender. A matrix display for this might look like the following:

Attributes	Types of Parents	
	Coaches	Spectators
Age range (list categories)		
Occupational type (list types)		
Gender Male Female		
Etc.		

Figure 15.3 Example of a matrix display.

Reprinted, by permission, from R.V. Russell and R. Bixler, 2005, Evaluation. In *Management of park and recreation agencies,* edited by B. van der Smissen et al. (Ashburn, VA: The National Recreation and Park Association), 676.

For more information on this topic, see "Group Discussion Ideas," option 3, in chapter 15 of the CD-ROM.

4. *Draw conclusions.* At last, make sense of what you have learned in the evaluation by inductively drawing together discrete bits of information to make a more conceptual whole. Verify the resulting understandings by checking for data quality and testing explanations.

Step 6: Preparing the Final Report

Now you are ready for the next to last step in the program evaluation process—preparing the final report. The final report summarizes the evaluation purpose, design, procedures, and findings. Based on both the findings and their interpretation, conclusions are developed and recommendations for changes are presented. The report might be used primarily within the organization as a guide for programming decisions. It may also be published in professional journals or presented at professional conferences. Regardless of where it is used, it is important that the report be clear and direct in linking the recommendations to the findings.

No evaluation is finished without a report, even if it is only a single page. Unless a report is made, the only beneficiary of the effort is the evaluator. The evaluation report communicates what has been done to answer the evaluation question as well as the resulting recommendations. A good report is factual and logical. Preparing a good report is hard work, and after the excitement of collecting and analyzing the information, report writing seems tedious. Yet there is no better way to share results and recommendations with those in positions to use them. For more information on this topic, see "More Options for Individual Programming Practice," option 1, in chapter 15 of the CD-ROM.

The evaluation final report should contain the following (Riddick & Russell, 1999):

* Orientation to the evaluation issue, question, or problem
* Background information, such as relevant literature from professional and research journals
* Methods and procedures used to gather the information to address the evaluation question or problem

---

Example of the Orientation to the Issue Section of an Evaluation Report

The purpose of this evaluation was to identify reasons for a low number of visitors to the community historical museum. Participation records kept by the museum director indicate a five-year decline in both the number of visitors who enter the museum and the amount of time visitors spend there. While it was assumed that publicity about the museum was at fault, casual comments made by several recent visitors suggest an investigation of whether the museum meets the interests of potential visitors was also warranted. Thus, this project studied both the museum's publicity strategies as well as potential museum visitor interests.

Adapted from Russell & Bixler, 1999, p.812.

---

* Results and analyses of the gathered information
* Conclusions that include both a summarization and interpretation of findings
* Recommendations for professional practice or management decision making

Many people have difficulty getting started when writing the first section of the report—the orientation to the evaluation issue. To give you an idea of how to begin, the box on this page shows an example. For more information on this topic, see "Can You Solve This Programming Issue?" in chapter 15 of the CD-ROM.

Step 7: Putting the Findings Into Action

The recommendations drawn in the final report need to be put into action. Even the most eloquently prepared report is worthless if the findings and recommendations it contains are not put to use. This evaluation step, then, is actually both the last and the first. Recommendations instruct both policy and practice decisions for future programs. Remember, the whole point of evaluation is to use data as the basis for suggesting courses of program action. Thus the evaluation is not finished until individuals in the

The Programming Process: Evaluation Steps

Evaluating the ability of this adult arts program, sponsored by the Westerville Parks and Recreation Department, to accomplish what it intends requires applying the seven steps of the evaluation process.

Let's apply what you've learned about the systematic evaluation process to Westerville's concern about acquiring measurable outcomes from their programs. Specifically, we demonstrate the evaluation steps for the adult arts programs, including ceramics, stained glass, and watercolor painting.

Step 1: Preparing an Evaluation Proposal

The program manager for adult programs, Laura Horton, along with several other members of her staff, prepares a written evaluation proposal that describes the intention for the study. Suppose they would like to know if the arts program participants have learned skills that have carryover value beyond the arts classes. They present the proposal to their supervisor, Phyllis Self, for approval.

Step 2: Designing the Study

The proposal specifies the research design they will use. Suppose they have chosen both the one-group pretest–posttest and survey designs. This means that before the start of the next beginner-level ceramics, stained glass, and watercolor painting classes, the new participants are given a questionnaire that asks about their participation in that art form at home, in neighborhood craft clubs, and in other situations outside the class. Then, a month after the conclusion of these beginning arts classes, the same participants are given the same questionnaire again.

Step 3: Selecting a Sample

Using a random numbers table, a simple random sample of 10 participants each from the beginning ceramics, stained glass, and watercolor painting classes is selected.

Step 4: Collecting Information

A four-question structured questionnaire is administered in person by Laura in each of the classrooms immediately before the start of the first class session. The sampled respondents were telephoned previously and asked to arrive 15 minutes early in order to complete the questionnaire. A month after the last class, the same sample of respondents is sent a blank copy of the same questionnaire via mail. A self-addressed and stamped envelope is included, and respondents are reminded via telephone if more than a week goes by without a response. Laura needs a response rate of 100 percent. To help confirm the findings, Laura also employs a nonreactive measure—for the next year she scans the local newspaper for art exhibit announcements that include class participants.

Step 5: Interpreting the Information Gathered

To interpret the questionnaire results, Laura calculates descriptive statistics for both sets of questionnaires. For example, a mean number of hours spent per week pursuing art outside of class can be determined for both before and after the class. To see if there is a difference, she might also calculate the inferential statistic using a t-test.

Step 6: Preparing the Final Report

Laura and her staff prepare a five-page final report of the findings. Suppose it was found that the beginner-level participants did increase the time spent on their art outside of class, but only slightly. Laura might then ask if the development of an art skill has to progress beyond the beginner level in order to affect participation beyond the program. One recommendation from this finding might be, therefore, to carry out the evaluation study again for those beginning participants who go on to participate in intermediate and advanced art classes.

Step 7: Putting the Findings Into Action

At the regular staff meeting for program managers convened by superintendent Phyllis Self, Laura discusses the report and solicits support to expand programming offerings to include intermediate and advanced art classes.

organization have been given specific assignments in order to act on the findings.

How might this be done? You have a variety of options for putting the evaluation results into action:

- Call a staff meeting to discuss the recommendations.
- Meet with your organization's policy makers.
- Prepare a popularized version of the report for the local newspaper.
- Give a presentation at a professional conference.
- Insert the results into the organization's program catalog.

Summary

This chapter presents the steps for carrying out a systematic program evaluation. You should understand the following key points:

- Evaluation requires time and effort, not only for collecting and analyzing the data but for planning and conceptualizing as well.
- First, an evaluation proposal is prepared, including plans for the study design and sampling method so that a focus and approach for the study are established.
- The evaluation study is implemented by collecting and interpreting information results.
- Finally, a report is prepared, and recommendations for making or changing program decisions, and plans ensure that the evaluation effort pays off.

Glossary

proposal—A written description of study intentions.

literature review—A summary of relevant information from studies conducted by others.

dissemination of study findings—How evaluation results and recommendations are to be communicated and implemented.

control group pretest–posttest—Both experimental and control samples are measured before the program and after the program, but only the experimental sample participates in the program.

one-group pretest–posttest—A sample receives a pretest before experiencing the program and a posttest after concluding the program.

survey—Respondents are questioned to determine their attitudes, preferences, and self-reported behaviors.

response rate—The percentage of those asked who answer a survey.

ethnographic study—Obtaining a complete understanding by intensely observing or interviewing about a program over a sustained period of time.

case study—A special kind of ethnographic study focused on a single individual, program, or agency.

content analysis—The study of the contents of a written, visual, or recorded document.

sample—A subset of everyone of interest.

representativeness—A sample is a reasonable likeness of those in the population.

simple random sampling—Produces a subset of respondents by pure chance.

stratified random sampling—Random sampling from subgroups formed according to common characteristics.

systematic random sampling—Every nth person is selected.

purposive sampling—Evaluators purposively seek out respondents they believe will fulfill the needs of the study.

snowball sampling—Like a chain reaction, identifying the next respondent in the evaluation based on the recommendation of the previous respondent.

questionnaire—A list of questions usually requiring selecting answers from a set of predetermined choices.

structured interview—A questionnaire administered orally.

unstructured interview—Orally administered open-ended questions.

focus group—A form of unstructured interview; a facilitated group discussion about a specific topic.

participant observation—Watching program participant behaviors from the vantage point of involvement with them.

continuous documents—Publicly available records, such as newspaper archives.

episodic records—Records that are more discontinuous and private, such as memos.

nonreactive measures—Data-collection strategies that do not alter the natural actions of people.

quantitative data analysis—Analyzing numerical information.

descriptive statistics—Tools that describe numerical information.

inferential statistics—Tools that analyze differences between numerical information.

qualitative data analysis—Analyzing nonnumerical information.

References

Babbie, E. (1998). *The practice of social research* (8th ed.). Belmont, CA: Wadsworth.

Buettner, L.L., & Fitzsimmons, S. (2002). AD-venture program: Therapeutic biking for the treatment of depression in long-term care residents with dementia. *American Journal of Alzheimer's Disease, 17*(2), 121-127.

Gall, M.D., & Gall, J. (1996). *Educational research: An introduction.* New York: Longman.

Miles, M.B., & Huberman, A.M. (1994). *Qualitative data analysis.* Thousand Oaks, CA: Sage.

Moore, N. (1987). *How to do research.* London: Library Association.

Riddick, C., DeSchriver, M., & Weissinger, E. (1991). A methodological review of research in Journal of Leisure Research from 1983 through 1987. Paper presented at the National Recreation and Park Association's Leisure Research Symposium, Orlando, FL.

Riddick, C.C., & Russell, R.V. (1999). *Evaluative research in recreation, park, and sport settings: Searching for useful information.* Champaign, IL: Sagamore.

Russell, R.V. (2005). Evaluation. In B. van der Smissen, M. Moiseichik, & V.J. Hartenburg (Eds.), *Management of park and recreation agencies* (2nd ed., pp. 655-677). Ashburn, VA: National Recreation and Park Association.

Russell, R.V., & Bixler, R. (1999). Evaluation. In B. van der Smissen, M. Moiseichik, V.J. Hartenburg, & L.F. Twardzik (Eds.), *Management of park and recreation agencies* (pp. 785-819). Ashburn, VA: National Recreation and Park Association.

Weiss, C. (1972). *Evaluation research: Methods of assessing program effectiveness.* Englewood Cliffs, NJ: Prentice Hall.

Appendix A: Accreditation Standards

Standards for Baccalaureate Programs in Recreation, Park Resources, and Leisure Services Established by the NRPA Council on Accreditation for Recreation, Park Resources, and Leisure Services Education

The NRPA Council on Accreditation for Recreation, Park Resources, and Leisure Services Education is sponsored by the National Recreation and Park Association (NRPA). The NRPA Council on Accreditation has established professional competencies for all students. The standards listed are ones the authors believe they have addressed in part in their chapters. The chapter numbers for each standard are in parentheses.

8.02 Understanding of the conceptual foundations of play, recreation, and leisure. (Chapter 1)

8.04 Understanding of the interrelationship between leisure behavior and the natural environment. (Chapter 3)

8.05 Understanding of environmental ethics and its relationship to leisure behavior. (Chapter 3)

8.06.02 Professional organizations (Chapter 2)

8.06.03 Current issues and trends in the profession (Chapter 3)

8.07 Understanding of ethical principles and professionalism. (Chapters 1 and 3)

8.08 Understanding of the importance of maintaining professional available resources for professional development. (Chapter 2)

8.09 Understanding of the roles, interrelationships, and use of addressing recreation, park resources, and leisure. (Chapters 2, 5, and 6)

8.10 Understanding populations. (Chapter 3)

8.11.01 Understanding of inclusive practices as they apply to: Operating programs and services (Chapter 4)

8.12 Understanding of the roles, interrelationships, and use of diverse leisure delivery systems in promoting: (Chapter 1)

8.12.01 Community development (Chapter 6)

8.13 Understanding of the variety community quality of life. (Chapters 1 and 4)

8.14 Ability to implement the following principles and procedures related to program/event planning for individual, group, and community quality of life: (Chapter 5)

8.14.01 Assessment of needs (Chapter 7)

8.14.02 Development of outcome-oriented goals and objectives (Chapter 8)

8.14.03 Selection and coordination of programs, events, and resources (Chapters 9 and 10)

8.14.04 Marketing of programs/events (Chapters 7 and 10)

8.14.05 Preparation, operation, and maintenance of venues (Chapter 10)

8.14.06 Implementation of programs/events (Chapter 12)

8.14.07 Evaluation of programs/events (Chapters 8, 14, and 15)

8.17 Ability to apply basic principles of research resources, and leisure services. (Chapters 6, 7, and 15)

8.20 Understanding of the principles and procedures of supervisory leadership. (Chapter 13)

8.21 Understanding of the principles and procedures of budgeting and financial management. (Chapter 10 and 12)

8.22 Understanding of the principles and procedures related to agency marketing techniques and strategies. (Chapters 7, 9, and 10)

8.24 Ability to apply current technology to professional practice. (Chapter 12)

8.27 Understanding the principles and practices of safety, emergency, and risk management related to recreation, park resources, and leisure services. (Chapter 13)

Appendix B: Accreditation Standards

Commission for Accreditation of Park and Recreation Agencies Standards

Charged with providing high quality recreation services and experiences, an increasing number of park and recreation agencies across the country are applying for the Agency Accreditation Program through the Commission for Accreditation of Park and Recreation Agencies (CAPRA).

CAPRA administers a rigorous program based on self-assessment and peer review using national standards of best practice to better promote the quality of agency services and delivery systems.

Agency accreditation is available to all entities administering park and recreation systems, including municipalities, townships, counties, special districts and regional authorities, councils of government and schools.

Agency accreditation is voluntary, but an essential piece to producing quality environments for communities to play, live, and grove.

1.2 Mission (Chapters 6 and 8)

1.3 Goals and Objectives (Chapter 8)

1.5 Relationships (Chapter 6)

2.0 PLANNING (Chapter 5)

2.1 Trends Analysis (Chapter 6)

2.2 Community Planning (Chapter 6)

2.3 Strategic Planning (Chapter 9)

2.4 Comprehensive Planning (Chapter 9)

2.4.1 Recreation Programming Plan (Chapters 5, 6, and 7)

3.3.4 Marketing (Chapter 7)

3.4 Management Information Systems, including Records Management (Chapter 12)

4.1.2 Staffing (Chapter 11)

4.1.3 Recruitment and Selection (Chapter 11)

4.1.4.4 Training, career development (Chapter 2)

4.2 Volunteers (Chapters 6 and 11)

5.1 Fiscal Policy (Chapter 10)

5.4 Budgeting Procedures (Chapter 10)

6.1 Programs/Services Determinants (Chapters 5 and 6)

6.2 Nature of Services/Programs Delivery (Chapters 4 and 11)

6.2.4 Programs/Services for a Fee (Chapter 10)

6.3 Objectives (Chapter 8)

6.5 Scope of Program Opportunities (Chapters 3 and 4)

6.6 Selection of Program Content (Chapters 4 and 9)

6.7 Types of Participation (Chapter 4)

9.0 RISK MANAGEMENT (Chapter 13)

10.1 Systematic Evaluation Program (Chapters 14 and 15)

Reprinted, by permission, from National Recreation and Park Association. For the complete list of Commission for Accreditation of Park and Recreation Agencies Standards, contact NRPA.

Appendix C: Certified Park and Recreation Professional Study Guide Criteria

The examination is one of the principal requirements for certification as a "Certified Park and Recreation Professional" (CPRP). It is designed to assess the base knowledge of job-related tasks common to entry-level professionals. The examination is administered under the auspices of the National Recreation and Park Association (NRPA) and the National Certification Board (hereafter referred to as NCB). A national job analysis was conducted in 1989, and again in 1999 and 2006, to identify the important core components of the leisure service profession. The NCB-appointed Job Analysis Advisory Committee conducted the study, which culminated in the test specifications. The test content outline serves as the blueprint for constructing the examination. There are three core components of the examination: general administration, programming, and operations management. The detailed test specifications for the programming component are included in this publication. At the time of publication, the CPRP Professional Study Guide criteria were under revision. For the most recent criteria, please visit www.nrpa.org. For more information about becoming certified for the examination, please contact the NRPA at 1-800-626-6772 or www.nrpa.org.

II. Programming – 49 items:

II.A Assessment (Chapter 5)

II.A.1 Assess target population program needs (e.g., community surveys) (Chapters 5, 6, and 7)

II.A.2 Assess individual participant needs (Chapters 5 and 7)

II.A.3 Assess resources (e.g., areas, facilities, supplies, equipment, fiscal) (Chapters 5, 6, and 7)

II.B Planning (Chapter 5)

II.B.1 Write purpose and goal statements (Chapters 5 and 8)

II.B.2 Develop individualized behavioral objectives (Chapters 5 and 8)

II.B.3 Analyze activities for individualized programming (Chapters 4 and 5)

II.B.4 Determine program and special event content (Chapters 4, 5, and 9)

II.B.5 Adapt activities according to the needs of participants (Chapters 4 and 5)

II.B.6 Develop individual participant plans (Chapter 5)

II.B.7 Comply with program accessibility standards (Chapter 5)

II.B.8 Coordinate activities, special events, and/or services with other agencies (Chapter 5)

II.B.9 Select program format (Chapters 4 and 5)

II.B.10 Develop recreation activities schedule (Chapters 5 and 10)

II.B.11 Develop management plan for program/special event delivery (Chapters 5 and 10)

II.B.12 Develop evaluation plan for programs and/or participants (Chapter 5)

II.B.13 Coordinate participant registration/reservations (Chapters 5 and 12)

II.B.14 Conduct participant program orientation (Chapter 5)

II.B.15 Develop risk management plan related to programs (Chapters 5 and 13)

II.C Implementation (Chapter 5)

II.C.1 Teach recreation skills (Chapter 5)

II.C.2 Provide direct leadership of leisure activities (Chapters 5 and 11)

II.C.3 Directly supervise recreation programs and special events (Chapters 5, 11, and 13)

II.C.4 Complete program follow-up activities (Chapters 5 and 11)

II.C.5 Provide follow-up programs for individual participants (Chapter 5)

II.C.6 Promote self-directed leisure activities (Chapter 5)

II.C.7 Refer potential participants to appropriate leisure services (Chapter 5)

II.C.8 Provide resource information on other programs or services (Chapter 5)

II.C.9 Facilitate use of equipment, supplies, services, and facilities (Chapters 5 and 10)

II.C.10 Promote exchanges among leisure resource providers (Chapter 5)

II.C.11 Negotiate prices and make arrangements for transportation, lodging, food services, etc. (Chapters 5 and 10)

II.C.12 Assure program compliance with standards and regulations (Chapters 5 and 8)

II.C.13 Complete program and participant reports and forms (including accident reports) (Chapters 5 and 12)

II.D Evaluative Research (Chapter 5)

II.D.1 Conduct program evaluation (e.g., formative and summative research) (Chapters 5 and 14)

II.D.2 Conduct participant evaluation (e.g., survey research) (Chapters 5, 7, 14, and 15)

II.D.3 Prepare comprehensive program report (e.g., finances, participant data, evaluation input) (Chapters 5, 14, and 15)

Reprinted, by permission, from National Recreation and Park Association. For the complete list of CPRP Study Guide Criteria, contact NRPA.

Index

Note: Page numbers followed by an italicized *f* or *t* indicate a figure or table, respectively.

About the Authors

Ruth V. Russell, ReD, is a full professor in the department of recreation, park, and tourism studies at Indiana University. She is a former trustee of the National Recreation and Park Association and a former president of the Society of Park and Recreation Educators. She has programming experience with San Diego Recreation and Parks Department, San Diego-Imperial County Girl Scout Council, a variety of Girl Scout camps, the Book Works retail store, Allied Gardens, and Chateau La Jolla Retirement Complexes. Dr. Russell is the author of numerous textbooks, technical reports, book chapters, and journal articles pertaining to recreation program planning.

Lynn M. Jamieson, ReD, is chair and full professor in the department of recreation, park, and tourism studies at Indiana University. Previously, she served as curriculum coordinator of the recreation administration program at California Polytechnic State University and spent 12 years in administrative positions as a recreation administrator, with special emphasis on recreational sport management. She has coauthored four texts and more than 50 articles about various aspects of management in leisure services.

CD-ROM User Instructions and System Requirements

System Requirements

You can use this CD-ROM on either a Windows®-based PC or a Macintosh computer.

Windows

- IBM PC compatible with Pentium® processor
- Windows® 98/NT 4.0/2000/ME/XP
- Adobe Reader® 8.0
- Microsoft® PowerPoint® Viewer 97 (included)
- 4x CD-ROM drive

Macintosh

- Power Mac® recommended
- System 9.x or higher
- Adobe Reader® 8.0
- Microsoft® PowerPoint® Viewer OS9 or OS10 (included)
- 4x CD-ROM drive

User Instructions

Windows

1. Insert the *Leisure Program Planning and Delivery CD-ROM*. (Note: The CD-ROM must be present in the drive at all times.)
2. Select the "My Computer" icon from the desktop.
3. Select the CD-ROM drive.
4. Open the "Start.pdf" file.

Macintosh

1. Insert the *Leisure Program Planning and Delivery CD-ROM*. (Note: The CD-ROM must be present in the drive at all times.)
2. Double-click the CD icon located on the desktop.
3. Open the "Start.pdf" file.

For customer support, contact Technical Support:

Phone: 217-351-5076 Monday through Friday (excluding holidays) between 7:00 a.m. and 7:00 p.m. (CST).

Fax: 217-351-2674

E-mail: support@hkusa.com